If ... c sphere is in a
ne ... to agree on the
ge ... These cultural
po ... beral attempt to
un ... nother form of
co ... civil liberties in
th ... en at the top of
Jü ... meaning of the
co ... and repeatedly
di ... ok at Habermas'
lif ... sk.

Fr ... e public sphere.
its ... Enlightenment,
m ... Vhereas his first
co ... blic-democratic
po ... de this cultural
In ... communication.
th ... s still central to
th ... can learn from
be ... es what needs to
he ... ore recent times
gl ... lic debates over
... n policy.

th ... re and rescuing
m ... ntroversial. For
pl ... a contemporary
H ... ohnson defends
co ... construction of

Pa ... iversity, Sydney.
Sh ... minist theory.

Routledge Studies in Social and Political Thought

Habermas

Rescuing the public sphere

Pauline Johnson

 Routledge
Taylor & Francis Group

LONDON AND NEW YORK

First published 2006
by Routledge
2 Park Square, Milton Park, Abingdon, Oxon, OX14 4RN

Simultaneously published in the USA and Canada
by Routledge
270 Madison Ave, New York NY 10016

Routledge is an imprint of the Taylor & Francis Group

Transferred to Digital Printing 2009

© 2006 Pauline Johnson

Typeset in Garamond by
Newgen Imaging Systems (P) Ltd, Chennai, India

British Library Cataloguing in Publication Data
A catalogue record for this book is available
from the British Library

Library of Congress Cataloging in Publication Data
A catalog record for this book has been requested

ISBN10: 0–415–36769–7 (hbk)
ISBN10: 0–415–54374–6 (pbk)

ISBN13: 978–0–415–36769–1 (hbk)
ISBN13: 978–0–415–54374–3 (pbk)

For John

Contents

Acknowledgements

First, thanks to Sandey Fitzgerald, who came to the rescue with her editing skills, making many useful suggestions. Maria Markus, friend and hero, thank you for your bracing comments on part of the draft. Other friends and colleagues have been there with a combination of support and helpful criticisms. I am indebted to my sister Lesley, Raewyn Connell, Viv Johnson, Cathy Phillips, Sean Scalmer and Michael Fine. Particular and heartfelt thanks to my daughter Harriet for emergency typing and expert advice in general. My greatest debt is to John Grumley. He knows all the many reasons why and how profoundly thankful I am.

Early versions of some of the chapters appeared in the following publications: 'Enlightenment and Romantic Legacies: Habermas' Postmodern Critics', *Contemporary Political Theory*, 2006; 'Are Our Utopian Energies Exhausted? Habermas' Radical Reformism', *European Journal of Political Theory*, 2004; 'Habermas' Search for the Public Sphere', *European Journal of Social Theory*, 2001; 'Distorted Communications: Feminism's Dispute with Habermas', *Philosophy and Social Criticism*, 2001.

1 Introduction

The plight of the public sphere

If we are to believe what sociologists are telling us, the public sphere is in a near terminal state. Our ability to build solidarities with strangers and to agree on the general significance of needs and problems appears to be under threat. Peter Self is worried that the 'public' is becoming something of a dirty word.[1] Zygmunt Bauman also has his sights set on defending the modern agora from systematic attacks. Michael Walzer thinks that a vital public culture is absent in contemporary multicultural America,[2] while Alain Touraine has repeatedly warned us about an accelerated crisis in public life.[3] What is this public sphere whose reputed imminent collapse is provoking such anxious concern?

John Dewey's concise definition suggests a starting point. 'The public', he tells us, 'consists of all those who are affected by the indirect consequences of transactions to such an extent that it is deemed necessary to have those consequences systematically cared for'.[4] Here the public is described as a particular, purpose-built, solidarity. It refers to a mode of interaction in which mutually dependent private individuals seek to build enabling interpretations of their shared circumstances and call for a general response to collectively significant needs and dissatisfactions. The modern public is not a collectivity drawn from organic, traditional solidarities. Rather, it designates a political process in which common cause is built through the search for solutions to problems initially encountered as private concerns. Dewey uses the term to refer to a concretely encountered mode of integration between private individuals endeavouring to respond politically to the socially induced character of their needs and their problems.

The modern public sphere suggests an evolved, democratized, interpretation of a modern humanist commitment to the production of self-directed, consciously shaped, futures. Conditioned by the historical appearance of demands for political rights of equal and atomized individuals in a mass society, it is a mode of interaction guided by a learnt conviction that in principle equal, but in fact relatively powerless, individuals can give concrete shape to the hope for an autonomous, self-determining life as a shared project. The public sphere refers, then, to processes of rational consensus-formation whose normativity is tied to a democratic interpretation of the aspiration towards self-shaped futures in an egalitarian and pluralistic age.

The public sphere suggests a mode of association that is distinguished by the particularity of its purposes. Whereas private forms of association endeavour to cement their exclusive character, an interest in building the shared grounds in terms of which the needs and points of view of strangers can become mutually intelligible is central to the goals of a public. Robert Putnam uses the terms 'bonding' and 'bridging' to describe the distinct purposes of private and public types of sociality.[5] A bonding mode of association tends to be inward looking and has exclusive intentions. Examples include 'ethnic fraternal organizations, church-based women's reading groups, and fashionable country clubs'.[6] 'Bridging', by contrast, describes the inclusive, outward looking purposes of a public that seeks to 'encompass people across diverse social cleavages'. The civil rights movement suggests a clear example.[7]

A practical interest in facilitating the efforts of mutually dependent private individuals to achieve self-determination is fundamental to the motivations of the modern public. This central purpose suggests a mode of interaction that is governed by the expectation that each will be allowed to try to demonstrate the reasonableness of his needs and of his points of view. A public mode of association must offer participating individuals the opportunity to establish the sense in which their concerns, needs and problems can be recognized as having generalizeable significances that are deemed amendable to active intervention by the collective. Participation in the public sphere is open to all those who engage in a process of mutual deliberation about what counts as equal and common in their perspectives, experiences, needs, and problems. This determination draws upon and builds recognition that concerns that have society-wide dimensions and significances require a general, political response.

Richard Sennett is clear that we need to make some distinctions about the purposes that structure different kinds of modern solidarities.[8] He is convinced that public life is under attack, but for him, this process is quite consistent with the bolstering of certain types of associational ties. In a recent study he looks at the shape of working lives in new capitalist societies and emerges with an interpretation of the social and political significance of different types of contemporary solidarities. Central to life in the new capitalism is the radical insecurity of a transient working population that can count on nothing in a 'flexible' working environment where constant risk-taking is rewarded and loyalties to professions and institutions ask for disappointment. This is an environment that endorses a particular type of association characterized by the temporary and superficial bonds of the 'work team'. Carefully engineered to suit the demands of the day, this is a form of solidarity that creates no new entity with its own capacity to initiate action. It simply facilitates the effective activities of its individual participants. The work ethic of the team 'celebrates sensitivity to others; it requires such "soft skills" as being a good listener and being cooperative; most of all, teamwork emphasizes team adaptability to circumstances'.[9]

The brainchild of new capitalism, the work team cannot satisfy the longings of insecure and isolated individuals living amongst the heightened risks of what Bauman has described as 'liquid modernity'. Sennett claims that the 'uncertainties of flexibility; the absence of deeply rooted trust and commitment; the superficiality of teamwork; most of all, the spectre of failing to make something of oneself in the world, to "get a life" through one's work' are the conditions for a newly intense longing for community.[10] This is a desire for a solidarity whose primary aim is that of self-protection. It is a defensive 'we', tolerated within the framework of new capitalism, that bases itself on the contrived homogeneity of a group constituted through its opposition to others: to immigrant groups, indigenous peoples, asylum seekers and the like.

The superficial solidarities of the work team and the contrived bonds of a defensively constructed 'we' do have some common features. In both cases the concept of solidarity prohibits an integral role to a spirited individuality aware of its dependence on others and keen to participate in building shared interpretations of problems and values. Solidarities formed by the efforts of private individuals seeking to achieve recognition for the generalized significance of their problems and of their particular points of view are, for Sennett, the basis upon which the 'dangerous pronoun' takes shape.[11] What is unsettling about this 'we' is that it suggests a public of private citizens who do not accept the limits of imposed or conventional descriptions of their needs, their circumstances, and their futures. Shared descriptions are rather built through the search for recognition engaged in by mutually dependent private individuals. Sennett insists that the give and take of argumentation and debate is an essential tool in building the democratic solidarities of a public. It is through argument, discourse, and debate that individuals are able to create the mutual understandings that permit recognition of the reasonableness of their viewpoints and the legitimacy of their claims upon shared resources. He stresses that agreements forged through argument and debate are inevitably stronger and more enduring than ties shaped by mere convention or convenience.[12]

The discriminations Sennett brings to an account of contemporary solidarities feature in other major attempts to identify the distinctiveness of the modern public sphere. Bauman, for example, is also interested in the fate of the peculiar mode of interaction in which private individuals seek to build collective interpretations of the significance of their problems and needs. According to him, the modern agora is a context 'where people meet daily to continue their joint efforts of translating back and forth between languages of private concerns and public good'.[13] For both Sennett and Bauman, what appears to be at stake are the procedures through which private concerns can offer themselves as specific interpretations of wider descriptions of the public good and hence as having legitimate claims upon shared resources. Walzer supports this general account of the distinctiveness of the modern public sphere. He makes the point that in contemporary multicultural America the associational life of collective private interests is actually quite strong.[14] An evolving multiculturalism has seen newly confident ethnic and cultural groupings voicing their distinctive needs and identity claims. What remain undeveloped, though, are the cultural expectations and democratic institutional arrangements that allow these localized problem–descriptions to explore and to test out their wider significance and to justify the legitimacy of their claims upon shared resources. A living, institutionally embedded, public culture needs to be secured in contemporary multicultural America.[15]

Anthony Giddens claims that the revival of social democracy is central to the political vision of the 'Third Way'.[16] He insists that the fostering of an active civil society is essential to a new politics that seeks an alternative to an Old Left that is 'dismissive of worries about civic decline'[17] and to the economic rationalist agendas of conservative governments. Theorists of Third-Way politics embrace a particular construction of the principle of civic activism as a social good. For Mark Latham, the new politics turns to the collective as a support to private initiatives committed to the self-managing of problems. According to him, the Third Way is a policy framework designed to 'support the work of social entrepreneurs: innovative projects that create new social and economic partnerships in disadvantaged neighbourhoods'.[18] Norman Birnbaum criticizes this aspect of Third Way politics. According to him, the Third Way wants the production of social bonds to appear as the moral responsibility of governments.[19] Government is to merely foster the self-managing of problems whose presumed local character remains uninterrogated. The specificity of the public as a mode of interaction that explores the systemic, generalized significance of specific needs and concerns is thereby missed.

Walzer makes the point that the apparently closed and tight bonds of particular local associations can provide the support and focus through which isolated individuals practice attitudes of civic engagement and learn to recognize the interdependence of their needs with claims raised by others. He goes on to suggest that, as long as they do not remain tied to a defensive construction of a supposedly homogeneous 'we', the solidarities of particular bonds can help sustain the complex double-sided motivations that nourish a vital democratic way of life. On the one hand, these bonds can promote the necessary confidence and self-consciousness of a particular point of view that is then able to take its self-interpretations into wider forums in which it can seek to describe their reasonableness and justice. At the same time, these local bonds can serve to reproduce and to extend the recognition of the mutually dependent character of private individuality that is also essential in building a modern public.

This constitution of a collective brought together by the mutual recognition of private individuals of their shared needs and by their search for generalized solutions contrasts with the description of inter-connectedness that binds the contemporary teams of the new capitalist workplace. These are collectives organized around the pragmatic effectiveness of pooling the resources of private actors who are left in no doubt that their concerns, problems, and futures are finally their own singular responsibility. The self-awareness of mutual dependence that is, for Dewey and others, essential to the formation of a modern public does not enter into a zero sum game with a commitment to the ideal of the unique, unrepeatable personality. Again, the peculiarity of the mode of interaction that forms the public sphere is decisive. The hermeneutic effort that is required to make the generalized significance of his needs and aspirations understood by strangers faces each participant in discourse with the task of expanding his own *self*-understanding. Each party in the interchange needs to reflect on the shared value commitments that can make its points of view and claims intelligible to the other.

The distinctive interactive and consensus-building processes of the modern public sphere give shape to how its 'architecture' (the relations of informal civil associations and formal decision-making centres) is seen to be ideally structured.[20] Because it neglects the need and problem-interpreting role of the public sphere, Third Way politics tends to describe one-sidedly the relations between initiating political centres and local associations that are called upon to self-manage already described concerns using their own resources. Dewey's account of the public as a dialogically produced interpretation of the political dimensions and ramifications of problems conceives the architecture of the public sphere differently. With the later Habermas and others, he advocates a decentred model.[21] This is a framework that recognizes the role of local associations, of specific publics, in hammering out descriptions of the shared character of particular unmet needs and dissatisfactions. It is also a model that recognizes the vital and specific contribution of the formal institutions of a political centre to the functioning of the public sphere. This account of the dialectics of issue-interpreting and problem-solving functions performed by a layered public sphere holds that the political centre ideally offers itself as a receptacle to, and as a testing ground for, descriptions of the generalized significance of need descriptions that are brought to it. This formal public must, Dewey and Habermas insist, constantly endeavour to justify the expectations of legitimate decision-making that the informal publics invest in it.

Perhaps we can get a clearer sense of what is at stake in the feared loss of a public sphere by turning to Alexis de Tocqueville's penetrating observations about the significant differences between types of modern artificial solidarities. As an aristocratic stranger visiting the evolving democracy of nineteenth-century America, Tocqueville was struck by the egalitarian and individualist interpretation of human freedom that was taking shape in the New World. This principle of privatism could, he noted, promote a longing for an exclusive type of solidarity. Tocqueville warned that the desire to protect narrowly conceived private interests could see the new society structured around the contestation between defensive coteries. He feared that this way of reacting to the vulnerability and powerlessness of independent private individuals might see the return of the use of associations as 'weapons' designed to secure advantage that had characterized a hierarchical aristocratic world.[22] Tocqueville insisted that a modern universalizing construction of liberty need not be encountered as the task of autonomous, isolated, and impotent individuals. Human freedom can be interpreted through a double allegiance to individuality and to egalitarianism as a mode of interaction in which self-directed private individuals seek to collectively build ways of life that reflect their considered priorities and agendas. For Tocqueville, a modern public draws upon egalitarian and individualistic commitments to produce a distinctive form of solidarity in which '[n]o one abjures the exercise of his reason and free will, but everyone exerts that reason and will to promote a common understanding'.[23]

Tocqueville saw that the prospects for egalitarian liberty would depend on whether modern populations could grasp the opportunities for forging types of interaction in which a liberal insistence on private right could cease to function as a dogmatic principle of self-assertion. Instead, individual needs and identity claims could seek to elaborate interpretations of their shared significances to build common cause. Considered in this light, it seems that the public sphere inhabits an ideological terrain responsive to main hopes and problems opened up by classical liberalism while representing a learnt reworking of these commitments. Specifically, the modern public sphere upholds a mode of interaction that seeks mediation between the liberal principle of private right and the republican ideal of a common good. This, Tocqueville hoped, would be a new kind of sociality in which practices of dialogue and debate allowed insights into apparently settled descriptions of particular aspirations and convictions, thereby loosening the burden of imposed traditional frameworks. It would also be a new kind of negotiated inter-subjectivity that would encourage the increased capacity for self-reflection embraced by the open and expanded personalities of the modern world.

Tocqueville's great fear was that the opportunity to build such participatory solidarities would be missed. He was deeply troubled by the prospect that self-absorbed and atomized individuals would enter into only calculating and instrumentalizing relations with each other. Relinquishing an active interest in securing the chosen character of their entwined futures, modern individuals might well find the conditions of their lives completely externally determined by centralized state power. This eventuality would have to be counted as a terrible loss of opportunities, as a waste of the potential to build democratic solidarities that would defend and expand the meaning of liberty in an egalitarian and pluralistic age.

For us, it might seem that the hopes that inspired Tocqueville's grim warnings have been all but crushed by the success of a neo-liberal project aimed at establishing the norms of market rationality as governing realities for the whole of contemporary social life. This is a conception of rationality that refers to the motivations of a self that is attributed with only a calculating disposition and with the desire to maximize its own desires and basket of needs. To its critics, this neo-liberal project aims at a world in which the main aspects of Tocqueville's nightmare prognosis of a life turned in on itself is lived by individuals who have been robbed of all insight into the costs involved.

The market as the new imaginary

The invasion of market values into domains of social and political life formerly governed by other types of priorities and expectations is no novelty in the histories of capitalist societies, yet many think that there is something qualitatively new afoot. Described as a dream of the 'market without edges', neo-liberalism is not, Thomas Lemke points out, to be construed as mere ideological rhetoric. As a 'political project that endeavours to create a social reality that it suggests already exists', it goes further.[24] Drawing on Michel Foucault's later writings, Lemke suggests that neo-liberalism rationalizes the overturning of two main features of classical liberalism. In the first place, it inverts a liberal model of the relationship between the state and the economy.[25] According to the neo-liberals, a powerful state does not define and monitor market freedom for 'the market itself is the organizing and regulative principle underlying the state'.[26] The second difference is that neo-liberalism refers itself to an organizing principle quite distinct from the point of reference that underpins the political framework of classical liberalism. The touchstone for the neo-liberal project of encoding the social domain as a form of the economic is *homo oeconomicus*: the economic individual who rationally calculates costs and benefits. Rather than locating itself in the ideal of natural freedom that we should all respect, 'it posits an artificially arranged liberty in the entrepreneurial and competitive behaviour of economic-rational individuals'.[27] Under the auspices of the practically 'uncontested hegemony'[28] of the neo-liberal project, market values insinuate themselves as the only terms in which we can justify our actions and rationalize our undertakings.

Long ago Marx described commodification processes as an obstacle to our capacity to recognize and to fully participate in the realization of the accumulated richness and diversity of humanity's historically produced and specific achievements. The critics of neo-liberalism fear that our ability to recognize commodification *as* a colonization process might succumb to the very effectiveness with which this process is now being prosecuted. The motivations of *homo oeconomicus* are now presupposed as the aspirations that guide the purposes and philosophies of a wide spectrum of our major social and cultural institutions. Critics of neo-liberalism suggest that commodifying imperatives are increasingly taking over from the idea of 'civic mission' that underpinned the provision of public goods such as education and health.[29] As part of this process of general commodification, the specific achievements and values to be colonized become re-described in terms of their advantage to prospective buyers. The customer too is primed up, made aware of new needs and previously unrecognized deficiencies. Bauman and others suggest that there is today no cultural good whose worth is not available to re-description in terms of the entrepreneurial/competitive motivations that offer the point of reference for economic rational conduct.[30]

Insinuating itself as a mere codification of an already existing social reality, neo-liberalism does not rely on a theoretically elaborated account of the advantages of the hegemony of market logics. Its naturalization of market rationality as an all-encompassing way of life attempts to re-appropriate competing expectations and values. The commitments of old liberalism to the ideals of self-advancement and self-development are taken out of the per-plexing realm of private interpretation and pursuit and repackaged as luxury items on sale to cashed-up consumers. 'Life politics', with its promise of a life lived well so long as it is mapped by 'self-help' recipes, reworks the old liberal ideals of the self-fashioned personality into terms consistent with the primacy of market rationality.

The new capitalism has been singularly effective in not appearing to rule out anything of value. Sennett, we saw, draws particular attention to the capacities of the modernized workplace to articulate the ideal of teamwork into its operations. Here, a commitment to the formation of rational/democratic solidarities is converted into the ideal of the self-managed unit. This turns out to be a strategy for forcing the group to negotiate its individual way out of troubles whose systemic character is simply denied. This colonization of rival value descriptions is again evident in the conversion of an ideal of hardy self-determining individuality into terms sympathetic to the ambitions and purposes of the market. The systemic production of a 'pseudo-individuality' by a consumer culture that appreciates and rewards those able to 'talk the talk' and 'walk the walk' of the self motivated, innovative 'type' has become thematic in what Bauman has described as the individualized society.

Faced with the naturalizing ideologies through which a neo-liberal project asserts itself, a critical sociology positions itself as ideology-critique. Bauman, Habermas, Touraine, and others want to expose the 'lie' at the heart of neo-liberalism's totalitarian ambition. The lie is that the universalization of market norms denies us nothing important. Moreover, neo-liberalism must not be allowed to get away with insisting that whatever lies outside the province of its 'realistic' description of our potentials was never really achievable in the first place. Bauman aptly describes the self-appointed mission of critical sociology as the attempt 'to enlarge and keep the width of that part of the human world which is subject to incessant discursive scrutiny and so keep it saved from the "no-choice" condition'.[31] This requires, in the first instance, a scrutiny of the ways in which our capacity to recognize choices can be systematically blocked by a project that offers itself as a representation of already achieved social realities.

Bauman believes that the success of market values in providing the horizons through which we interpret our world and its prospects turns on the ability of neo-liberalism to persuade us to live with the tensions of a deep structural and experiential paradox. He stresses that there is no real gain for the principle of robust self-determining individuality in the 'individualized society'. This is a society divided into 'winners' and 'losers' who are held singly responsible for their destiny. Yet this is also a world that makes no secret of its fateful, externally determined character. 'Winners' must remain on alert, aware that no safety-net will be extended should they stumble, while 'losers' too need to equip themselves to respond to the unpredictable demands of chancy circumstance. In the 'game of life we all play' choice is reduced to a description of the necessary gamble involved in each move in a game in which the 'dice may be loaded' and the 'odds are being piled against the players'.[32]

How can our consent to go on playing this game be accounted for? Bauman is clear that 'no brainwashing' is required.[33] All that is needed is a diffuse but ubiquitous world-interpretation able to persuade us that we have no alternative. This conviction is partly carried by the moral imperative of 'self-reliant individuality'. Each individual is to become an entrepreneur managing his own capital. Ruled out by this imperative is that recognition of the mutual dependencies of vulnerable private individuals that Dewey considered vital to the formation of a modern public. Encountered as the private trials of 'failing' individuals, problems in the individualized society cease to be described as shared concerns amenable to political, rather than merely technical or administrative, solutions. Obstructed also is that self-consciousness of private individuality as the site of particular perspectives, points of view and need interpretations which forms the basis of the argumentatively constructed 'we' described by Sennett. The other side of the paradoxical self-responsibility of the entrapped individual is the diminishing capacity for an individuated will on the part of solitary personalities who fear their survival depends on a slavish adherence to ascribed rules of the game. It seems that only the degraded, superficial solidarities of the team and the defensive construction of private groupings are available to the diminished energies and fearful psychologies of isolated individuals.

What is taking place here is, of course, no mere failure of nerve on the part of individuals who increasingly feel unable to raise reasonable claims on behalf of an individuated point of view. A conformist spirit that blocks the formation of argumentatively achieved understandings reproduces itself via the compelling character and reach of engineered solidarities imposed by centres of corporate power. Nowhere is this process more clearly demonstrated than in the workings of the contemporary mass media. Noam Chomsky has recently commented that the media techniques he referred to in the late 1980s as producing the 'manufactured consent' of populations to poorly understood agendas of corporate centres are still very evident.[34] The old Frankfurt School critique of the anti-democratic character of the publicity functions appropriated by a corporatized media remains relevant. Max Horkheimer and Theodor Adorno predicted that media as big business would inevitably construct its audience not as a collectivity of private individuals capable of rational argument and debate but as a mass of isolated and passive consumers of pre-packaged messages aimed at the reproduction of relations of power. Removed from its service to the elaboration of transparent 'truths', 'publicity', Habermas insists, is appropriated by private interests determined to 'sell' themselves to compliant consumers.

Squeezed on the one side by conformist solidarities engineered by instruments of corporate power, the democratic opinion and will forming processes of the public sphere are threatened on the other by the mobilizing capacities of fundamentalist convictions. Fundamentalism suggests a closed system of beliefs that seeks to offer 'fundaments in a modern world where there are none'.[35] Hostile to the requirements of accountability demanded by a modern public sphere, fundamentalism reacts against the rationalizing expectations of Enlightenment.[36] This revival of a forceful fundamentalist attack on the deliberative processes and consensus-building aspirations of democratic decision-making takes secular as well as religious forms. Critics of recent US foreign policy have noted the irony of corporate interests that seek to trademark 'democracy' as a creed useful as sanction for their global interventions while at the same time undermining the institutional frameworks of democratic consultation and rational debate in international politics and undercutting conditions vital to the preservation of civil liberties within democratic nation states.[37]

Habermas has commented that, in the present context, the project of building a vital public sphere might well have 'the ring of an empty formula'.[38] If, as critics of neo-liberalism fear, the framework of market rationality has insinuated itself as the new reality of our times, it could seem that the sociologist who holds faith with the democratic ambitions of the public sphere is a mere dreamer. Yet something needs to be said about the distinct ways that the realism of an attempt to defend the normativity of the modern public sphere might be assessed.

Michael Hardt is amongst those who insist that the realities of the neo-liberal epoch have undermined the viability and the effectiveness of any attempt to rescue the public sphere.[39] He suggests that these imperatives have subverted the preconditions of an active civil society empowered to influence the agendas of sovereign authority in democratic nation states. A post-liberal 'society of control' has seen the drying up of the motivational sources that had fuelled the normativity of a modern public sphere.[40] The normative core of a modern public, with its hopes for a life lived freely in accordance with chosen commitments made rational and accountable by processes of discussion and debate, is negated in a society dedicated to the production of 'self-disciplining subjects' who encounter the expectation of autonomous individuality only as the burden of an unsupported self-responsibility. Others insist that we can be sober about the practical chances for successfully pressing the claims of a public sphere in a society increasingly governed by market rationality while maintaining that its normativity is not yet extinguished. Despite everything, we are still able to recognize the public as a vital cultural ideal, everywhere on the defensive but crucial nevertheless. It seems that for Bauman, Sennett,

Walzer, and Stephen Bronner[41] the over-determined and ambiguous achievements of liberal democratic histories have not been overrun to the extent that the 'society of control' thesis suggests. If we are not yet entirely blind to the paradox described in Bauman's account of the individualized society, it is because we still have some residual hope that the ideal of the self-directed, autonomous life might mean more than simply a skilful handling of the cards dealt to us.

Walter Benjamin once commented that 'the fact that "everything just keeps on going" is the catastrophe'.[42] A seemingly realistic accommodation to the flow of events can indicate compliance in the suppression of things we value and the blocking of yet unrealized potentials. Habermas insists that a determination to rescue valued and still latent liberal democratic cultural potentials does not involve a backward-looking nostalgia. It suggests only a selective and critical appropriation of endangered legacies as the basis from which we can build desired futures. He would agree with Bauman's suggestion that the task of the sociologist is to promote the critical scrutiny of an ambiguous world and so keep it saved from the 'no-choice' condition.[43] For both, this involves bringing home the claims that the unrealized promises of the modern public sphere continue to make upon us.

Rescuing the public sphere

Although the public sphere encompasses a certain ensemble of informal/formal structures and institutions, neither Bauman nor Habermas reduce the project of rescuing it to a defence of particular concrete, political, or social forms within liberal democracies.[44] The idealized expectations of the public (that private individuals can arrive at rational consensus about the justice of claims upon shared resources) have underpinned, but cannot be reduced to, many of the practical achievements and institutionalized arrangements of modern democratic cultures. They have made possible: the constitutional and the welfare states, civil action directed at institutional reform, and the humanizing sociality of multicultural societies that seek both the expansion of understanding between, and the increased self-understanding of, private individuals. By placing itself as interpreter to the normativity of the public sphere, a critical sociology is positioned to interrogate the sometimes limited and distorted character of concrete attempts to realize the potentials of this ongoing cultural resource.

The idealizing expectations of the modern public sphere have left deep marks upon us. Its norms are embedded in the institutions and in the complex cultural histories of democratic societies. Habermas has emphasized their historically conditioned and institutionally located character. According to him, the expectation that private individuals could argumentatively construct the terms of mutual understandings made its first significant appearance in the cultural landscapes carved out by a European bourgeoisie. Open to a new sense of the multiplicity of concrete personalities and committed also to building solidarities able to contest the authority of traditional ties, the ambitions of an aspiring bourgeoisie first entrenched themselves in a range of cultural institutions in: the German *Tischgesellschaften*, the English coffee houses, and the French salons. In these cultural associations Habermas identified a set of expectations for dealing with the claims of others that would later forge a presence in the political institutions of liberal democracies. This was a mode of interaction in which participants undertook to conduct themselves without regard for social status, believing that the authority of the better argument should be allowed to prevail. A commitment to the principle of publicity advocated the opening up to free discussion and critique, values upheld by all manner of cultural beliefs. Finally, this newly emerging 'public' insisted on a principle of openness and inclusion. Ideally, all were permitted to participate in interactions in which the only restriction was a willingness and a capacity to submit to the norms of argumentative discourse.

Today significant, if dispersed, voices calling for the defense and rejuvenation of a modern public sphere are making themselves heard within a lively debate over the core commitments of contemporary critical theory. No unified project is taking shape here but there are signs of a trend. Not so long ago, a more comprehensive critique of the cultural legacies of democratic Enlightenment, fashioned in particular by Foucault, seemed to set the framework for a critical diagnosis of the present. This was a perspective that discovered an undifferentiated repressive logic within the histories of bourgeois modernities. From a contemporary point of view, the ground appears to have shifted. In the space of a few decades, the institutions of the welfare state that were targeted by this critique as the key instrumentalities of modern power, have been all but dismantled. In the context of an increasingly globalized social order whose supposed 'self-evident' necessities are being represented through neo-liberal frameworks, we have seen major figures in English-language sociology insisting on the need to critically appropriate endangered liberal democratic potentials. This is an interpretation of the task of contemporary critical sociology that refuses to collude with the mandated realism of neo-liberal ideologies and rejects Hardt's claim that 'under present conditions' any invocation of the normativity of democratic processes can 'only remain empty and ineffectual'.[45]

In this context it seems useful to look in a systematic fashion at what Habermas has been saying for the last four decades about the meaning of the public sphere, its ongoing importance and relevance, and the challenges facing its defense. This vast *oeuvre* has investigated the historical preconditions of the public sphere, has explored its transcendental preconditions, has diagnosed its crises, and has sought from a multiplicity of angles to remind us of its ongoing claims. An English-speaking audience, now attending with new interest to the highly contested question of the contemporary relevance and significance of liberal democratic achievements and potentials has, I suggest, much to learn from Habermas' lifetime of work on this topic.

While only one of Habermas' major texts includes the 'public sphere' in its title, the task of interpreting and defending the idealizing expectations embedded in the institutional arrangements of bourgeois modernity has never been far from his central purposes. For Habermas, the critical theorist must battle against ideologies that block our appreciation of the ambiguous potentials of modernization processes. This is no mere contemplative, theoretical, interest. A conception of an engaged critical theory has been reflected in a life that, together with its enormous scholarly endeavours, has found time for the responsibilities of the public intellectual. Habermas has always offered himself as a critic in the public sphere.[46] His determination to seize opportunities for entering into public discussion about the choices available to the present was evident in his student days. Habermas was an active participant in a post-war German student movement that saw the goal of a democratized University as a preliminary to a programme of major reform in the institutionalized priorities of German society.[47] Since those distant days, Habermas has made his views known on many controversial topics, from a lively interchange with leftist student radicals in the late 1960s, to a critique of right wing 'distortions' about the recent fascist German past in the 'historians dispute' of the 1980s, and most recently engagements with the aspirations of current American foreign policy. A willingness to engage with the particular issues thrown up by contemporary politics is, for Habermas, a central responsibility of the critical theorist. He repudiates the suggestion that any general theory is 'supposed to be able to solve all of life's problems' and stresses that the theorist needs to be able to 'visit [already] "disassembled" problems that have their place in very different contexts'.[48] In recent years, Habermas' important contributions to ongoing discussions about German unification, over the future of European political solidarities, on the problems of asylum seekers, multiculturalism, and on the Gulf and the Iraqi Wars have been quickly translated into English.

There is a recognizable Habermasian stamp to these interventions. He consistently reviews what is happening in a traumatic present in the light of its impact upon not yet fully realized, and irreplaceable, cultural capacities and political potentials. His 1993 public address on the politics of asylum for European refugees stressed that a radical Right Wing response threatened the fragile civility achieved in post-war Germany.[49] His more recent 'Interpreting the Fall of a Monument' considers the contemporary turn of American foreign policy to pre-emption from the standpoint of its damaging consequences for a meaningful and effective world public sphere.[50] Where does this heightened awareness of the fragility of civilizing achievements come from and what fuels Habermas' unflagging determination to remind us of their vulnerability? His response as a young teenager to the disclosure of the horrors of Nazi Germany gives a clue:

I sat before the radio and experienced what was being discussed before the Nuremberg Tribunal; when others, instead of being struck silent by the ghastliness, began to dispute the justice of the trial, procedural questions, and questions of jurisdiction, there was that first rupture, which still gapes. Certainly it is only because I was still sensitive and easily offended that I did not close myself to the fact of a collectively realized inhumanity in the same measure as the majority of my elders.[51]

What also comes through in every piece is the conviction that we might yet be able to win a 'second chance'. To earn this we must use our experience of the catastrophes we have lived through to learn to recognize what is valuable to us and what is required if we are to avoid a continuum of disasters. Learning processes must be guided by an ongoing critical appropriation of those traditions and legacies best able to protect and carry chosen potentials forward. The terms of Habermas' current intervention into debates over the political future of Europe and International relations illustrate the hopes he invests in our capacity to learn from catastrophe and to reshape the future. He argues that arresting the disastrous history of nationalism in European states requires the formation of trans-national political centres that seek to re-appropriate democratic political traditions fostered within the nation states and to replace the unifying function performed by *volkish* mythologies by a programme of democratic welfare reforms with an internationalist scope.[52]

Habermas' interest in the past is, as already mentioned, far from nostalgic. He thinks that we need to be discriminating about the ambiguous significance of modern achievements and it is here that he departs most strikingly from what he regards as the one-sided pessimism of Adorno, his early mentor. For Habermas, we have choices because our history is not shaped by any single imperative. Modernization has been an ambiguous journey and the authors of the *Dialectic of Enlightenment* offered us insight into only one of its trajectories. Adorno and Horkheimer suggested that the historical Enlightenment's vision of a humanity able to steer its future by converting capricious nature and unruly history to its own controlling purposes had turned from a hope for human freedom into the nightmare of an unleashed will bent on domination. Habermas does not, on the one hand, dispute the Frankfurt School's portrait of the barbarous consequences of a world in which a capacity for rational control has become identified with the determination to regulate, order, and subdue all interference to a governing instrumental will. However, he insists that an Enlightenment commitment to rationally controlled futures also needs to be appreciated as a commitment to opening our guiding purposes to processes of reflection and deliberation. A self-directed future means not just the effective pursuit of illusions of total control but also a future that is guided by an inter-subjective will that has formed itself through processes of critical scrutiny, deliberation, and negotiated consensus-building. This, for Habermas, is the central insight of the tradition of democratic Enlightenment that is also our legacy. Stressing the ambiguities of an Enlightenment heritage, Habermas reminds us that, even if instrumentalizing imperatives have been appropriated by the mighty alliance between the market and administrative power, we can still choose to rescue and reconstruct the neglected potential of democratic Enlightenment.

Accused sometimes of writing in a dry and technical style, Habermas does not think it is his place to attempt to produce the energies needed to seize the opportunities that critical theory clarifies for us. All that theory can do is to try and bring before us, in a systematically elaborated form, commitments that we have made to ourselves and to our futures. Over the years, Habermas has attempted to reconstruct from many angles the claims that the public sphere makes upon us as our own neglected potentials. We have unleashed these expectations and should not surrender them without a struggle.

A critical theory for our times?

Amongst the various lines of critique that swirl around Habermas' social and political writings, one major theme is taking shape within the recent English-language literature. While the seminal status of his work is generally conceded, Habermas is often seen to be too conservative, too interested in saving the severely compromised institutional achievements of liberal democracies, and too willing to let limited expectations legitimated by liberal ideologies supply the ideal of emancipation that underpins his critical theory.[53] There are some differences in the way that the critique is set up. Omid Payrow Shabani thinks that Habermas' critical impulses have been eroded in later writings that make 'too many concessions to the "real-existing" political order of liberal–democratic states'.[54] Martin Morris, to take a different example, suggests that Habermas' dedication to reinvigorating democratic Enlightenment upholds a complacent politics based on consensus, accommodation, and reconciliation.[55] Martin Matustik is dismayed at those aspects of Habermas' thinking that seem to betray the commitments of a 'safe democratic reformist',[56] while Joel Whitebook is suspicious of the 'new sobriety' that supposedly characterizes Habermas' reformulation of critical theory.[57]

What brings the critics together is the suggestion that Habermas is too little the utopian to be able to sustain a critical theory project. The contents of the ideal of emancipation that informs his critical intentions are seen to be absorbed either from a normalizing Enlightenment commitment to reasoned consensus that ultimately betrays the claims of unreconciled difference, or from legitimating liberal ideologies that sanction existing institutional structures. Against perceptions of his anti-utopianism, this book will attempt to show that Habermas' critical theory anchors itself not only in achieved normative and constitutional demands, but also in an interpretation of unmet cultural needs whose satisfaction requires a radical reconstruction of the priorities, arrangements, and imperatives that today govern really existing liberal democracies.

Habermas can be referred to as a modern utopian in the sense set out in his major essay from the mid-1980s titled 'The New Obscurity: The Crisis of the Welfare State and the Exhaustion of Utopian Energies'.[58] For us moderns, he says, 'utopian thought fuses with historical thought'. In our times, utopian energies suggest a practical critique of present social and political arrangements that is anchored in an interpretation of 'alternative life possibilities that are seen as inherent in the historical process itself'.[59] There are, Habermas tells us, clear 'remnants of utopianism' in a project that, mindful of the collapse of totalizing socialist ambitions, dedicates itself to the democratization and extension of the welfare project. This is an undertaking that wants to know 'how much strain can the economic system be made to take in directions that might benefit social needs, to which the logic of corporate investment is indifferent'.[60] Habermas stresses that a commitment to democratizing the welfare project suggests an interpretation of the unrealized normativity of a public sphere whose achievement would require a far-reaching reorganization of the normal business of liberal democratic societies. Welfare programmes would need to be constituted as means to the realization of a plurality of ends set by the democratic problem interpretations of active citizens who are confident that the structures and arrangements of a decentred public sphere can permit recognition of the generalized significance of their particular claims. Habermas has recently stressed that a utopian attempt to rescue the democratic potentials of modernity's ambiguous rationalizing legacies also calls for a radical reconstruction of transnational relations in a globalizing era. Amongst other things, this is an ambition that would require the transnationalization of democratized welfare policies.

Critics tend to overlook the real critical power Habermas teases out of the ambiguous idealizations and the structural potentials of liberal democratic societies. However they do have an important point to make. The complaint that Habermas has himself described the alternative life possibilities thwarted by contemporary realities in terms that are too narrow and one-sided seems justified. His attempt to revive the ambitions of democratic Enlightenment represents a response to only one type of unmet cultural need for autonomy that has been unleashed by modernization processes. The irreducible significance of other, particularly Romantic, interpretations of the frustrated hopes and longings of modern individuals needs to be brought into view by a critical theory sensitive to the complexity of our radical motivations. As Habermas' various post-modern critics have stressed, a Romantic interest in the free self-expression of unreconciled particularity finds intolerable, and cannot be willingly recruited to, the rationalizing demands of democratic Enlightenment.

The accusation that Habermas fails to appreciate the inassimilable distinctiveness of Romantic longings seems to be right. It is, however, a mark of their own totalizing conception of the type of radical needs able to support critical theory that recent critics typically represent Habermas as an anti, rather than one-sided, utopian thinker. They have tended to judge the value commitments that underpin his theory from the point of view of standards borrowed from a distinctive and limited way of thinking about the alternative life possibilities loosened by modernization processes. This book will put forward a critical theory framework that seeks dialogue and mutual recognition between these two different kinds of emancipatory interests.

The one-sidedness of Habermas' conception of the value commitments that anchor a contemporary critical theory appears to be the outcome of an important tension in his conception of the purposes and tasks of critique. He considers it necessary and possible to seek universal justification for the values that underpin critical theory while at the same time representing the theory as a clarification of unmet cultural needs that seek articulation as concrete demands. I will argue that the undertaking to provide universal justification for the commitments upheld by the theory, the attempt to provide philosophical support to its rationality claims, needs to be clawed back to reveal the critical and evocative power of Habermas' efforts to defend a particular set of cultural potentials bequeathed by the ambiguous legacies of European Enlightenment.

2 The structural transformation of the public sphere

Habermas begins his search for the public sphere with the German publication of *The Structural Transformation of the Public Sphere: An Inquiry into a Category of Bourgeois Society (The Structural Transformation)* in 1962. This had its origins as a *Habilitationschrift*[1] that Habermas had intended to submit to Max Horkheimer and Theodor Adorno at Frankfurt. However, Horkheimer, who disliked its general drift, blocked the process and it was finally successfully submitted to Wolfgang Abendroth at Marburg. At one level, it might seem a bit surprising that Horkheimer felt so at odds with the general tenor of the book. As Habermas was to later remark, the standpoint adopted in the last chapters suggested a diagnosis of the chances for a democratic future for the West that bore all the marks of Horkheimer and Adorno's own bleak view of modernizing trajectories.

Experiencing first-hand the atrocities of totalitarianism and viewing with despair developments in bureaucratic capitalism, Horkheimer and Adorno had come up with a deeply pessimistic analysis of a world governed by systematic alliances between economic and political power that used a corporatized culture to manufacture a compliant public. Cohering in the aftermath of the Second World War, the thesis of a fully administered society saw frightening structural similarities between fascist Europe, Stalinist Russia and, Roosevelt's America: all were regimes that had delivered a potent mix of economic, political, and cultural power into the hands of ruling elites. In the end, Habermas' early work seemed to endorse the essentials of this grim sociology. The young Habermas finally reaffirmed that the world of monopoly capitalism had seen the effective triumph of 'staged and manipulative' publicity that worked in favour of combined corporate interests.[2]

Yet, Horkheimer was by no means wrong to discern a real parting of the ways. The agreement that *The Structural Transformation* eventually reached with the sociology of the administered society was actually a registration of the disappointment of the main ambitions driving Habermas' early work. An acutely sensitive member of a generation that has been described as a 'second degree witness to the Holocaust',[3] Habermas' moral personality has been shaped by the conviction that we need to learn from disaster. Determined to place critical theory at the service of this learning process, he was early preoccupied by the question of how liberal democratic principles could be rescued and radicalized in Germany after the era of fascism. What attracted Habermas to the idea of the public sphere was its potential as a foundation for a society based on democratic principles. He wanted to consider the possibility that contemporary welfare state societies could reform themselves in line with a critical re-appropriation of the concept of a democratic public that had emerged in the classical phase of the development of bourgeois societies. The rediscovery in the last chapters of the seeming truth of Adorno's account of an 'unholy alliance' between administrative state power and monopoly capital appeared to signal the frustration of this quest. Only later, after the experience of the New Left and the counter-culture of the late 1960s, would Habermas forge a sociology that registered fully the tensions within welfare state societies that might be exploited to engineer their democratic self-reform. Subsequently he would develop the explicit critique of the one-sided interpretation of modernization processes embraced by Adorno and Horkheimer. Yet the basis for the coming decisive break was already very apparent in the project undertaken by the *Habilitationschrift*.

The Structural Transformation describes the transformation and virtual destruction throughout the nineteenth and twentieth centuries of the ideals of a rational public sphere that grew out of eighteenth-century bourgeois cultural institutions in Britain, France, and Germany. As Adorno's assistant throughout the 1950s, Habermas sympathized with the diagnosis of the paradoxical character of modernization processes in which technical rational progress turned out to deliver unfreedom and domination.[4] However, as yet unsystematized, misgivings about the unrelieved character of the narrative of the distorted realization of reason in history structure his enquiry into the legacies of the bourgeois public sphere. Habermas thinks that chances may well have been missed and wants to know if in a post-liberal era democracy is still possible. He frames this as a question about the possibilities for effectively reconstituting the ideal of a reasoning public that had been the achievement of eighteenth-century Europe under radically different socio-economic, political, and cultural conditions.

Described as 'one of the most influential books for the incipient opposi-tional movement at German Universities',[5] the significance of Habermas' more hopeful diagnosis of ambiguous modernizing potentials and his search for capacities in the present able to promote a radical self-reform of society was not lost on a generation of West German radicals. No longer wholly identified with an instrumentalizing intent, enlightenment reason, for *The Structural Transformation*, appears also as a commitment to reflection and to public deliberation over chosen ends. Here again the emancipatory hopes borne by reason are seen to fall victim to modernizing pathologies. Yet Habermas looks upon this wounding trajectory not simply as the necessary outcome of deeply paradoxical tendencies within rationalizing ambitions themselves but as a specific product of sociological circumstances that have permitted the over-bearing domination of an instrumentalizing reason.

Accordingly, Habermas begins a search for countervailing conditions and tendencies within the present, a quest that pushes up against the limits of the sociological framework he had inherited. At odds also with the totalized frameworks of his old mentors, Habermas' book bravely insists that for us 'the past is not closed'. It is not closed because modernization has followed ambiguous trajectories and we have something to learn from a diagnosis of the frayed hopes for a critical public. The dialectic of Enlightenment is to be interpreted not simply as a fateful path but as a story of self-misunderstandings, betrayed opportunities, and neglected potentials. This is an account of the histories of Enlightenment that discovers real analytic limits in the borrowed critical theory framework that the early Habermas tries to work within.

The rise of the bourgeois public sphere

The Structural Transformation focuses on the genesis and course of development of bourgeois political life from the mid-seventeenth century through to the mid-twentieth century. In particular, it considers this historical development from the standpoint of the elaboration and the structural transformation of its normative ideals to see what we might learn from this flawed history. Habermas wants to make explicit the meaning of these normative ideals and to reflect upon how they contribute to the essential informal core of a democratic society. This was exceptional territory for a figure emerging from a critical theory tradition schooled in a Marxist disdain for the 'merely' ideological character of bourgeois democratic principles. In opposition to this heritage, Habermas felt confident that the 'rational kernel' of radical expectations that underpinned the self-justifying dimensions of bourgeois democratic ideals might be analytically distinguished and its ongoing normative importance clarified. If the elements of truth and emancipatory potential were to be recovered from the ideological dimensions of the bourgeois ideal of a reasoning public, it was vital that the genesis of this political doctrine in practices of cultural critique and contestation be rediscovered. The central chapter in *The Structural Transformation* on 'The Bourgeois Public Sphere: Idea and Ideology' is preceded by chapters on 'Social Structures of the Public Sphere' and 'Political Functions of the Public Sphere' which attempt to analytically reconstruct the cultural, social, and political sources of the idea of a bourgeois public sphere.

The early chapters explore the social conditions under which a mode of interacting that suggested that private persons could agree about matters of public importance, not simply out of deference to traditional authority, but through the give and take of reasoned discourse, took shape within modern European history. Habermas wants to show that the critical norm upheld and formalized by institutions of bourgeois political democracy gave particular formulation to expectations that had emerged within the complex cultural and social histories of Western modernization. The bourgeois public was a new type of association whose function of preserving and protecting the private individuality of its members required that the principle of privacy should be articulated as a norm that governed their manner of interacting. The socio-cultural conditions for this novel type of solidarity were set up by revolutionary changes in the structures of modern life brought forward by a burgeoning market-based economy.

The major consequences of the progressive emancipation of economic life from the grip of traditional political regulations throughout the eighteenth century are well known. The feudal powers of church, prince, and nobility, which were the carriers of a representative publicness, disintegrated and the bourgeois nation state became the sphere of public power while society emerged as a realm of private interest and activity. Old political ties could no longer effectively regulate an economic life that had been revolutionized by long-distance trade and commercialization. The de-politicization of the economy broke the claims of local regulations that had hitherto determined the process and outcome of commercial transactions, exposing all individuals, in wholly unprecedented fashion, to the unintended consequences of private transactions. The economic activity that had become private had to be oriented toward a commodity market that expanded under public direction and supervision. The economic conditions under which this activity took place lay outside the confines of the single household: 'for the first time they became of general interest'.[6]

With the de-politicization of the economy and the increasing centralization of political power, newly constituted private individuals, 'self-made' men of a rising bourgeoisie, sought each other out, conscious of their evolving, shared autonomy and mindful also of its vulnerability. The emergent self-awareness of the generalizable interests of private individuals was promoted and expressed by the rise of a bourgeois press. The publication of 'news' via journals and newspapers facilitated the consciousness of a novel public made up of private persons able to inform themselves about matters of importance and able to air and share their concerns with distant others. A vibrant urban culture arose in the course of the eighteenth century to offer a new space to the emerging self-consciousness of this new public. City life with its lecture halls, museums, public parks, theatres, meeting houses, coffee shops, and the like formed a spatial environment for a new mode of association between individuals who were not called upon to sacrifice their anonymity. This was a novel form of association in which private individuals entered into an enjoying, exploratory companionship freed from the observance of rigid political ties and from the traditional bonds of status and privilege. Released from these old unities, the new solidarity of private persons had to constitute itself as a public fashioned out of the sharing of information and opinions and tastes, hence as a public dependent on the presses, publishing houses, lending libraries, and literary societies.[7]

This self-conscious, dynamic allegiance saw its *raison d'etre* as a shared appreciation of, and as a fortification for, the private autonomy of the bourgeois householder. This organizing purpose shaped the mode of intercourse characteristic of an evolving public sphere. The norms governing public discussion expressed faith in the possibility of arriving at consensus, not on the basis of the suppression of the private autonomy of its participants, but precisely as a measure of their united commitment to the principle of the private autonomy of each.[8] The classic modern public sphere was anchored in the anxious aspirations of a particular, bourgeois, subjectivity and articulated these preoccupations as the norms by means of which the rationality/reasonableness of points of view raised in public interchanges might be assessed. Habermas' account of the normativity of the bourgeois public sphere attempts to reconstruct and critically weigh up the processes through which the exclusive aspirations of a subjectivity shaped by the concerns of a social class managed to offer themselves as the norms of a mode of interaction distinguished by its open and inclusive character.

The autonomous subjectivity that sought recognition in a bourgeois public had its origins, Habermas tells us, in the new kind of self-conscious association fostered by a domestic life that considered itself emancipated from economic and political bonds. '[B]efore the public sphere explicitly assumed political functions in the tension-charged field of state-society relations, the subjectivity originating in the intimate sphere of the conjugal family created, so to speak, its own public.'[9] The intimate sphere that was demarcated by the self-enclosure of a patriarchal conjugal family yielded a new psychology of the human being as a private subjectivity.[10] Here the private person was constituted as simply a 'human being, that is, [as] a moral person'.[11] The bourgeois family had a double-sided significance in the construction of this new sensibility. On the one hand, it produced a domain of private autonomy that demanded freedom from the domination of external socio-political constraint. In this regard, the 'right to autonomy' of the human being that underpinned the bourgeois household was an ideology that supported and cloaked the class character of the bourgeois demand that entrepreneurial commercial activities be emancipated from all political controls and directives.[12] At the same time, this insisted upon right to autonomy affirmed by the conjugal family also became a living source of a new self whose passionate examination of its complex psychological states craved acknowledgement. This new self appeared to be established spontaneously by free individuals and to be maintained without coercion. Resting on the 'lasting community of love on the part of the two spouses: it seemed to permit that non-instrumental development of all faculties that marks the cultivated personality'.[13]

Despite the self-contradictory character of the *patriarchal* family's self-image as a sphere of 'humanity-generating closeness', this was no mere ideological illusion. Notwithstanding the entrenched hierarchies that structured the independence of this type of family, it also loosened expectations about a particular kind of intersubjectivity based on a loving intimacy. This expectation of a sympathetic reception between self-disclosing personalities was also the typical mode of intercourse for an eighteenth century 'world of letters'.

Here a psychologically emancipated bourgeois self sought to extend a 'community of love' via the exchange of letters as well as in the reading of psychological novels and novellas.[14] These were 'experiments with the subjectivity discovered in the close relationships of the conjugal family'.[15] They helped to push forward the ideal of an expansion of self-insight via exchanges with other selves: '[f]rom the beginning, the psychological interest increased in the dual relation to both one's self and the other: self-observation entered a union partly curious, partly sympathetic with the emotional stirrings of the other I.'[16] Habermas underlines the distinctive interactive character of intercourse in the early bourgeois literary salons. Unlike their earlier aristocratic counterparts, the new salons extended the original principle of intimacy by revealing the subjectivity of each individual in the presence of the other, thus linking privacy to publicity.[17] The heart of salon sociability was conversation, the rules of which were more dialogical and egalitarian than those prevailing in the hierarchical milieu of the court.[18]

The expectation of a patient, willing comprehension of sympathetic fellows and the luxury of an expressive mode of self-presentation that shaped the apolitical literary public sphere could be sustained as long as private individuals only sought to communicate about their subjectivity.[19] As soon as privatized individuals began to communicate in their capacity as property-owners keen to influence public power in their common interest, the discursive norms through which the literary public had shaped the idea of the shared humanity of private persons had to be reconfigured. However, what did not alter for an emergent politicized public was the expectation that private individuals could communicate their particular points of view via a discursive process that would respect their individuality. For Habermas, the functional conversion of the idea of the shared humanity of private persons that had been shaped in the literary public into the norms of a public in the political realm involved the attempted resolution of two essentially conflicting roles that had been assumed by the private individual:

> The fully developed bourgeois public sphere was based on the fictitious identity of the two roles assumed by the privatized individuals who came together to form a public: the role of property owners and the role of human beings pure and simple.[20]

A new polemical purpose began to organize an emergent political public sphere. As it became interested in contesting entrenched powers, the new public of private individuals had to constitute itself as a rival principle of authority. Against the reliance on princely authority on secrets of state and on the untested legitimacy of tradition, it insisted on the promotion of legislation based on accountability, on *ratio*.[21] The distinctive authority of a public of private individuals articulated itself through three related norms.[22] First, reasoned argumentation, not the status or authority of the speaker, was to be the sole arbiter in debate. As a description of a communicative interaction that recognized only the shared autonomy of its participants, the public sphere was in principle disinterested in any appeal to rank and position. Habermas admitted that this was an expectation that was not 'actually realized in earnest in the coffee houses, the *salons*, and the societies'.[23] Second, nothing was to be protected from criticism. Once the reasoned opinions of private individuals were allowed to vie with the authority of church and court as the arbiters of taste and good judgment, areas previously unquestioned became problematized. This profane airing of matters artistic, religious and political points to the essentially critical bent of the bourgeois public sphere. Finally, constituting themselves as a form of association predicated upon a shared interest in the autonomy of private individuals, the norms of the public sphere were intolerant of all cliquish inclinations in which merely private interests might seek to assert their combined weight and influence. The issues discussed 'became "general" not merely in their significance, but also in their accessibility: everyone had to *be able* to participate'.[24]

These novel discursive norms provided the grounds of a new principle of legitimate authority. This was not a mere change away from a secretive arbitrariness in political judgments towards argumentative publicity. It also meant a shifting of a political role from the citizen as an actor in the political realm, to 'the more properly civic tasks of a society engaged in critical debate (i.e., the protection of a commercial economy)'.[25] A public sphere of private citizens first began to assume political functions during the eighteenth century in Great Britain in a drawn-out contestation between state and society.

> Step by step the absolutism of Parliament had to retreat...Expressions like 'the sense of the people' or even 'vulgar' or 'common opinion' were no longer used. The term now was 'public opinion'; it was formed in public discussion after the public, through education and information, had been put in a position to arrive at a considered opinion.[26]

Gradually this respect would tip over into a new interpretation of the sources from which formal political and legal decision-making structures derived their legitimacy. The struggle of the bourgeois for political ascendency demanded that legislative power defer to the authority of informal, collective processes of opinion and will formation of an active civil society. *'Public debate was supposed to transform* voluntas *into a* ratio *that in the public competition of private arguments came into being as the consensus about what was practically necessary in the interest of all.'*[27]

For the eighteenth-century public sphere, the principle of universal access did not yet require the sacrifice of particular points of view to the demands of a generalizable interest that nineteenth-century liberalism was to exact from the disinterested 'citoyen'. Because at this stage of its development the bourgeois public sphere, domain of the 'homme', sustained the assumption of a shared interest, the individuality of its participants was not constituted as the competitiveness of private wills that must be bracketed out by a contrived impartiality. Given a presumption of shared values articulated through the discursive processes of the public sphere itself, private individuals were able to confront each other, not as rivals but as discussants, ready to persuade and open to persuasion. At the same time, the eighteenth-century political public sphere constituted itself as a purposeful domain of activity with a mode of interaction directed by an interest in the defence of private autonomy and by a commitment to the principle of the legitimate consensus that emerged out of argumentative dialogue. In argumentatively articulating a point of view, actors in the political public sphere called for recognition of the rationality and the legitimacy of their claims. Particularity was constituted not as an absolute which endlessly revealed its presence, but as a contingency which, dependent on the maintenance of a specific mode of intercourse, was made to seek to reproduce the norms of a reasonable relationship each time it articulated its claims. The discursive procedures themselves embodied those values of voluntariness, critical enquiry, and self-reflexiveness necessary to the articulation and to the defence of the principle of private autonomy.

The question of normativity

The bourgeoisie sought to justify the rightness of its political ascendency by insisting on the universal character of the normative sources it appealed to. This was a dominance that referred itself to the norms of a mode of interaction that asserted the principle of reciprocity and openness. What seemed so valuable about this mode of interaction was its attempt to draw together a respect for the plurality of private individuals with an interpretation of their shared interests that could supply a criterion against which the reasonableness of their claims might be assessed. It was this project of harmonizing the claims of the idea of the 'common interest' with the affirmation of the principle of plurality that Habermas sought to preserve and to recharge with contemporary significance. However, he first needed to review the ideological terms in which this amalgam had been forged by the early bourgeois public sphere. Once it was admitted that certain mandatory constructions of private autonomy clung to the norms of interaction that underpinned the bourgeois public sphere, the fraudulence of its professed openness could not be ignored. The plausibility of its central commitment to the principle of publicity was at stake for '[a] public sphere from which specific groups would be *eo ipso* excluded was less than merely incomplete; it was not a public sphere at all'.[28]

Throughout the nineteenth and the twentieth centuries the supposed universality of the bourgeois public sphere, its belief in a description of 'shared interests' which drew only on the self-recognition of the 'human being as human being', was decisively challenged by excluded populations. By Marx's time, a class of wage earners had clearly unmasked deep assumptions that contradicted the bourgeois public sphere's own principle of universal accessibility:

> [T]he equation of 'property owners' with 'human beings' was untenable; for their interest in maintaining the sphere of commodity exchange and of social labor as a private sphere was demoted ... to the status of a particular interest that could only prevail by the exercise of power over others.[29]

Once its idea of a universal abstract humanity was exposed to reveal the bourgeois character of the 'homme', belief in a homogeneous public composed of private citizens engaged in rational–critical debate seemed irreparably damaged. A socialist, and later a feminist critique, was able to propose, moreover, that the representation of the conjugal family as the site for the formation of the human being as such freely acting in a bourgeois public masked the deep entwinement of the domestic sphere with specific class and patriarchal interests. Actually, the self-image of an emancipated intimate sphere

> collided even within the consciousness of the bourgeoisie itself with the real functions of the bourgeois family. For naturally the family was not exempted from the constraint to which bourgeois society like all societies before it was subject. It played its precisely defined role in the process of the reproduction of capital ... As an agency of society it served especially the task of that difficult mediation through which, in spite of the illusion of freedom, strict conformity with societally necessary requirements was brought about.[30]

Despite the layers of ideological contamination that infiltrated a bourgeois determination of the public sphere, Habermas insists that an enduring, utopian significance clung to the values articulated through its procedural norms.

> Although the needs of bourgeois society were not exactly kind to the family's self-image as a sphere of humanity-generating closeness, the ideas of freedom, love, and cultivation of the person that grew out of the experiences of the conjugal family's private sphere were surely more than just ideology.[31]

The image of a human subjectivity bent on constant self-reflection, attracted to voluntariness and to a self-development acquired through reciprocal relations, assumed a significance that outran the bounds of the bourgeois family. This excess seeped into the modes of interaction upheld by a critical, reasoning discourse and elaborated itself through the procedural norms of the bourgeois public sphere. Critical theory under Habermas now acquires the task of clarifying the rational kernel of the idea of a critical public.

The substantive contents which had tied the idea of the 'human being as such' to the specific person of the bourgeois property owner and patriarch of the conjugal family needed to be dissolved leaving only such descriptions of the discursive process as might admit universal access.

The supposition of *The Structural Transformation*, which proved to be particularly contentious for Habermas' feminist critics, is that the procedural norms of the bourgeois public sphere can be exempted from any distorted ideological content.[32] As we will see, Habermas emphasizes that the principle of discursive rationality upheld by the early public sphere had lost massive ground, yet he insists that the frailty of its idealizations does not simply expose the irredeemably corrupted character of the normative claims raised by the principle of discursive rationality itself.[33] Rather the decline of the normative power of this idea is to be explained in terms of its vulnerability to the momentous sociological changes that characterized the development of modern capitalist societies. Whether the public sphere can reshape its supporting institutions to accommodate these developments was the un-Adorno like question that confronted the Frankfurt School inspired sociology of the final chapters.

Structural transformation

The bourgeois public sphere constituted itself as a public of private people gathered together to articulate the needs of society with the state. In this way it was considered part of the private realm.[34] The course of the nineteenth and twentieth centuries saw tendencies towards the reintegration of public and private domains resulting in the structural transformation of the public sphere away from the principle of rational–critical debate on the part of private people. This reconstruction, that finally eroded the basis of the conditions that had underpinned the bourgeois public, was made possible by an exploitation of the professed commitments of a bourgeois public itself.

Its governing ideology of universal access saw the public sphere swell with the claims of needy populations whose specific demands would finally unmask the ideological assumptions which, de facto, had organized that experience of a 'common humanity' vital to its functioning.[35] As indicated earlier, Habermas suggests that the growing recognition throughout the nineteenth century that deep class divisions were required by the logic of capitalist economic development exposed the illusory character of the public sphere's professed openness. It had invited all to participate as autonomous subjects on the basis of the assumed generalized capacity of private subjects to satisfy their needs through their own endeavours, an ability that the market actually only distributed to a privileged elite. The unmasking of the ideological character of the idea of the 'justice immanent to commerce', and a consciousness of the structural character of a class-divided society, meant that private autonomy might no longer be assumed as universally available, depending only on the industry and fortune of the specific individual.[36]

In this new context, the public sphere could not presume the private autonomy of self-sufficient participants. It had to learn to cope with the publicity-seeking demands imposed by new claimants persuaded that their needs would never be satisfied by the mechanisms of the market.

The bourgeois public sphere proved vulnerable to new demands placed on its principled commitment to universal access that would expose the ideological character of its formulation. This process brought about a radical transformation of the public sphere, eroding the conditions under which it had constituted itself as a domain of rational–critical debate between private individuals. The 'old basis for a convergence of opinions . . . collapsed'[37] and with this criteria for determining the rationality of deliberations about the common good folded also. The principle of the autonomy of private, self-reliant, subjectivity that had been the criterion turned out to be sustained by an ideological equation between the *homme* and the *bourgeois*. Once disadvantaged populations took up the invitation of universal access, 'private autonomy' ceased to appear as an already achieved attribute and irrupted as a frustrated demand through which unequally placed actors confronted each other. It could, then, no longer serve as the basis for assessing the reasonableness of diverse points of view. A 'public' populated by contesting and unequally resourced interests 'completely lacks the form of communication specific to a public'.[38]

The structural transformation of the public sphere from a site of rational–critical debate into a forum for the publicizing of unmet needs saw mounting pressure for a renegotiation of the terms of the society/state divide that had underpinned the bourgeois public sphere. By about the middle of the nineteenth century,

> it was possible to foresee how, as a consequence of its inherent dialectic, this public sphere would come under the control of groups that, because they lacked control over property and therefore the basis of private autonomy, could have no interest in maintaining [the social reproduction of life] as a private sphere.[39]

Once confidence in the 'justice' supposed immanent to the market had been undermined, a liberal conception of the role of the state as mere 'nightwatchman' for an already constituted private autonomy could no longer be sustained. Its appointed task of securing conditions necessary to the autonomy of private actors required the liberal state to adopt a new interventionist role. The state expanded its activity, adding a whole series of new functions to its old duties. 'Besides the traditional functions of maintaining order . . . it began to assume formative functions as well.'[40] Of a different order to the tasks of providing protection, compensation, and subsidies to economically weaker groups, a post-liberal state assumed the task of influencing and guiding changes in the structure of society.[41] Finally, 'the state also took over the provision of services that hitherto had been left to private hands'.[42] A repoliticized or refeudalized social sphere was formed 'in which state and societal institutions fused into a single functional complex that could no longer be differentiated according to criteria of public and private'.[43]

Paradoxically, given its goal of supporting a troubled liberal project of supplying public protection for private autonomy, an interventionist welfare state eroded the power of those domains of bourgeois life that had been the grounds upon which a self-interpreting private individuality took shape. The family was swept into the self-transformation of bourgeois society. As the family's distinctive role in upbringing and education, protection, care, and guidance lost out to newly empowered public authorities, its importance as a socializing agent was decisively undermined. In turn, a functionally weakened family became incapable of providing frameworks of orientation for strong subjectivities able to 'mix it' in public debate over the character of general interests. Instead the 'quiet bliss of homeyness' of a family turned into a consumer of income and leisure time helped to complete the work of producing dependent psychologies undertaken by the various bureaucratic and administrative agencies of a society increasingly administered by alliances between state and business.

As the state intervened with an ever-expanding agenda into society, it became the friendly host to the most powerful, well-resourced, and effectively advertised private interests. Here we encounter another collapsed axis of the structural differentiation between the private and public domains that had underpinned the bourgeois public sphere. The interpenetration of state and society not only saw the erosion of the conditions that had shaped the private autonomy of the participants of a bourgeois public, the public functions of the state were overwhelmed by the clamouring of powerful private interests. This latter process was signalled by the denigration of the democratic credentials of parliament which became the 'public rostrum' for special interests that required a degree of public credit.[44] The packaging of corporate interests that sought to influence rather than persuade was the conspicuous task of a modern media industry that had both amplified and exploited the transformation of a public sphere from a setting of rational–critical debate into an arena for advertising.[45] Publicity now became the tool of a media machine that constructed its audience, not as private individuals capable of rational argumentation, but as passive consumers of messages which, utilizing strategies of repetition, seduction and disavowal, relied upon and reproduced relations of power.[46]

The structural transformation of the public sphere had already set in by the end of the nineteenth century. The institutional separation between private and public domains, which had underpinned the ideal of a reasoning public made up of private individuals with a seemingly secure sociological basis, had been seriously undermined and would later utterly collapse. Habermas has never been tempted by liberalism's 'realistic' response to these transformations.[47] The liberals conceded that a pluralistic and relativist age had lost the capacity to identify the generalizable interests of private individuals in such a way as to provide a criterion for reasoning in public. To them, tolerance for a difference whose claims, finally inaccessible to argumentative support, might only be dogmatically asserted, was all that remained of the normativity of the modern public sphere.[48] While Habermas also recognizes that the old basis for a convergence of opinion has collapsed, he refuses to break faith with the ideal expressed in the public sphere. He will not concede that liberal pluralism can accommodate a degraded idea of modern democracy guided only by pragmatic agreements forged by driving bargains, negotiating compromises and, 'doing deals'.

A glimmer of hope

Habermas' extended presentation of the decay of the bourgeois public sphere is interrupted by the hopeful purposes that inspire his project. He conceives of the bourgeois public sphere as an ideological anticipatory form that 'transcend[ed] the status quo in utopian fashion'.[49] The challenge is to discover an immanent tendency in modern society toward a re-institutionalization of the public sphere. This would have to be a trend that could resist the processes that have conspired to unseat the hopes of democratic Enlightenment. At this point in his thinking, Habermas considers that this would need to be a tendency that could claw back the bad totalities that had all but obliterated the structural separation between the private and the public that appeared to him as the condition of a modern public sphere.

The Structural Transformation has no bold or systematically elaborated solutions and there is no search in it for an agent able to carry the incomplete project of a public sphere forward. Instead Habermas looks to some ambiguous developments in welfare state societies that might be grasped as opportunities to reconstruct the democratic hopes that had sustained the bourgeois public sphere. He notes two possible scenarios for the future in relation to the displaced democratic ideals of the bourgeois public sphere.[50] Welfare state programmes could either represent an acceleration of the erosion of the principle of the public sphere or they could help to rescue and re-establish this ideal, placing it on footings appropriate to the realities of late twentieth-century societies. We have seen that at this stage he is persuaded that dominant trends suggested that those policies of the welfare state that were supposed to supply the factual conditions for an equal opportunity to exercise negative freedoms paradoxically run the risk of impairing individual freedom. Because welfare state policies tend to reduce private individuals to the consumers of public wealth, they 'make room for a *staged and manipulative* publicity displayed by organizations over the heads of a mediatized public'.[51] The welfare state might prove, namely, an enemy to that principle of private autonomy essential to the reproduction of a vibrant critical public sphere. Yet Habermas is, at the same time, hopeful that the welfare project could be constructed as a support to the structural differentiation of the autonomy of the private individual. If the welfare project could make good its promise to mete out the conditions of economic justice that had eluded the market, the private individual could enter into the public sphere as the bearer of points of view and problem interpretations that invited rational deliberation. The erosion of a normatively loaded idea of the public sphere could be avoided if the welfare state committed to establishing the conditions necessary to the realization of these utopian hopes. Habermas', at this stage, very Arendtian perspective charged the welfare state with the task of ensuring that negotiations concerning the reproduction of life did not become the essential business of the public sphere.[52] The 'not unrealistic' hope of the early 1960s was that the increasing affluence of industrially advanced societies might see the welfare state successfully adopting a redistributive function and in this case 'the continuing and increasing plurality of interests may lose the antagonistic edge of competing needs to the extent that the possibility of mutual satisfaction comes within reach'.[53]

This latter account of the capacities of welfare state programmes to secure the private autonomy deemed necessary for the reproduction of a modern public sphere was to be later significantly reconstructed by Habermas into a systematic analysis of the need for a democratization of the welfare project. This subsequent position would suggest that a modern public sphere needs to reconstitute itself as a site in which the goals of private autonomy and public autonomy realize their *interdependence*. However, at this early stage, Habermas is persuaded that what is needed is not a reconfiguration of the norms upheld by the bourgeois public sphere but only an attempt to reground them in terms appropriate to the demands of the present. If a welfare project could secure the conditions of private autonomy as a basic right then the elite character of the bourgeois form of the public sphere that had been restricted to independent subjects able to make free use of their reason could be relinquished. He stressed that the paradox between the goal of securing the conditions of private autonomy and the paternalistic methods of the welfare state can be lessened. To this end, the principle of publicity needs to be brought to bear to ensure the internal democratization of the bureaucratic organizations and agencies of the welfare state.[54] This internal democratization will require accountability and transparency in all the dealings of corporate bodies that presumed to act in accordance with public welfare. In the relatively unpolitical context of the 1950s and early 1960s, Habermas thinks that the only real hope for democratization resides in opening up to scrutiny the internal organization and agendas of existing powers and in a renegotiation of their relationships.

The Structural Transformation discerns some ambiguous trends in welfare state democracies that might support residual norms of a modern public sphere. Habermas suggests that the claims of solidarities based on reason are encountered as a 'constitutionally institutionalised norm' weakly present in the political institutions of liberal democracies. This norm has survived the structural transformation of its social bases in the ideologies of classical bourgeois society and now still functions to 'determine an important portion of the procedures to which the political exercise and balance of power are factually bound'.[55] Legitimate state power in post-liberal welfare societies 'continues to count on the liberal fictions of a public sphere in civil society'.[56] It seems that, in the end, an intact public opinion is still the only accepted basis for the legitimation of political domination. This normativity continues to be reinforced by the constitutional institutions of large democratic social-welfare states. However, the structural transformations within modernizing processes have placed the efficacy of this legacy in grave danger. The ideal of critical publicity is now but a feeble competitor to processes that have hijacked the concept of publicity to describe the activities of self-promoting private interests. Remnants of the ideal of critical publicity in the constitutional norms of liberal democracies do not change the fact that '[t]he communicative network of a public made up of rationally debating private citizens has collapsed'.[57]

According to *The Structural Transformation*, even if traces of the expectations set in motion by a classical public sphere remain, a historicizing and relativistic twentieth century has to part with the old ways of justifying this normativity. If the ideal of reasonable communications between private subjects is to be made plausible for us, it has to be freed from its reliance on the idea of universal human attributes. Contemporary modernity has inherited a set of norms of interaction that enjoin certain virtues: accountability, listening and responding to the viewpoint of the other, and the attempt to build the grounds for reasoned argumentation. In the expectations of critical self-reflection and in the openness to reasonable argumentation built into the norms of communicative interactions of a reasoning public, we continue to recognize the normative force contained in the idea of the classical bourgeois public sphere. Habermas is persuaded that an interest in retrieving the contemporary normative significance of a commitment to a reasoning public does not need to be afraid of the ideological contamination of its early bourgeois formulation. The normative load no longer appeals to the type of autonomous subjectivity shaped by the bourgeois family as its grounds. With its rearticulation via the procedural norms of a communicative interaction, the particularity of this alleged universalistic idea of subjectivity is expunged.

Habermas' more recent reflections on this early formulation of his ongoing campaign to bring before us the normative claims of a public sphere comment on its failure to grasp the necessity of reconceptualizing in a more radical fashion the presumptions built into a normativity born within eighteenth-century European society. In particular, his contemporary works challenge the conviction that rescuing the normative value of the public sphere requires a reconstruction of the conceptual and structural separation between private and public meanings of autonomy that had supported a bourgeois public. Not only did *The Structural Transformation* fall short in its efforts to rework an ideological formulation of the normativity of a modern public sphere, it was, Habermas tells us, unable to adequately and in systematic fashion assess the practical opportunities within ambiguous welfare state democracies that might be exploited to defend and radicalize this cultural potential. In the end, his first approach to the task of rescuing the public sphere could only suggest a contrast between an 'idealistically glorified past and a present distorted by the mirror of cultural criticism'.[58]

Insights of the feminist critics

Feminists have been among the most vigorous and useful critics of Habermas' first effort at defending the ongoing normativity of a modern public sphere. Their concerns have given particular focus to reservations about his early failure to fully confront the ideological equation between *bourgeois* and *homme* carried by the self-interpretations of a bourgeois public sphere.[59] Feminists have argued that, far from establishing the universal accessibility of its discursive processes, the principle of separation between private and public domains that informed the self-understanding of the bourgeois public sphere confirmed its de facto closed character.[60] To them, the supposition that the idea of the critical public sphere requires a separation between private and public rests upon a repressive attempt to render some human attributes and modes of interaction foundational, beyond the realm of public discussion. This process of essentialization happens in both directions. If the procedural norms that govern interaction in the public domain are never tested against the claims of private dissatisfactions, then these norms can only finally entrench and absolutize certain forms and styles of intercourse as foundational, expressive of supposedly fundamental human attributes. At the same time, by quarantining 'private' concerns, Habermas' early efforts to shore up a division between public and private have been seen to require a repressive essentialization of sets of power relations generated out of, and legitimated by, the conjugal family.

Seyla Benhabib and Joan Landes argue that Habermas' critique of the ideological self-representations of the bourgeois family did not penetrate far enough.[61] While he sought to unmask the extent to which the specific idea of subjectivity produced in the bourgeois family complemented and was functionally adapted to the needs of the capitalist economy, Habermas was insufficiently critical of the particular gendered values that clung to this production of human subjectivity. To these critics, the suggestion that the family provided an empathetic mutuality that fostered the self-development of the individual is a patriarchal myth that obscures the reality of the sacrifice underpinning this 'community of love'. For Landes, the exclusionary character of the values embodied in this conception of subjectivity is not dispelled by their reconstitution into the terms of the procedural norms governing interaction within the public sphere. She insists that the articulation of the self-understanding of this idea of subjectivity through the norms of rational argumentation still carries into the public sphere main aspects of that gendered ideological equation of *homme* and *bourgeois* that characterizes the self-representations of subjectivity in the bourgeois family. Landes maintains that the self-understanding of the liberal public sphere fashioned in eighteenth-century Europe, and heralded by Habermas as the kernel of the modern democratic idea, was *in principle*, not just in practice, closed and exclusionary. This particular self-representation of the public constituted itself in direct opposition to a 'woman-friendly' salon culture.[62] Consequently, a new, austere style of public speech and behaviour was promoted, a style deemed 'rational', 'virtuous', and 'manly'. On this reading, Habermas championed a bourgeois public sphere that privileged certain, argumentative ways of talking and, hence, builds closure and exclusivity into its discursive norms.

Geoff Eley and Mary Ryan generalize this criticism, affirming that there can be no reconstruction of supposedly universal discursive norms that does not finally collude with the assertion of a certain regime of power.[63] Habermas' search for a single public sphere is regarded with deep suspicion. It, supposedly, falsely reduces the democratic principle to procedural norms governing one particular investment in the search for recognition and dogmatically opposes the publicity of a discursive rationality, in which subjects use processes of argumentation to achieve recognition for the justice and intelligibility of their claims, to the publicity of expressive communication in which selves seek to disclose the uniqueness of their 'worlds'.[64] Nancy Fraser also insists that Habermas' defense of the normative priority of the consensus-building procedures of a public sphere is necessarily unresponsive to the radical diversity of needs and identity claims raised in multicultural democracies.[65] In egalitarian societies, a multiplicity of publics is, she insists, preferable to a single public sphere. Fraser thinks that a conception of a modern public sphere that invests normativity in a particular mode of interacting with others is inadequate to the pluralistic motivations and commitments upheld by the ideal of a modern democracy.[66]

Dena Goodman takes a different view. She has no problem with Habermas' claim that democratic purposes require that the dominance of certain generalized discursive processes be upheld and pursued.[67] Marginalized needs and interests must be allowed not just to express their differences but also to demonstrate the reasonableness of their claims upon public goods. The search for rational consensus between estranged parties is essential to the legitimation of previously unrecognized needs and problems. Feminism, Goodman points out, has been a major beneficiary of these rationalizing functions of the modern public sphere. The claim is illustrated historically. While she confirms Landes' claims that the feminized character of a salon culture was finally sacrificed to a public sphere that privileged robust, argumentative ways of talking, Goodman maintains that this process did not suggest the engulfment of one type of democratic public by another, more aggressive and powerful construction. She insists that the feminized elite world of the salon was an environment that was too infiltrated by norms of courtly discourse to support the democratic formation of public opinion.[68] This was a world of decorous conversation guided by a *salonniere* dedicated to 'keeping it within the bounds of politeness'. The transfer of the public sphere from the domain of the salon culture into the male-dominated cafes, coffee houses, the lodges, and the museums, did see a new exclusion of upper-ranking women. Yet, Goodman points out, this process also saw gains for the expectations of reciprocity and conversational justice between strangers, democratic norms that were central to the formation of modern feminism itself. Against a feminist critique of the supposed essentially gendered character of the discursive norms upheld by a bourgeois public sphere, Goodman agrees with Habermas that utopian dimensions of these expectations spilled out from the ideological husk of an elite masculine domain and acquired generalizable significance as the procedures through which marginalized claims and points of view could seek to establish their reasonableness.

Yet criticisms voiced by Landes and Fraser at the early formulations of Habermas' abiding conception of the modern public sphere as a 'single text' do have a point. As I see it, the real weakness of the early version is that it did not describe the architecture of the public sphere in sufficiently differentiated and complex terms. Only in his later writings does Habermas break decisively from a liberal model of a society bifurcated into private and public domains to describe the public sphere as a flow of contents from struggles to attain private autonomy occurring in civil society up towards the formal decision-making institutions of liberal democracies that are now to be included as a part of the functioning of a decentred public sphere.[69] The importance of this emphatic shift away from a liberal construction of a structural division between the private and the public domains towards a model of their mutual interdependencies is particularly clear in the radicalized terms of Habermas' later call for a democratization of the welfare project. We have seen that in the early days he had been content with advocating a welfare state programme that, in meting out economic justice denied by an anarchic market, could hope to secure the private autonomy deemed necessary to the exercise of reason in the public domain. In later chapters we will consider his mature investment in a democratic welfare project that charges public powers, not merely with the task of providing a safety net for the economically marginalized, but with responsibility for responding to the agenda-setting efforts of private struggles to establish the generalizable significance of a diversity of particular needs.

Even though Habermas' early work insists, against the viewpoint of classical liberalism, that the modern public sphere described the mode of reasoning enacted between private, not merely political, actors he still imbibes the liberal conviction that the public sphere can only be rescued if it is relieved of responsibility for the crushing weight of unmet needs for autonomy. His feminist critics have helped to disclose the ways in which prejudicial assumptions can encrust an account of the public sphere formulated as a set of reasoning procedures abstracted from the struggles of specific need and identity claims. In particular, they have suggested that as long as the public sphere is frozen into a set of discursive procedures, an illegitimate equation between the codes through which the rationality of arguments are recognized and the supposed authority of a particular type of subjectivity will inevitably make itself felt. We will see later that Habermas now admits the necessity of theorizing the procedural norms of a public use of reason in terms that fully take on board a feminist critique of the ways in which an appeal to the credentials of certain 'styles' of self-presentation may actually betray the commitment to the formation of rational solidarities.[70]

Recharging the public sphere with contemporary relevance

In the final stages of *The Structural Transformation*, the residual liberal leanings of Habermas' model of the necessary separation between the private and public domains coalesce with the pessimism of the administered society thesis to effectively block any systematic analysis of the potentials in the present for a revitalized public. It turned out that a framework that supposed that modern democracy required a structural separation between private struggles for autonomy and public deliberations over shared goods worked in with the dogmatic elements of the administered society thesis that only admitted the possibility of a repressive downward motion of an integrated state and corporate power on a compliant, individualized society deemed incapable of supporting any civil activism of public importance. In the political climate of the 1950s and early 1960s it is not surprising that Habermas was not able to bring himself to invest hopes in the radical potentials emerging out of civil society. 'At the time', Habermas writes, 'I could not imagine any other vehicle of critical publicity than internally democratized interest associations and parties. Inter-party and intra-associational public spheres appeared to me as the potential centres of a public communication still capable of being regenerated'.[71]

As Jean Cohen and Andrew Arato have pointed out, the trouble with this minimalist formulation of democratic hopes that limited itself to a rebalancing of existing powers is that it did not suggest a mechanism or process whereby critical publicity might be restored.[72] A coherent account of rescuing a critical public sphere would need, in the first instance, to rework Habermas' early sociological framework to bring into view the wider importance of civic struggles aimed at achieving recognition for the legitimacy of particular need and identity claims for the revitalization of a democratic culture. The normative underpinning of the bourgeois ideal of a critical public would also need to be subjected to a more searching interrogation and reworked into a new understanding of communicative rationality freed from the ideological assumptions of a liberal model.

Later writings have offered a more positive and systematically elaborated account of what a project committed to the reappropriation of a critical public involves. This is an advance that does not specifically depend on a more moderate estimation of the obstacles that confront the task. As we will see, Habermas' current sense of the likely prospects for an emancipatory self-reform of an era dominated by globalizing markets and politically gutted nation states is not less gloomy than his early account that had believed that bureaucratic capitalism was the virtually insuperable threat. The point is not that Habermas is now more optimistic but rather that he has clarified his interpretation of the normativity of a modern public sphere and has, accordingly, a rather different diagnosis of the conditions required for its realization.

Habermas' sociological reflection upon the democratic potentials of civic activism has only taken shape in response to the critical fractures that a New Left and counter-cultural politics opened up within liberal democracies. However, it was not just the sociological basis of his search for a contemporary public sphere that needed to be renegotiated. Habermas' own later self-reflections suggest that he needed to interrogate further the normative claims that had been taken over from existing idealized accounts of a critical public. For, if 'cultural goods are spoils that the ruling elites carry in their triumphal parade',[73] ideology critique had to 'go deeper' to find its normative foundations. It is, in large part, these ideologically critical intentions that inspired a more philosophical turn in Habermas' search for the normative foundations of a critical theory of society. The search for normative foundations had to recognize that it could not simply attempt to 'de-ideologize' the class-bound aspirations of an elite without taking on board some of its central contaminating influences. This acknowledgement has contributed to the dramatic rethinking of the project of critical theory that culminated in the theory of communicative action.

3   The theory of communicative action

Only after the publication of *The Structural Transformation* does Habermas begin to clarify the nature and the extent of his differences with the later Adorno and Horkheimer. The disagreements are fundamental, encompassing differing accounts of the tasks of a contemporary critical theory as well as distinct analyses of significant sociological trends in capitalist democracies. We have seen that the relatively unthematized character of these differences with the older generation of the Frankfurt School had left its mark in some major conceptual tensions within *The Structural Transformation*. At this early stage, Habermas was neither completely reconciled to the way that Adorno and Horkheimer had conceived the contemporary character of critical theory nor yet ready to formulate the terms of a clear and unequivocal break.

The young Habermas had inherited a potent critique of the Hegelian underpinnings of Marx's account of the capacities and tasks of critical theory. A politically disappointed older generation of the Frankfurt School had relinquished the idea that critical theory could achieve a direct linage between theory and praxis. The collapse of their early Marxist hopes persuaded the authors of the *Dialectic of Enlightenment* that reason in history had no liberatory potentials, it was only the instrument of a relentless interest in self-preservation. While deeply influenced by this retreat from totalizing theory to negative dialectics, Habermas cannot accept Adorno's abandonment of the search for an objectively grounded and practically motivated critical theory. The inclinations of *The Structural Transformation* are towards a retrieval of critical theory as a reflection on unrealized historical potentials. However, while it jettisoned any idea of a historical telos, the early work failed to make explicit any alternative sociology of modernity, nor arbitrate amongst existing cultural options. Habermas is increasingly persuaded that, if it is to ground its normativity away from a parade of legitimating ideological categories, ideology critique must become more self-reflexive about its categories and their normative origins than his earlier framework had allowed. At the same time, he continues to insist that a critical theory has practical motivations that require it to engage with the potentials immanent in everyday forms of life. Since Marx's reliance on a Hegelian philosophy of history is no longer viable, how is the double-task of a practically motivated critical theory that is able to justify the rationality of its normative claims to be negotiated? After *The Structural Transformation*, Habermas tries to locate an alternative construction of the tasks of a contemporary critical theory within the terms of a re-appropriated Kantian transcendentalism. The following discussion will review aspects of this journey from Hegel to Kant as Habermas attempts to sustain an immanently praxial dimension for a rationally justified critical theory of society.

Redoing the normative foundations

For Habermas, the task of restoring credibility to the rationality claims raised by critical theory is set by the historical defeat of Marxism. The 'accommo-dation' of the proletariat to liberal democratic capitalism suggests the historical irrelevance of Marx's attempt to view his critical theory as a clarification of the historical mission of a revolutionary class. According to this critique, the contemporary helplessness of Marx's version of critical theory is not simply a matter of the now implausible character of the philosophy of history that underpinned it and the obsolescence of his sociology of bourgeois society. In the end, Marxism articulated itself too uncritically with the terms in which bourgeois modernity had interpreted its own essential dynamism. This much of Habermas' views is in deep agreement with the later Frankfurt School's account of the crisis in Marxism. However, Habermas goes still further. Marxism, he supposes, fails as a critical theory with contemporary relevance because, recognizing only one axis of continuity that could make sense of modernizing trajectories – the instrumental, purposive, rational one – it is unable to specify the normative grounds upon which rational deliberations could be made about present potentials deemed *worthy* of being carried forward into a self-shaped future.[1] Marxism is guilty of a 'normative deficit'. It does not set out the criteria against which the irrationality of the direction that capitalist development had taken could be spelt out.

The later Frankfurt School's powerful critique of the authoritarianism of a hegemonic 'technocratic consciousness' included a decisive challenge to Marx's nineteenth-century faith in the essentially progressive character of modernity's assault on nature and on parochial traditionalism. Deeply marked by the rise of European totalitarianism and appalled at the repressive consumerism of bureaucratic capitalism, Adorno and Horkheimer proclaim the dark 'truth' of the will to domination lurking in a civilizatory reason. According to the authors of the *Dialectic Enlightenment*, modernization means the progressive liberation of means–ends calculative reason from the service to any purposes that can seek independent justification. Released from any legitimating ends, the means have asserted themselves in a terrifying affirmation of the uncontested reign of instrumental imperatives. Habermas wholeheartedly agrees with Adorno and Horkheimer that, reduced to a mere instrument of technical mastery and control, reason loses its connections with emancipatory interests and becomes affirmative. 'Emancipation by means of enlightenment is replaced by instruction in control over objective or objectified processes'.[2] Yet he does not accept their estimation of what this distorted dialectics means for the status and role of contemporary critical theory. For Adorno, the triumph of technocratic consciousness, with its threatened 'metamorphosis of critique into affirmation' requires critical theory to turn itself into a 'negative dialectic' that renounces the positivity of all rationalizing ambitions that are simply counted as an ambition to reconcile, control, and subdue recalcitrant otherness. In the face of reason's search for closure, critique, Adorno proclaims, should take the point of view of unreconciled particularity.

Seyla Benhabib points out that Habermas views the dilemma facing the future of critical theory in the wake of this 'total critique' in stark terms: '[e]ither the empirical diagnosis of the one-dimensionality of social and cultural rationalization processes must be revised, or critical theory must admit to its own historical impossibility'.[3] Habermas opts for the former. For him, it is not simply the principle of particularity itself but the ideal of an interactive rationality enacted *between* particular subjectivities that is principally threatened by the triumph of a technocratic consciousness interested only in controlling modes of integration. Habermas' defence of the appeal to reason sustained by contemporary critical theory is based on a differentiated appreciation of rationalizing trajectories unleashed by modernization processes.

Denouncing the triumph of a technocratic consciousness, Habermas still commits critical theory to the project of a 'rational society'. He sets his sights not on a critique of instrumental reason as such, but on its expansion 'to the proportions of a life form, of the "historical totality" of a life world'.[4] Adorno's totalizing critique of an authoritarian reason placed critical theory at the service of a 'fallen nature', reason's other. For Habermas, by contrast, critical theory clarifies and defends an embattled alternative construction of civilizatory reason. Repudiating Adorno and Horkheimer's diagnosis of the developmental logic of modern rationalizing imperatives as one-sided, he replaces this interpretation with an account of the complex, radically unequal, relations between ambiguous rationality potentials systematized by modernization processes.[5]

Habermas was later to refer to *Knowledge and Human Interests* (1968) as one of the major 'guideposts' on the way to his mature critical social theory.[6] This study takes decisive steps in the conceptual elaboration of a differentiated conception of reason able to supply a discriminating critique of instrumental reason and an explicit normative basis for critical theory. Formulating its critique of instrumental reason as a critique of reason per se, the later Frankfurt school obscured the distinct interests articulated in a diverse typology of human knowledges. In particular, it bought into a positivistic blindness about the irreducibility of an interest in reflection and self-reflection.[7] These were assumed to be mere instruments of a technocratic interest in subjugation, not a relatively independent human motivation.

According to Habermas, we can, and do, rationalize our activities in terms of a commitment to self-reflection on our purposes as a *primary* interest that cannot be simply assimilated into the instrumentalizing impulses of a mastering will. This is a self-reflection that springs from the requirements of our communicative interactions with others, hence from the concrete needs of socially situated subjects.[8] Like all other knowledges (those guided by practical as well as technical interests) an interest in reflecting upon our goals is historically and socially rooted. Yet Habermas also locates these as anthropologically deep-seated interests of the human species. Knowledge-guiding interests arise from the 'actual structures of human life'.[9] Specifically, all knowledge-generating interests are tied to the purposes of humans as tool-making and language-using animals. Humans must not only manipulate and control nature, they also need to build understandings with each other through the use of language.[10] It is from this latter orientation to a world not only mastered but also rendered intelligible that Habermas derives a primary, emancipatory, interest in the capacity to open our goals and purposes up to processes of reflection, scrutiny, and review.[11] The ability to reflect critically on our own presuppositions is emancipatory because it allows us to free ourselves from constraints imposed on us by non-natural, that is, human causes. It is fundamental because the capacity for critical self-reflection that is articulated and built through our dialogic interactions is deemed a condition of possibility of knowledge in general.

Habermas attempts to ground the objectivity of the commitments articulated in a critical theory of society in a reconstructive analysis of an emancipatory interest without which, not only our practices of critical self-reflection, but human knowledges themselves, would not be possible. This project bears the heavy imprint of Kant's transcendentalism. For Habermas, the emancipatory interest in autonomy and self-responsibility upon which the critical standard of self-reflection is based is implicit in the very structure of human communication and can thus be 'apprehended a priori' with 'theoretical certainty'.[12] But he is very clear that the interest reconstructed by critical theory is only of a 'quasi' transcendental character. The full unfolding of these cognitive interests is a potential that is only realized in history and only reconstructable after the event of this development. Modernization processes have systematized and rendered explicit certain distinct modes of rationalization but a pathological modern development threatens to engulf our capacity to rationalize our actions with respect to the goal of critical self-reflection by a one-sided focus on a world rationalized in accordance with technical interests.

The 'linguistic turn' that Habermas was to give to his attempt to ground the normativity of a critical social theory is, Robert Holub points out, already evident in the afterword to *Knowledge and Human Interests* where he admits that 'the paradigm of language has led to the reframing of the transcendental model'.[13] This reframing was supposed to suggest a final overcoming of the subjectivist biases of a Kantian problematic. By shifting the focus of his reconstructive analysis from an interest in the idealizations supposed implicit in distinct kinds of knowledge claims towards a reconstruction of the presuppositions that make possible the everyday use of language to communicate, Habermas intends to finally abandon the philosophy of the subject by working an account of an idealized mode of *intersubjectivity* into his description of the normativity upheld by a critical theory of society.

Habermas now begins to insist that a critically enlightened perspective articulates itself through theoretical reflection on the contrast between idealizations supposed implicit in the communicative functions of language and their distortion in the instrumentalizing interactions deemed normal in a pathological capitalism.[14] Such a hermeneutic

> connects the process of understanding to the principle of rational speech according to which truth would only be guaranteed by that kind of consensus which was achieved under the idealized conditions of unlimited communication free from domination and could be maintained over time . . . it is only the formal anticipation of an idealized dialogue . . . which guarantees the ultimate sustaining and counterfactual agreement that already unites us; in relation to it we can criticize every factual agreement, should it be a false one, as false consciousness . . . To attempt systematic justification we have to develop . . . a theory which would enable us to deduce the principle of rational speech from the logic of everyday language and regard it as the necessary regulative for all actual speech however distorted it may be.[15]

Habermas insists that this formulation of a normatively charged critical theory retains all the capacity to distinguish between what people are and what they might be, all the 'interest in future conditions'[16] essential to the project. Yet while this early formulation does refer to an idealizing account of the conditions of constraint-free communication, to an 'ideal speech situation', this, Thomas McCarthy points out, was not meant as an image of a future in which communicative interactions aimed at a pure democratic consensus would replace calculating exchanges governed by an instrumentalizing reason. The 'ideal speech situation' merely proposes a formalized account of the norms of interaction that appear rational from the standpoint of the communicative purposes implicitly embraced by the users of language. Unlike a classical utopianism that ascribes a telos that we are committed to bring about, Habermas' critical theory affirms an ideal whose claim to rationality refers to the already implicit purposes of everyday users of language in their efforts to make themselves understood. Habermas always insists that his critical theory offers only a reconstructive analysis that wants only to 'prove what we already tacitly assume'.[17]

Critical theory helps both at an individual and at a societal level our efforts to reflect upon the conditions that must be observed if we are to make ourselves understood by differently placed others. Implicit undertakings can become delineated as explicit value commitments whenever language users are called upon to formalize the conditions under which interrupted communicative interactions can be renewed. Individuals as well as societies show their maturity by their accumulation of insight into their problems and by their capacity to deal with them at higher levels of abstraction.[18] Moral and historical development is measured in terms of our capacities to reconstruct, on a new, chosen and self-reflexive basis, meanings that have been thrown into crisis.[19] The regulative idea of a true consensus raised as the goal of participants in rational discourse is not, then, the discovery of the theorist wielding the tools of 'reconstructive science'. The theorist only gives expression to and helps clarify the regulative norms immanent to everyday acts in which we arrive at understandings with others. Habermas considers that the idealized speech situation governed only by an interest in making ourselves understood is not locked within the theorist's grasp. It is a 'piece of ideality' that can also fall within the practical self-awareness of concrete actors as they problem-solve their way through the challenges of communicating in a complex modern world.

As already noted, Habermas wants to try and rescue contemporary critical theory as a practically motivated and objectively justified normative perspective. A central objection could be raised that the 'ideal speech situation', which finally carries the normative load of this version of critical theory, is only able to avoid an idealist construction of its contents by contriving to anchor itself as an expression of an immanent progress in our self understandings whose course of development is underwritten by the covert return of a philosophy of history. In other words, the proposed re-unification of the practical motivations and the rational grounding of critical theory only works to the extent that Habermas allows a repudiated account of an emancipatory telos, supposed immanent to the progress of history, to creep in the back door. The point can best be made if we look at a major conceptual tension that surfaces in *The Legitimation Crisis* (1975).

Redoing the sociology

The Legitimation Crisis suggests a real departure from the sociology of the administered society that had so influenced *The Structural Transformation*. We saw that the work of the early 1960s described how the united operations of state and commercial power in organized capitalist societies use consumer culture and bureaucratic planning to engineer the repressive overcoming of contradictory capitalist structures. By the early 1970s, Habermas disputes key aspects of Adorno and Horkheimer's account of the seamless effectiveness of this alliance. He now suggests that something of Marx's claim that the basic contradictions of capitalist society issue in destabilizing crisis tendencies is still relevant in contemporary capitalism. On the one hand, Habermas agrees that Marx was wrong to suppose that a self-reforming capitalism would not be able to find ways of containing the impact of major economic contradictions. Yet in the politically charged climate of the late 1960s and early 1970s it seemed that the later Frankfurt School was also mistaken in supposing that this meant the end of all crisis tendencies. For Habermas, the new crisis tendencies of capitalism, located not in the economic but in the socio-cultural spheres, appear as a side effect of its successes. The spread of administrative rationality that accompanies the expanded activity of the state in bureaucratic capitalism produces an increase in the need for legitimation, for justification of government intervention into new areas of life.[20] This new authority seems unable to produce new meanings equipped to offset the destabilizing impacts of its challenges to the traditional sources of cultural validity. This process of disorientation and the search for building new cultural interpretations that is provoked by it have the unintended effect of undermining the civil privatism that appears necessary to the smooth reproduction of the reign of bureaucratic capitalism.[21] From the vantage point of the early 1970s, Habermas thinks that

> the 'syndrome of civil and familial–vocational privacy' is being undermined by (among other things) certain changes in the dominant mode of social-ization, changes producing motivational patterns and value orientations that are incompatible with the requirements of the economic and political systems.[22]

The reorganization of lived contexts by the intrusions of bureaucratic and administrative systems tests out the capacities of conventional ideologies to supply interpretative frameworks able to make sense of the changes and provokes the need for new, reflected upon and negotiated understandings. In this sense, Habermas suggests that the legitimation crisis of late capitalism opens up potentials for a re-politization of the public sphere.

However, Thomas McCarthy discovers an important tension between the role that *The Legitimation Crisis* actually attributes to critical theory and Habermas' explicit proclamations about the merely reconstructive, not positive, status of claims raised by contemporary critical theory.[23] There is, McCarthy points out, a predictive dimension to the legitimation crisis thesis. It locates crisis tendencies 'pregnant with the future' within disruptions to the lived experiences of state capitalist societies. While Habermas supposes that the legitimation crisis opens up potentials for a re-politicization of the public sphere, ultimately, McCarthy contends, his critical theory is unable to locate an organized social movement able to grasp these potentials and to carry them forward in terms deemed appropriate by the theory.[24] The theory is not, in other words, able to set itself up in an interpretive relationship with any 'situationally engaged' struggles for enlightenment. As Dietrich Bohler suggests, the theory finally equates its essentially emancipatory interests in autonomy with the 'formal interest' in freedom presupposed by the theoretical enlightenment in which emancipation is understood as the overcoming of dogmatism by exercising our potentials for self-reflection.[25]

McCarthy and Bohler unearth a dichotomy that, at this stage, scars Habermas' conception of the role of critical theory. As already noted,

Habermas considers critical theory as a 'reconstructive science', as one that seeks to raise to the level of reflection the intuitive, pre-theoretical knowledge of linguistically competent subjects.[26] To establish itself as rationally grounded critique, Habermas determines that critical theory has to be able to establish the universality of the interests it commits itself to; these must be traceable 'beyond the threshold of modern societies'.[27] Habermas also insists that a contemporary critical theory must answer to Marx's insistence that the world needs to be changed, not just interpreted. As engaged theory, it has to be able to identify itself as a clarification of emancipatory motivations of certain concrete actors. Habermas' early inability to mediate these two sets of purposes that will continue to shape his view of the task of critical theory is, for McCarthy, exemplified by the tendency in the *Legitimation Crisis* to implicitly confer some kind of unaccounted for quasi-necessity on a portrait of the evolution of a practical, critical consciousness. Only by appearing to suppose that objective trends within the present are colluding to bring on a re-politicization of the public sphere can Habermas seem to close the gap between the idealized constructs and the social and political realities that theory claimed as the object of its clarifications. It appears that, at this stage, Habermas' critical theory, despite its explicit disavowals, secretly relies on the residual support of an unacknowledged historical teleology.

Yet *The Legitimation Crisis* marks a real advance in the complexity of Habermas' diagnosis of modernizing processes. It brings into view capabilities whose significance was obscured by the stark one-sidedness of the administered society thesis. Already introduced in *On the Logic of the Social Sciences* (1967) as part of the complex archeology of human experience, Habermas now carries the concept of the 'lifeworld' into an analysis of historically dynamic modernization processes.[28] Coined by the phenomenological tradition initiated by Edmund Husserl, the notion of the lifeworld refers to the pre-interpreted and pre-reflective background against which our everyday life unfolds. *The Legitimation Crisis* attempts to make use of this concept for a theory of social life and of the processes of modernization. The 'lifeworld' introduces an account of the necessity of our communicative interactions into the theory. 'Our intersubjectively shared, overlapping lifeworlds lay down a background consensus, without which our everyday praxis simply couldn't take place.'[29] Habermas is especially interested in the way that these communicative interactions are rationalized, formalized and, made explicit in those contexts where they were no longer automatically reproduced. The concept of the lifeworld allows him to look at modernization processes as an expansion of discursive capacities for reflection on taken for granted contents. As intuitively available shared background knowledges are problematized, they must be renegotiated in the efforts of concrete subjects now assuming the discursive roles of speakers and interlocutors. This discursive mode of integration was left out of the administered society thesis whose view of modernization processes recognized only the downwards totalizing power of unified economic and administrative systems.

In this first view of a modern society differentiated into dynamic relations between distinct and opposed modes of integration (between symbolically related speaking and hearing subjects) and the steering capacities of self-regulating economic and administrative systems,[30] Habermas puts in place the ingredients of a powerful and systematic critique of capitalist modernity from the point of view of its suppression of the historical potentials for democratic self-reform. At the same time, he sets up the terms for an analysis of those dynamics within modernization processes that enable concrete actors to discover for themselves the rationality of interactions that are aimed at arriving at communicatively achieved understandings.[31]

The theory of communicative action

The two volumes of *The Theory of Communicative Action* (1981) have been described as an attempt to bring 'to a provisional conclusion the intellectual efforts of twenty years of reflection and research'.[32] Habermas supposed that this work would only appeal to a specialized audience interested in the technicalities of its proposal to systematically reconstruct the orienting values behind critical theory's diagnosis of the pathologies of bourgeois society. This is a project for those 'who have a professional interest in the foundations of social theory'.[33] At the same time, it also represents a major contribution to, and a clear theoretical explanation of, Habermas' ongoing attempt to system-atically reconstruct the norms of democratic Enlightenment and to bring these before us as our own neglected and unrealized potentials.

Balancing modernity's rationality potential

For Adorno and Horkheimer, contemporary history had seemed to corroborate the worst of Max Weber's fears. As they saw it, the triumph of reason appeared as the victory of an instrumental rationality committed to the promotion of control of human beings over nature, the objective social world and of the individual human being over others. However, as Habermas struggles against this immobilizing pessimism, he also turns to Weber as a 'point of departure'.[34] He thinks that Weber can be used to supply the germ of a theory of history able to contest Adorno's 'cul de sac of despair'. Adorno, his pupil insists, had failed to make the most of the distinctions drawn in Weber's account of rationalizing processes of modernization.[35]

Weber's analysis of the progressive rationalization of modern life had tried to grasp a whole complex of tendencies related to scientific and technical progress and its effects on the institutional framework of traditional society. The tendencies include: the extension of the areas of society subject to crite-ria of rational decision, the progress of industrialization, the expansion of administrative and bureaucratic control, the radical devaluation of tradition and the progressive secularization and disenchantment of the modern world.[36] However, dominant in this account of modernizing tendencies is the process of societal rationalization: the expansion of a functional and instrumental reason that defines modernity as a purposive calculation of the relations between means and ends. This process aims at achieving the subjugation of the world to chosen human interests and treats as rational the strategic actions that conform to this aim. This description of modernity's rationality emphasizes the appearance of a critical, suspicious attitude towards merely received goals that henceforth could be the chosen ends in a world of disenchantment.

For Weber, societal rationalization gives a much-circumscribed account of the hopes for a self-directing humanity embraced by Enlightenment. The unity of a world described in terms of traditional religious world-views has crumbled and we inheritors of Enlightenment are compelled to choose between value standpoints that can claim no authority external to their own cultural spheres. However, in the final analysis, values cannot be rationally grounded and rationality is reduced from the servant of the ideal of a self-directing humanity to an interest in calculating the relations between means and ends. The gain in the transparency of the implications of chosen goals is paid for by a loss of orientation. For Weber, the progress of societal rationalization amounts to the dominance of a goal-oriented rationality, to the ascendancy of administrative efficiency and to the quest for entrepreneurial advantage.[37] The Enlightenment ambition to a self-legislating future for humanity has turned out to be an 'iron cage'.

Habermas considers this analysis of the trajectory of Enlightenment reason a fatefully one-sided point of view that neglects the potentials of Weber's own insight into the significance of the separation of the spheres that is the hallmark of the modern cultural achievement. He argues that while there were actually two notions of rationalization in Weber, cultural and societal rationalization, Weber unconsciously allowed the second concept to completely dominate his understanding of the historical process of rationalization as a whole. As mentioned, Weber, on the one hand recognizes the emancipatory potential of the process of rationalization insofar as it dissolves the hold of traditional world-views and allows scope for individuals to give shape and meaning to their own lives through a chosen commitment to rationalized value spheres. The modern individual can choose between the 'warring Gods' of science, art, politics, and eroticism. In Weber's reconstruction of the trajectory of rationalization processes, the emancipatory dimension of this process of cultural rationalization is swamped by the galloping processes of societal rationalization in which modernization is equated with the expanding orbit and influence of a purposive or instrumentalizing reason.[38] Habermas thinks that this subsumption of the theme of cultural rationalization into that of societal rationalization was a grave distortion in Weber's account. The emancipatory potentials of the processes of cultural differentiation it describes remained under-theorized.[39]

What is needed is a paradigm that allows us to describe the differentiated relations to the world achieved by modern individuals in the context of the fragmentation of the value spheres. The thesis of the 'iron cage' underestimates the emancipatory effects of the processes of cultural differentiation that allow modern individuals to test their world from a number of points of view.[40] No longer in the grip of a fateful religious world-orientation, modern individuals can interrogate descriptions of their world from the point of view of their objectivity, normativity (rightness), and their authenticity.

On this interpretation, cultural differentiation offers a place to a new kind of rationality that also shapes a modern experience. This is a world in which all assertions, descriptions, claims, and propositions are contentious, open to criticism and review on the basis of their conformity to idealized and differentiated descriptions of their validity. Modernizing rationalization produces, then, the possibility of open and self-reflective personalities and the novelty of a mode of interaction in which all belief and knowledge claims can be opened up for rational criticism and publicity. Hence, rather than describing modernization as a loss of meaning, we can more appropriately refer to the potential development of new communicatively elaborated meanings. According to this analysis, modern individuals are oriented in the world not simply as strategic but, above all, as communicative actors. Their actions are coordinated not only through egocentric calculations of success but through acts of reaching understanding. 'In communicative action participants are not primarily oriented to their own individual successes; they pursue their individual goals under the condition that they can harmonise their plans of action on the basis of common situation definitions.'[41] This insight into a new more comprehensive understanding of modern rationality was lost to Weber because he was fixated on the problem of Western uniqueness and its underpinning distinctive societal rationalization. Adorno and Horkheimer followed Weber down this road and, according to Habermas, thereby sacrificed a discriminating, dialectical perspective on the achievements of modernizing processes that could anchor their own critical impulses.

The mature position reached in the *Dialectic of Enlightenment* viewed the evolution of Western civilization as the story of the historical unfolding of self-preservative instrumental reason. This critique of instrumental reason was unable to appreciate the other side of Enlightenment because it failed to fully value the significance of the processes of cultural rationalization.[42] Armed one-sidedly with the concept of instrumental reason as the key to the understanding of the civilizatory process, Adorno and Horkheimer underplayed the ambiguous potentials of bourgeois society. In particular, their reconstruction of the process of civilization as the unconstrained self-assertion of a subjectivity bent on control and mastery neglected the gains in individualist patterns of identity formation, the opportunities for democratic decision-making and for universalistic notions of morality and law that are also instantiated by processes of cultural rationalization.[43] Adorno and Horkheimer were 'unable to appropriate the systematic content of Weber's diagnosis of the times and to make it fruitful for social–scientific enquiry' partly because 'they did not take seriously enough Weber's studies on the rationalisation of worldviews, or the independent logic of cultural modernity'.[44]

Habermas' theory of modernization attempts to redress this imbalance and to reinvest critical theory with the capacity to reflect upon the pathological tendencies of capitalist modernization. Two steps had to be taken to affect this paradigm shift. First, Adorno and Horkheimer's equation of the civilizatory process with the evolution of a purposive–instrumental reason must be supplemented by a conception of the humanizing character of our capacities for communicative action. Second, using only the methodologies of the 'reconstructive sciences', the systemic imbalance between communicative and instrumentalizing action that is built into the processes and structural arrangements of capitalist society needs to be diagnosed as a deformation of a potential for reasons embedded in the evolution of human cultural practices.

An unbalanced appreciation of Weber was not the only legacy that inhibited Adorno's ability to discover any immanent normative grounding for a diagnosis of pathological modernizing tendencies. *The Theory of Communicative Action* expands Habermas' account of the contribution that a 'normative deficit' in Marx also played in limiting modern critical theory's interpretation of the meaning of reason in history.[45]

Struggling against the normative deficit in critical theory

The Theory of Communicative Action builds on Habermas' earlier critique of the supposed equation in Marx of the burgeoning productive forces of bourgeois society, which saw the rapid expansion of new capacities, skills, talents, and needs, with the cause of social emancipation as such.[46] For Marx, this expansion of productive powers represented the measure of progress against which must be judged the alienating and obsolete social relations of production in capitalist society. What, for Habermas, is wrong with this attempt to conceptually anchor a diagnosis of bourgeois alienation is that it allows us to suppose that the instrumentalizing imperatives built into the escalating productive forces of capitalist society have an essentially progressive, emancipatory tendency. Once the supposed bearer of this dynamic potential loses its historical momentum, a tradition of Marxian critique finds itself unable to discriminate between the dynamic processes operating within bourgeois society. If, namely, critical theory describes only one single set of potentials within modernization processes, the failure of the agent that was supposed to endow these with emancipatory significance leaves the theory bereft of any grounds that might anchor its critique of the pathological dimensions of the dynamism unleashed by modernization processes.

This deficit needs to be made good and critical theory recharged with a normativity that does not simply appeal to the 'other' of a repressive reason. According to Habermas, critical theory can only defend itself by elaborating a diagnosis of modernity complex enough to allow us to determine those immanent tendencies likely to promote the realization of value commitments that the theory also helps us to appreciate. For him, the double-task to be performed by the contemporary critical theorist begins with an appreciation of the two dimensions of modernity's rationalizing processes. Rationalization at the level of an extension of the capacities for mean-ends calculations on the one hand facilitates the growing mastery of nature from the standpoint of instrumental control. Yet this description of modernity's rationality potentials needs to be distinguished from rationalization at the level of the frameworks of communicative interaction that aim at removing restrictions on free communication and encouraging self-reflection and socio-political emancipation.[47] Habermas thinks that contemporary critical theory must, in the first instance, allow modernizing achievements neglected by the Marxian tradition to come fully into view.

This critique of a narrow interpretation of modern rationality potentials calls to account a distorted 'philosophy of the subject' that has, Habermas supposes, dominated modern philosophy since Descartes.[48] This rejected paradigm promotes a narrow concept of human self-formation viewed as a process aimed at the emancipation of a particular self-asserting will. An overly rationalist formulation of the process of self-constitution accorded a privileged status to the formative power of knowledge while Marx shifted the emphasis to other dimensions of the self-forming capacities of human subjectivity.[49] Marx discussed those activities that not only act upon and appropriate the world but also transform our contexts, opening up new ways of doing things and expanding our potentialities. What remains obscured in all these interpretations of a dynamic self-constituting humanity is the vital role played by the communicative actions between subjects. For Habermas, if we want to know how human beings form themselves we need to consider not simply the way that they act on their environment but the constitutive power of their communicative interactions as well.

Volume Two of *The Theory of Communicative Action* draws upon George Herbert Mead's perspective on the communicative socialization of individuals according to which the process of self-constitution is tied to language and culture.[50] We develop and exercise our unique species power for self-formation through our embeddedness in communicative interactions with others. Our capacities for self-reflection and rational deliberation are increased and our interpretive horizons constantly expanded by the effort we must make to have ourselves understood by others. This attempt to describe the self-constituting capacities of human subjects as a product of their activities as language users sees itself as a transformation of the normative foundations of contemporary critical theory. Under this description, the emancipation of a humanizing potential for self-development is conceived, not in terms of a project aimed at the liberation of self-asserting subjectivity, but as a commitment to realizing the potentials of communicative interactions between subjects.

Habermas maintains that the utopian perspective of self-realizing human potential 'ingrained in the very conditions of the communicative socialisation of individuals, is built in the medium of the reproduction of the species'.[51] We misunderstand our thirst for autonomy unless we grasp this as an inter- est in the potentials of our interactions with others. The process of acquiring a self and of building its expanding possibilities draws upon no special talents or virtues but only on our capacity to use language properly. The competent user of language understands that the goal of reaching mutual understanding requires that each participant in discourse learn to adopt the standpoint of the other. Language only works as effective communication to the extent that dialogic partners suppose that it is possible to build a generalizing description of a shared interest that does not dissolve the individuality of each point of view but only expands all of them and makes them mutually intelligible.

This idealizing presumption is a 'counterfactual' whose significance lies in the supposition of its achievability and desirability. If we begin to theorize the presumptions of communicative processes, we arrive at a description of autonomous self-constituting subjectivity that does not refer to the aspira- tions of any cultural or historical type but appeals to a mode of interaction whose worth is, implicitly, grasped by all. Let us imagine, Habermas writes,

> individuals being socialized as members of an ideal communication community; they would in the same measure acquire an identity with two complementary aspects: one universalizing, one particularizing. On the one hand, these persons raised under idealized conditions learn to orient themselves within a universalistic framework, that is, to act autonomously. On the other hand, they learn to use this autonomy, which makes them equal to every other morally acting subject, to develop themselves in their subjectivity and singularity. Mead ascribes both autonomy and the power of spontaneous self-realization to every person who, in the revolutionary role of a participant in universal discourse, frees himself from the fetters of habitual, concrete conditions of life.[52]

Yet Habermas is not satisfied with the terms in which Mead describes the critical potentials of the idealizing propositions that formed the counterfactual conditions of our use of language. These idealizing presumptions are not sim- ply to be identified with the acquired motivations and explicit commitments of language users. Of significance, rather, is the counterfactual character of the undertakings implicit in the communicative act. This is a description of rational action that makes itself known in the breach. The goal of reaching understanding requires of competent language users that they recognize the necessity of responding to challenges to their claims with reasons designed to support their validity. Rational speakers have to be able to say why their claims should be thought of as true, as right, or authentic. It follows, then, that our capacity to raise communicative rationality as a value, as a normatively charged commitment, is provoked in those peculiar circumstances in which the effort to build rational solidarities is both presupposed and, at least potentially, rendered contestable at the same time.

At this juncture, Habermas' critical theory branches into two, conceptually entwined, directions. On the one hand, the theory moves to a detailed discussion of the norms of communicative interaction. Elaborated in a series of essays written throughout the 1980s, the discourse ethics offers a detailed reconstruction of the ideal of communicative rationality that is supposed to be implicit in our use of language. Here Habermas wants to thematize the kind of ideal this is and to suggest that we can understand our value commitments, our potentials, and ourselves better if we clearly grasp its significances and implications. This body of work and its consequences for Habermas' proposed re-interpretation of the normativity of the modern public sphere will be examined in Chapter 4. For now, I want to review a second avenue of enquiry opened up by the communicative action theory. The rest of this chapter will look at Habermas' attempt to describe the patholog-ical tendencies of contingent modernizing processes that see a historically achieved delineation of our capacities for communicative rationality under attack from the over-developed and powerfully supported ambitions of an instrumentalizing reason.

Ambiguous modernization processes

The Theory of Communicative Action wants to 'introduce a theory of commu-nicative action that clarifies the normative foundations of a critical theory of society'.[53] It intends doing so without any contrived appeal to the standpoint of an emergent revolutionary subject or to the return of a repressed/excluded set of human powers. This repudiation of the search for a subject able to carry its normative load is a requirement that is built into the presuppositions of Habermas' critical theory. The theory does not offer itself as a third person account of what historical actors 'ought' to think because it stands as an idealization of a type of interaction between subjects in which reference to external authority is deemed irrelevant.[54] Critical theory thematizes the nor-mative authority of democratizing modes of interaction between speakers and hearers and, as such, it hopes to provide the 'focussing power of a magnifying glass'[55] on inchoate claims that an interactive rationality makes on concrete actors situated in the vortex of ambiguous modernizing tendencies.

Habermas clearly repudiates the idea that the practically motivated, engaged character of his critical theory is dependent in any strong sense on setting up an expressive relationship with an already constituted bearer of its emancipatory hopes. Yet he certainly considers that his critical theory does connect with existing determinations of radical needs that project themselves beyond the perverted priorities of administered modern societies. We will see that Habermas thinks that his social theory is able to both respond to and offer an account of the emancipatory motivations of a generation of actors for whom building rational solidarities is a real goal. However, in *The Theory of Communicative Action*, purposes other than a concern with outlining the self-critical potentials immanent to late capitalist society take centre stage.

At this juncture, Habermas' theory of modernity adopts its primary agenda from a critical engagement with a Western Marxist theory of reification. He supposes that his principal task is to respond positively to a critique of the crisis in Marxism and to furnish a contemporary critical theory with an alternative way of framing its critical orientation. Habermas no longer uses the language of alienation that had been shaped by Marx's philosophy of history but describes what he called the pathologies of modernity. Pathological developments are seen to be distortions that arise from the dominance of certain trajectories in the rationalization of the lifeworld that, according to Habermas, drives modernization processes.

We have already briefly considered the first use that Habermas made of the concept of the lifeworld in his efforts to reorient a critical theory of society. This capacity of the concept is considerably elaborated in the mature critical theory of the early 1980s. Described as a 'source of situation definitions that are presupposed by participants as unproblematic',[56] the lifeworld is the 'nexus' of meaning that makes it possible for speakers to talk about the same thing. While the naivety of this background of shared knowledges is tested in a complex and pluralistic modernity, the condition of understanding it had provided needs to be put on a new, self-conscious, footing. When the task of social integration depends less on tradition and more on the interpretative capacities of individuals and their greater commitment to the negotiation of agreements, there are great risks of disagreement and increasing pressure to create relief mechanisms that promise an increase in efficiency and a reduction in the possibility of breakdowns.

A system mode of integration is one that is governed by impersonal rules and formal calculations. It can offer relief to concrete, communicatively achieved, integrations that have become over-burdened and dysfunctional. Relief mechanisms take two basic forms. One involves the condensation of communicative action in the sense that lifeworld knowledges are rationalized, not replaced. 'Every step we take beyond the horizon of a given situation opens up access to a further complex of meaning, which, while it calls for explication, is already intuitively familiar.'[57] Here we see the uncoupling of world interpretations from the immediacy of lifeworld contexts into systems that render their communicative functions more dense and abstract. An example of this kind of uncoupling of systems from the lifeworld is in the mass media, where communicative processes are released from the provincialism of local contexts and a broader area of public discussion emerges. The second form of relief mechanism involves the complete replacement of communicative interaction by the steering mechanisms of money and power that uncouple action coordination from language and the lifeworld and submit it to quasi-automatic subsystems. Here Habermas has in mind the economic and administrative systems that provide the basis for modern functional coordination of action beyond the lifeworld. They bypass the individual's own interpretative acts and self-responsibility with the creation of almost norm-free systemic structures.

Unlike Marx, who tended to view the automaticity of the market in terms of the reification of the world of commodities that dominated living labour, Habermas does not consider that the uncoupling of the subsystems from the lifeworld is in itself problematic. This does not automatically signify the subjugation of the lifeworld to the imperatives of the functional systems. The institutions that anchor the economic and administrative subsystems in the lifeworld, institutions like civil and public law and political representation, ideally offer a two way channel for the influence of the lifeworld on the organized functional systems and vice versa.

The Theory of Communicative Action does not have much to say of an explicit character about the place of a public sphere as a coordinate in this newly complex account of the internal dynamism of modern societies. However, there is much here that is of real relevance to a reworked account of the public sphere as a practical, critical, presence within dynamic modernization processes. The concept of the rationalization of the lifeworld as a process in which the actions, interpretations, and practices of individuals are detached from taken-for-granted normative contexts and submitted to examination, critique, and negotiation, places an account of the formation of the public sphere within the terms of an analysis of unexceptional processes of modernization. Thus reinterpreted, the concept of the public sphere is freed from the specific historical conditions of an eighteenth-century mode of intercourse and becomes anchored in an account of the everyday efforts of concrete subjects attempting to establish effective ways of coordinating their actions in complex modern societies. Yet, while *The Theory of Communicative Action* does the detailed work of retheorizing an account of the public sphere as a (vulnerable) mode of rationalizing interactions grounded within ambiguous modernizing processes, at this stage in the development of Habermas' theory of modernity, the public sphere does not really feature as a fully concretized and institutionally structured presence. It remains the task of *Between Facts and Norms*, the major work of the 1990s, to configure the concrete dimensions of the public sphere in liberal democratic societies and to fully elaborate the critical potentials of its normativity. Yet these later developments in Habermas' analysis of the functioning and the potentials of a modern public sphere rely upon the key insight of this more systematized concept of the rationalization of the lifeworld: that ambiguous modernization processes make for the concrete everydayness of expectations that we can forge rational solidarities with strangers.

The 'rationalization of the lifeworld' entails that knowledges, no longer simply legitimated by the authority of convention and tradition, refer themselves to particular types of validity recognized as governing specific modes of human activities and needs. These arenas of validity around which the differentiated meanings of modernity congeal are in no way simply 'found' or 'given'. They are objective in the sense that they make sense of certain kinds of behaviours (the norms of science are not to be confused with those of art and politics). Yet they still need to be *made* in the sense that concerned or involved publics are required to seek agreement about their formulation, to debate the appropriateness of achieved descriptions of validity claims, and to recommend new conceptualizations. For Habermas, then, the fragmentation of the world into various, partly institutionalized, and partly ideologically described, systems of meaningful activities is the site of a historically new mode of social integration in which understandings, no longer simply taken for granted, must be communicatively achieved. The 'rationalisation of the lifeworld' is an axis of development that describes an accumulation of interpretative freedoms constrained by an interest in arriving at explicit agreements about the meaning and significance of specific human behaviours and endeavours.

Rationalizing the lifeworld releases the rationality potentials of the mutual understanding in language through which the everyday communicative practice of the lifeworld context is achieved. As the zones of what is considered unproblematic shrink,[58] the rationality potentials of these communicative processes are actualized. A growing pressure for rationality is set in motion as fractured and problematic lifeworlds put the mechanism of mutual understanding under strain, increasing the need for achieved consensus and for the expenditure of interpretive energies.[59] The 'parcelisation' of meaning into the differentiated systems suggests an increasing detachment from the social structures through which social integration takes place. As already mentioned, according to Habermas, this process of increasing detachment by system organizations from the communicative modes of integration of the lifeworld contexts follows two different trajectories and the pathologies of an alienated modernity can be traced to the predatory expansion of *one* of these paths of development.

The modern public sphere actualizes and affirms the rationality potentials embedded in the everyday communicative practices of the lifeworld. At this stage, Habermas situates the public sphere within the lifeworld set in motion by processes of rationalization. This mode of interaction, which aims at building agreements through processes of offering and responding to reasons, is seen to have its unextraordinary roots in the normal functioning of modernization in which traditional meanings become problematized by the differentiation of functional roles in an increasingly complex modernity. An informal public sphere emerges as modern individuals become growingly conscious of an achieved capacity to make explicit the agreements that underpin the norms that guide their behaviours and modes of action. The public is bound to the private sphere because both 'are communicatively structured spheres of action, which are not held together by systemic means'.[60]

However, as already noted, Habermas is not persuaded that the anonymous, rule-governed modality of the systems is a mode of integration that is necessarily functionally opposed to the discursive interactions of the public realm. Indeed he insists that morality and the law can offer themselves as mechanisms of relief tailored to articulate and to protect the normativity of communicative action from the ever-present risk that interpretative freedoms simply dissolve into debilitating open conflict.[61] By no means ignoring the processes through which legal and political power could acquire their own systems logic in capitalist democracies, Habermas wants to correct a one-sided sociology that sees only the 'totalitarian features of the Enlightenment tradition and its social embodiments'.[62] The complex functioning of the law and political institutions within capitalist democracies can only be made sense of if we acknowledge that these systems also perform a role in formalizing communicative tasks that the lifeworld is unable to fulfil in a complex modernity.[63]

Habermas stresses the ambiguous possibilities of the separation of rule-governed, anonymous processes of system integration from the normative density of the lifeworld that characterizes modern development. Unlike the older generation of the Frankfurt School, he insists that there is nothing essentially pathological about the rise of an instrumentalizing reason. This is a mere description of what is required by a system mode of integration that has been 'largely disconnected from norms and values'.[64] He emphasizes that discriminations need to be made here about the distinctive kinds of relations that develop between the instrumentalizing logics of the system and the communicative interests of the lifeworld. While particular manifestations of a system mode of integration (the subsystems of law and media) may hold themselves finally accountable to the communicative power emanating from the lifeworld, other subsystems do not seek to legitimate their coordinating power with reference to the intentions and will of those who were affected by their jurisdiction. Habermas suggests that, since Adam Smith, 'the classic example of this type of regulation is the market's "invisible hand"'.[65]

Pathological consequences of the uncoupling of system and lifeworld arise when communicatively achieved agreements are colonized (replaced) by the alien rationalizing imperatives of a functional mode of integration. In these circumstances the coordination of action built upon the interacting points of view of those involved is interrupted by a mode of action coordination that takes only the requirements of the system into account. Integration is achieved by the assertion of the power of the media against the linguistically attained coordination of action in lifeworld processes. Mainly interested in the general structure of this colonizing relationship, Habermas does indicate some concrete circumstances in which we might recognize its pathological effects. The deforming impacts of this colonization of one form of modern rationality by another are experienced in moves towards a 'profit-dependent instrumentalization of work in one's vocation', in 'the market dependent mobilisation of labor power' and in 'the extension of pressures of competition and performance all the way down into elementary school'. It can be felt also in 'the monetarisation of services, relationships, and time' and in the 'consumerist redefinition of private spheres of life and personal life-styles'.[66] The penetration of money and bureaucratic power into the communicative structures of everyday life tends to deplete existing, non-renewable cultural resources that are needed to create and maintain personal and collective identities.

Habermas' analysis of the forms of juridification utilized by welfare states illustrates the ambiguities involved in the double-sided interchange between system and lifeworld. The expression 'juridification' refers 'quite generally to the tendency toward an increase in formal (or positive, written) law that can be observed in modern society'.[67] On the one hand, juridification of social relations describes the relief that is extended by legally sanctioned administrative power to overburdened communicative interactions. In this capacity, the extension of juridical power into everyday life can assume the complexion of a 'freedom guaranteeing juridification'. It can help to recast the unmet needs of marginalized populations as legal rights and in general serve to bridle the economic system.[68] At the same time juridification also functions as a pathological colonization of lifeworld contexts by system integration because it inevitably displaces communicative action as the mechanism for the self-interpretation of needs and as the basis for coordination action.[69] Experts intervene with their juridical or administrative means into social relations that become formalized and reconstructed as individualized 'cases'. Formal, individualizing and universalizing judgments that cannot deal with contextual complexities disempower clients by pre-empting their capacities to participate actively in finding solutions to their problems. At this stage in his thinking, Habermas considers this paternalistic dimension of the juridification process a necessary consequence of the welfare state.[70] This, as we will see, is an emphasis that shifts with the later account of the prospects for a democratization of the welfare project.

Old problems of a new critical theory

Habermas insists that, because he failed to sufficiently theorize modernity as a play of tensions between instrumentalizing and communicative rationality potentials, Weber was unable to account for why the unrestrained growth of bureaucratic systems should be regarded as a pathological path of development.[71] The later Adorno also failed to discover any point of view other than irrationalist longings from which the pathologies of an instrumental reason gone wild might be characterized.[72] At the time of *The Theory of Communicative Action* Habermas thinks that, by describing modern pathologies in terms of the colonizing processes of instrumentalizing system-demands on a communicative lifeworld rationality, social theory can rediscover an immanently critical standpoint. He claims that

> a theory of capitalist modernisation developed by means of a theory of communicative action ... is *critical* ... of the reality of developed societies in as much as they do not make full use of the learning potential culturally available to them, but deliver themselves over to an uncontrolled growth of complexity ... this increasing system complexity encroaches on non-renewable supplies like a quasi-natural force; not only does it outflank traditional forms of life, it attacks the communicative infrastructure of largely rationalised lifeworlds.[73]

An instrumentalizing reason that has become dominant follows a 'highly selective pattern' that seems to thwart goals of 'building institutions of freedom that protect communicatively structured areas of the private and the public spheres against the reifying inner dynamics of the economic and administrative systems'.[74]

The utopia of an emancipatory reason promised by Enlightenment was 'never a mere illusion'.[75] The critical theorist is not engaged in the task of peddling 'glossy ideals' disconnected from the immanent self-understandings of concrete actors. His task is to engage in a kind of 'metacommunication' with the self-reflexivity that is embedded in each deliberative act of communication, underscoring the rationality potentials it confirms. This could happen because

> [t]he same structures that make it possible to reach an understanding also provide for the possibility of a reflective self-control of this process. It is this potential for critique built into communicative action itself that the social scientist, by entering into the contexts of everyday action as a virtual participant, can systematically exploit and bring into play outside these contexts and against their particularity.[76]

Critical theory challenges a fatalistic accommodation to a one-sided pattern of modern development. Habermas insists that '[t]he transposition of communicative action to the media-steered interactions and the deformation of the structures of a damaged intersubjectivity are by no means pre-decided processes that might be distilled from a few global concepts'.[77] Hope lies in the recognition that the ideologies through which bourgeois society has sought legitimation (principles of individual and mutual self-development and of democratic decision-making) remain capitalist modernity's misdescribed and neglected, but still objective possibilities.

Throughout the late 1970s, it seemed that the 'silent revolution' of a 'new politics'[78] was recovering something of these rationality potentials while remaining rather blind about their systemic character and, hence, about their universal significance. *The Theory of Communicative Action* discerns a common thematic in diffuse and shifting patterns of contemporary protest movements.[79] Resistance had broken out, not so much in locations identified by traditional socialism (work and exploitation), but 'along the seams between system and lifeworld'.[80] In the Federal Republic of Germany, sites of protest had been built up by the early 1980s around environmental and peace issues (including the theme of the North–South conflict), single and local issues and around minorities (the elderly, gays, handicapped, and so forth).[81] As Habermas sees it, these diffuse patterns of protest are unified in their resistance to systems intrusions into the rationality potentials of diverse lifeworld contexts. They aim at recapturing the capacity and the right to the self-interpretation of needs by affected parties against growing consumerist and bureaucratic imperatives. Yet, for Habermas, the inability of these diffuse sites of resistance to autonomously thematize their common ambitions is a weakness and a source of vulnerability. To the extent that it particularizes concerns and problems which it fails to recognize as generated by the systematic frustration of a rationality potential, this politics of protest can mistakenly describe itself as a longing for the return of traditionally described lifeworlds. If the protest movements fail to describe their ambitions in universalizing terms, in terms namely of a specific appropriation of the principle of the right to a discursively elaborated needs interpretation that is also an achievement of legal and moral structures in liberal democratic societies, then the danger is that their reaction to ascribed need-interpretations imposed by the economic and administrative systems will assume the merely reactive character of a withdrawal into a conventional description of needs and identities.[82]

At this time Habermas thinks that only the feminist movement had managed to consistently avoid 'overburdening the communicative infrastructure' and reflect upon the connection of its particular reaction to the colonization of the lifeworld to generalized commitments held up by the framework of liberal democratic law.[83]

> Its struggle against patriarchal oppression and for the redemption of a promise that has long been anchored in the acknowledged universalistic foundations of morality and law gives feminism the impetus of an offensive movement, whereas the other movements have a more defensive character. The resistance and withdraw movements aim at stemming formally organized domains, and not conquering new territory.[84]

Critical theory is supposed to clarify the character of present threats and opportunities. Specifically, the systematic character of its reflections should be able to illuminate the fault lines in the relations between system and lifeworld that inspirit the protests of the new social movements. In doing so, it offers a kind of political education that contests the limited defensive tendencies embraced by the protest movements. The critical theorist suggests that the needs for autonomy that galvanize these struggles requires an united effort directed at rebalancing modernity's ambivalent rationalizing potentials. The integrated interpretative framework provided by critical theory allows the movements to recognize that the damage to subjectivities and to intersubjective relations they are protesting against are the specific consequences of the society-wide failure and pathologies of capitalist modernities.

The attempt to suggest expanded frameworks of self-interpretation for political struggles of the day is only one dimension of the task Habermas gives to the critical theorist. His view is that a contemporary critical theory must marry its efforts to connect up with practical, emancipatory motivations with an attempt to justify the universality of its normative claims. I argued that McCarthy was right when he insisted that the sociology of *The Legitimation Crisis* is unable to find an adequate path through the two burdens Habermas places on his critical theory. It might be worth revisiting this line of argument to situate some of the conceptual problems that continue to mark the more mature critical theory of *The Theory of Communicative Action*.

The Legitimation Crisis suggests that critical theory helps to clarify the significance of vulnerabilities in ideological attempts to legitimate capitalist imperatives. In this way, the theory presents itself as a contribution to the emancipatory motivations of certain concrete actors. At the same time, Habermas also offers his theory as a rationally justified critique, as a theory whose normativity is grounded in claims that can be traced 'back beyond the threshold of modern societies' and hence justified universally and without reference to ideological categories of the present. Specifically, the 'reconstructive science' seeks to elaborate idealizations that are deemed implicit in the communicative functions of language. However, as we saw, Habermas does not want references to an 'ideal speech situation' to function as galvanizing images of a primary commitment to democratic interactions distorted by the instrumentalizing logics pushed by bureaucratic capitalism. It seems that other pathways from a conception of the rationally justified character of its normative claims to the emancipatory functions of critical theory need to be found. *The Legitimation Crisis* appears to 'solve' this problem by sliding in a dogmatic re-affirmation of a quasi-necessary emancipatory purposiveness that is supposedly working its way through the contingencies of history.

By the time of *The Theory of Communicative Action*, the break with Marx is more explicit and complete. However, it seems that the conceptual advances that had been supposed to help negotiate the tension between the twin tasks of critique only see the old problem reappear under a new description. *The Theory of Communicative Action* again fails to negotiate the double burden of an engaged theory that seeks to represent itself as a critique that is justified with respect to universal, not ideological, criteria. It turns out that, as it was then formulated, the concept of the rationalization of the lifeworld is unable to mediate between the two tasks of critical theory. It is even caught between their competing imperatives.

As we saw, Habermas uses the idea of the rationalization of the lifeworld to concretize the modernizing process whereby individuals learn to build rational solidarities from the ruins of conventional agreements. This is a learning process that takes place within a particular cultural tradition. Cristina Lafont points out that the concept of the rationalization of the lifeworld is, therefore, 'in danger of merely reconstructing the self-understanding of this particular tradition, illicitly excavating it to a supposedly universal dimension'.[85] The danger is there because Habermas cannot really sustain the double vision required by his critical theory. The theory offers itself as a reflection on the self-understandings acquired by particular, located subjects as they attempt to rationalize their lifeworlds. It also offers a reconstruction of the supposed universality of these rationality potentials in undertakings that are claimed to be implicit in the communicative dimensions of each linguistic act. It seems, then, that the immanent self-understandings of the situated communicative actors have recovered a way of orienting to each other that has a universal value. In the end, as Axel Honneth and Hans Joas point out, *The Theory of Communicative Action* suggests that 'there is an inde-structible moment of communicative rationality anchored in the social form of human life'.[86]

The objection that Habermas imports an anthropological dimension into his account of the universality of our potentials for an interactive rationality is a familiar one in the secondary literature. Chapter 4 will explore the terms in which this claim can be made to stick as an important critique of key aspects of the theory of communicative action. I will argue that the attempted negotiation of the two distinct tasks that the theory sets itself (clarification of the immanent self-understandings of located actors and self-justification of the universal credibility of its normative claims via reference to counterfac-tually assumed commitments of the 'abstract' community of language users) is the site of significant conceptual confusions. A narrowed conception of the task of the theory of communicative rationality as a real contribution to the re-interpretation of the neglected potentials of a particular cultural tradition is required.

Perhaps, in part, Habermas' tension-laden construction of the role of crit-ical theory can be traced to difficulties that attend his project of formulating a critical theory able to fill the boots left by the 'crisis of Marxism'. Because *The Theory of Communicative Action* still works within agendas set by Marxism and by its reference to a philosophy of history, Habermas considers that crit-ical theory has to justify the rationality of its normative claims universally. This means that, at this stage in the development of his *oeuvre*, the capacities of the concept of the rationalization of the lifeworld as a novel interpretation of the unrealized capacities of a particular cultural tradition, can not fully surface.

Habermas has since recognized that, by taking its cue from an attempt to renegotiate a Marxian perspective on the pathological character of capitalist processes of modernization, *The Theory of Communicative Action* failed to give the emancipatory potentials of the rationalization of the lifeworld their due weight and attributed a misleading status to colonization processes. Indeed, in the Preface to the 1985 German edition of *The Theory of Communicative Action*, he relinquishes the concept of the colonization of the lifeworld as a source of confusion about the purposes of the theory.[87] The concept of system colonization of the lifeworld suggests an image of fixed historical processes that distorts the theory's efforts to enter into clarificatory relations with a present rendered mobile by the concrete struggles of social actors. The 1985 Preface stresses that *The Theory of Communicative Action* had been particularly concerned to find an adequate reformulation for a Marxian theory of reification. Once Marx's philosophy of history has been repudiated, critical theory needs to find a new basis from which to ground its challenge to modernization pathologies. A thematization of colonization by media driven systems of lifeworld rationality was supposed to carry the critical burden of the new diagnosis of reification processes. Yet Habermas later saw that, seeming to identify fixed relations and historical processes that were 'predecided from the start', the colonization thesis was at odds with his own attempt to break from the monological philosophies of history embraced by older versions of critical theory. Modernization is an ambiguous process and its potentialities need to be recognized and chosen by concrete historical actors. The colonization thesis seemed to confer an automatic status to a selective path of development. As such, it was a construct that 'failed to utilize the whole range of potential contributions of the theory'. The question as to 'which side imposes limitations has to be treated as an empirical question which cannot beforehand be decided on the analytical level in favour of the systems'.[88]

How far down do tensions in Habermas' conception of the role of critical theory go? In the next chapter I will argue that his attempt to locate the rational justification of the commitments carried by critical theory outside the vagaries and ambiguities of contingent cultural choices is the site of significant conceptual problems in Habermas' project which can only serve to cloud the capacities of the theory to render self-conscious the significance of important 'wishes and struggles of the age'. Later chapters will broach the question of how Habermas' concerns about the apparently parochial character of a critical theory agenda that offers itself only as a reflection of the learning processes of a particular cultural tradition might be addressed without resorting to an attempted philosophical justification of the universality of its normative commitments.

4 Discourse ethics and the normative justification of tolerance

The reconceptualization of the normative foundations of critical theory undertaken by *The Theory of Communicative Action* has guided Habermas' project of social enquiry ever since. According to him, shifting the normative reference of critical theory away from the frustrated aspirations of particular subjects onto an account of the unrealized potentials of a certain mode of interaction permits the de-transcendentalization of critical theory's philosophical roots. Critical theory, Habermas supposes, can now free itself from its former dependence on abstract descriptions of supposedly essential human motivations and position itself as a reflection on the normativity that concrete subjects themselves invest in a mode of interacting that occurs in their everyday acts of communication. The theory does not, thereby, forfeit its claims to objectivity. The standards of critical judgments are not to be turned over to the subjective tastes of empirical actors but are to refer to procedural norms whose rationality is implicitly affirmed by every interaction that aims at achieving mutual understanding. This account of the normative reference of critical theory implicitly democratizes ethics. A communicative ethics does not place concrete individuals as the passive recipients of judgments about how they might act reasonably in a complex and pluralistic social environment. It offers itself as a clarification of the wider significance of the norms of reasonable interactions that are, at least implicitly, present in the communicative practices of the everyday.

Habermas' discourse ethics describes itself as an ethics of and for modernity.[1] He means that it is an ethics for a time in which an enormous plurality of ethical frameworks, together with the systematic invasion of commercial imperatives and administrative power into lifeworld contexts, seem to challenge the very possibility that we can undertake to live in accordance with common norms for the regulation of reasonable conduct. Habermas is convinced that an ethics based on principles of discourse is a better way of negotiating the real difficulties that face the formulation of a contemporary ethics than has been made available to us by a conventional liberal framework. While the discourse ethics shares liberalism's interest in finding a way to talk about our agreed purposes in terms that accommodate the realities of multicultural and value plural societies, Habermas rejects the supposed ideological assumptions carried by a liberal approach. Conventional liberalism holds that a civilizing solidarity between privatistically motivated subjects requires only a legally sanctioned commitment to the defence of private right. Discourse ethics reacts against this as a legitimating standpoint that presumes the already achieved autonomy of self-sustaining private individuals. The normative underpinning of discourse ethics is not a conception of the shared interests of an already *acquired* autonomy but rather the procedural norms of a communicative interaction that is rationalized by a common interest in *achieving* autonomy. The following chapter will review Habermas' efforts in a series of essays published in the 1980s to establish that we can better grasp the unrealized potentials of liberal democratic ideals if their interpretation is wrested from conventional liberal frameworks and reworked by an ethics of discourse.

Nothing in the past or present of European history has made Habermas hopeful that the automatic reproduction of liberal democratic expectations of a civilized, tolerant, and decent way of life might be counted on. Principled modes of coordinating actions are under terrible strain to compete with the steering capacity of money and administrative power and these embattled norms need to be clearly elaborated and rationally defended. Habermas supposes that by re-interpreting these commitments through the framework of the theory of communicative action we can discover better, more persuasive, reasons for preserving and extending them. While the liberal tradition can take credit for its advocacy of principled commitments able to bind diverse modern societies, Habermas considers that its account of these shared values typically offered sanctuary to some narrow and deeply prejudicial convictions. It turns out that the ideal of autonomous subjectivity that liberalism represented as a common interest within a pluralistic society is formulated in terms that presume the motivations and privileges of a quite particular, self-sustaining, private individual. By contrast Habermas insists that discourse ethics does not presuppose a self who is able to meet its own needs. Rather, it affirms and clarifies the value invested in a mode of interaction through which subjects can attempt to have the reasonableness of their unmet needs and frustrated identity claims recognized.

On the one hand, discourse ethics hopes to bolster the claims of the liberal democratic ethic of toleration by re-interpreting this normatively charged description of the self/other relation to disclose attractive possibilities that are obscured by a liberal account. Habermas' theory offers to justify and to reinforce the claims of this embattled ideal by disclosing its overlooked and desirable dimensions. He suggests that a discourse ethics can supply us with more compelling reasons for why we need to defend the liberal democratic ideals of respect for autonomy and toleration of difference than those that conventional liberalism has come up with. This is a re-interpretation that would require more of us by way of substantial reforms in our social practices and institutional arrangements. We will see that Habermas also supposes that a discourse ethics is superior to a liberal ethical framework because, while it offers a universally relevant justification of an ethics of tolerance, it does so in terms that avoid all metaphysical presumptions.

In my view, some part of Habermas' claimed advantages of a discourse ethics re-interpretation of liberal democratic morals ought to be conceded. The discourse ethics does manage to exclude some of the legitimating ideological aspects of a liberal interpretation of tolerance and it does open up attractive new egalitarian and emancipatory meanings of this ideal. However, I will also suggest that discourse ethics does not completely succeed where conventional liberalism has failed. In the end, the discourse ethics cannot persuasively demonstrate the non-metaphysical, universal grounds of the rationality it upholds. A short exposition of the main tenets of the discourse ethics will be followed by a discussion of the insightful ways in which Habermas uses this framework to reconstruct the potentials of the principle of tolerance as a mode of regulating conduct in a liberal democratic society. I will argue that this kind of justification of the theory, in terms of its enriched interpretation of the potentials of particular cultural norms, needs to be distinguished from the problematic dimensions of Habermas' efforts to justify the validity of his communicative ethics universally.

An ethics of and for modernity

Rejecting the proposition that a modern ethics can assume a priori the motivations and central aspirations of sovereign individuals, discourse ethics tries to reconstruct the shared interests that social subjects betray through the way in which they seek to co-ordinate their interactions. It has its starting point in the observation that, despite our perceived and, at times keenly felt, differences, we humans continue to discursively engage, interact, and arrive at broad agreements with one another. This generalized communicative capacity does not call upon any special talents or philosophical commitments. Communicative interaction is not, to Habermas, a contingent, optional mode of inhabiting the world; it is essential to our human identity. He makes the point that, because individuals acquire and sustain their identity by appropriating traditions, belonging to social groups and taking part in social-izing interactions they do not have the option of long-term absence from the contexts of action oriented toward reaching an understanding. This would mean regressing to an unsustainable monadic isolation and disorientation.[2] Under modern conditions of cultural and social pluralism, we can no longer count on a shared ethos to sustain our interactions and are, accordingly, required to look to norms of interaction to which all mature agents could freely assent. The discourse ethics is, then, principally concerned to reconstruct the procedural norms implicitly affirmed by competent speakers as the grounds for their communicative interactions.

The point was made earlier that, for Habermas, the norms thematized by the discourse ethics are a mere reconstruction of certain undertakings implicitly embraced by every competent speaker in the pragmatic dimension of each linguistic act. In so far as speakers wish to engage in a process of reaching reciprocal understanding, they are implicitly raising grounds in terms of which the validity of their utterances may be understood and, in principle, criticized by their hearers. From our present point of view, the significant consideration is that, according to Habermas, in making such a claim the competent speaker always undertakes to argumentatively defend the criticizable validity claims raised by his utterance. Communicative rationality is, thereby, supposed to feature as a universal presumption of the pragmatics of human language itself.[3]

William Outhwaite has reiterated that this recognition of the claims of an idealized rational communication is not presented by Habermas as a positive value towards which competent speakers can aspire. The concept of an ideal speech situation, which idealizes completely transparent communicative interactions, is not, he writes, meant as a 'concrete utopia which would turn the world into a gigantic seminar'.[4] This idealization is a regulative idea that betrays itself only negatively in the context of the disappointment of expectations invested in the communicative functions of language. These expectations are concretely embedded within the procedural norms implicitly affirmed by all rational users of language. Discourse ethics views itself, then, as an attempt to reconstruct those procedural norms implicitly affirmed by all competent speakers that might be explicitly appealed to in an attempt to restore the conditions for a continuation of disrupted communication. In those contexts in which speakers can arrive at no broad agreement in the interpretation of the facts and can call upon no shared understanding of cultural traditions, we are 'left with no alternative except to locate the normative basis for social interactions in the rational structure of communication itself'.[5] As Habermas sees it, this conception of the function of the theory points to its self-limiting character.[6] Discourse ethics refers to a 'negatively damaged life instead of pointing affirmatively to the good life'.[7] The discourse ethics conceives its own motivating interest as an investment on behalf of systematically frustrated needs for personal autonomy. It repudiates the 'postmodern' proposition that, in the face of seeming intractable difference and the apparent loss of the grounds for communicative interaction, we have the choice of simply 'going off in peace'.[8] Interpreted as a generalized strategy, this is not 'a meaningful choice', for 'there are problems that are inescapable and can only be solved in concert'.[9] For discourse ethics, the critical theorist has to attempt to identify those general principles to which oppressed and estranged difference can appeal in its efforts to have the rationality of its need and identity claims recognized.

Habermas refers to the central commitment of the reconstructive project undertaken by the discourse ethics as the principle (D). (D) is intended as a procedural principle of argumentation that would show how a determinate range of practical issues can be decided in a way that is mutually beneficial to all participants. This principle states that '[o]nly those action norms can claim to be valid that meet (or could meet) with the approval of all affected in their capacity *as participants in a practical discourse*.[10] (D) does not pretend to specify the terms in which normative validity is to be decided in all cases. It seeks jurisdiction only in those circumstances in which the question of normative validity is up for dispute with a range of competing interpretative perspectives and interests claiming priority. In such circumstances, (D) maintains that the legitimacy of proposed norms has to be determined by ensuring the free agreement of all who might be affected by its general observance.

This principle of impartial adjudication of disputed claims in no way requires a bracketing of the particularistic interests of each speaker. On the contrary, in the discourse ethics the question of validity makes the self-interest of each into a criterion against which the validity of the norm might be decided. As Habermas sees it, 'every single participant in argumentation remains with his "yes" and "no" a court of final appeal: no one can replace him in his role of one who pronounces on criticizable claims to validity'.[11] At the same time, the procedural principle of argumentation holds that 'even those interpretations in which the individual identifies needs that are most precisely his own' are open to a revision process as the social nature of what is most individual is opened up to public discussion.[12] The observance of the principle of impartial adjudication formulated by (D) requires, then, that the participants in the discourse undertake a process of 'ideal role taking', described as a procedure of 'checking and reciprocally reversing interpretative perspectives under the general communicative presuppositions of the practice of argumentation'.[13] The descriptive terms in which each individual conceives his interests has to be open to criticism by others. Our needs and wants are interpreted in the light of cultural values and hence are always components of intersubjectively shared traditions. The revision of values used to interpret needs and wants therefore cannot be a matter for individuals to handle monologically.[14]

The process of ideal role taking described under principle (D) identifies those procedural norms that must be observed if we are to discover what we inhabitants of a heterogeneous social universe share and how we are to identify that range of doing things that require our solidaristic recognition.[15] This discovery of inter-subjectively shared traditions should involve no imposed construction of the terms of substantive agreement nor suggest a primary orientation towards consensus. Rather, according to the theorization of the discourse principle, the building of shared traditions emerges as a kind of by-product of the struggle for recognition waged by individuals in a heterogeneous modernity. Habermas makes the point that, from the fact that persons can only be individuated through socialization (i.e., they can only interpret their own needs and formulate their aspirations in the light of available cultural descriptions), it follows that their seemingly most individual reasons for action can be open to public discussion and to the elaboration of those shared traditions upon which they implicitly rely.

Habermas insists, however, that this kind of substantive agreement over what might count as 'good' reasons in support of the diverse need interpretations and action plans of persons in a complex modernity is by no means the only terms in which intersubjectively shared traditions might be discovered by processes of discursive interaction. In the absence of such agreements, the participants can 'rely on the "neutral" fact that each of them participates in *some* communicative form of life which is structured by linguistically mediated understanding'.[16] In such circumstances, the participants in the discursive process discover their shared humanity with those others who, recognized as the bearers of different descriptions of the good life, are never-theless seen to be able to formulate these diverse descriptions as reasons in defence of their need for self-sovereignty.

This is the province of the (U) principle. In those cases where profound differences in forms of life and life projects block any substantive experience of intersubjectively shared traditions of a lifeworld in common, the scope of solidaristic recognition shrinks back to the level of a common assent to the idealizing presuppositions implicit in the abstract rules and principles which govern the integrity of discourse. Habermas makes the point that in 'the course of the development towards multiculturalism within particular societies and toward a world society at an international level', we have been compelled to retreat to a more formalistic proceduralist understanding of the terms of solidaristic recognition. While this retreat to the terms of such solidarities as might be achieved under the governance of the principle (U) suggests a dramatic truncation of the range of questions that can be answered rationally from the moral point of view, it also seems that 'finding a solution to these few more sharply focused questions becomes all the more critical to co-existence and even survival in a more populous world'.[17]

Habermas has continued to insist on the difference in the status of the (D) and the (U) principles.[18] (D) is a reconstruction of the discursive procedures whereby the shared horizon provided by the lifeworld of a particular socio-cultural group might be redeemed and offered as grounds from which a disturbed consensus might be re-established. (U), by contrast, appears as a completely formal account of those generalizable principles of discourse which are implicitly affirmed in any appeal to the (D) principle. (U), that is, holds that a contested norm cannot meet with the consent of the participants in a practical discourse unless all affected can *freely* accept the consequences and the side effects that the *general* observance of a controversial norm can be expected to have for the satisfaction of the interests of *each individual*. In those circumstances in which a substantive shared horizon cannot be reconstructed, (U) identifies the terms in which the normative basis for social interactions can be located in the rational structure of communication itself.

Having identified some of the components of Habermas' discourse ethics we can now turn to a discussion of its significance for a re-interpretation of our cultural options. The need for a rational defence of a liberal democratic ethics is, Habermas insists, becoming growingly evident as competing modes of integration become ever more powerful. In the mid-1990s he observed that the liberal virtue of tolerance had increasingly become a 'diminishing resource'.[19] While complex societies *rely* more and more upon a legally non-coercible mutual toleration of forms of life and worldviews that represent existential challenges for each other, for a neo-liberal epoch 'this require-ment...is increasingly experienced at the subjective level as an unreasonable demand'.[20] As Habermas sees it, the threat that this mounting disaffection with the expectation of tolerance poses to the stability of unwieldy modern societies suggests that the demand itself 'requires a normative justification to a growing degree'. It is up to critical theory to reconstruct those terms in which the 'reasonableness' of the expectation of tolerance can be recognized. According to Habermas, this is a task that, in some measure, requires us to understand and appreciate better the unrealized potentials of cultural ideals over which liberalism has claimed jurisdiction. Let us see if he has been able to offer a justification for the principle of toleration that is both better, more rationally compelling, than a conventional liberal account and that avoids some of the problems that confronted it.

Reworking the tolerance principle

Joseph Raz points out that liberalism appeals to the principle of private autonomy as the grounds of an ethics of toleration. Indeed, according to him, the 'duty of toleration, and the wider doctrine of freedom of which it is a part, are an aspect of the duty of respect for autonomy'.[21] John Stuart Mill's trea-tise *On Liberty* formulated the 'simple principle' that 'over himself, over his own body and mind, the individual is sovereign'[22] as the basis from which the immorality of intolerance as a denial of self-sovereignty could be formulated. Yet it seems that a liberal attempt to interpret and to advocate an ethics of tolerance through a primary commitment to the ideal of private autonomy yields a potential paradox. Does an interpretation of tolerance construed as an injunction to forbearance towards a trumping private autonomy oblige us to accept things believed to be morally wrong? His determination to negotiate a way out of this seeming conundrum provokes Mill to offer a discriminating account of the meaning of the ideal of private autonomy upheld by a liberal ethics of tolerance.

The capacity of the ideal of tolerance to sustain interpretations other than a dominant liberal formulation was discovered a generation ago by Herbert Marcuse.[23] He described a liberal account of this ideal as an ideological standpoint that was non-partisan 'inasmuch as it refrains from taking sides – but in doing so...actually protects the already established machinery of discrimination'.[24] By construing tolerance as a passive state of forbearance for an already constituted private subjectivity, the 'democratic argument for abstract tolerance' refuses to admit the public significance of claims made on behalf of the unmet needs and the dissenting points of view of private individuals. Marcuse goes on to suggest that this liberal construction of toleration as a merely passive virtue is a deformation of its early modern interpretation as an active state. On the eighteenth-century Enlightener's active construction of this principle, '[t]he toleration of free discussion and the equal right of opposites was to define and clarify the different forms of dissent: their direction, content, prospect'.[25] On this account, toleration refers to undertakings between discursive partners committed to building understandings between those who are different. By contrast, armed with its rigidly interpreted principle of division between public and private domains, liberalism seeks in the observance of the ideal of toleration not clarification for, but a quarantining of, the point of view of the dissenting voice. The discourse ethics attempts to elaborate and to formalize an active construction of the principle of tolerance as the rational norm of a mode of interaction between subjects for whom autonomy appears as a mutual goal. In this sense, the (D) principle opens up critical potentials within the ideal of tolerance that are obscured by its liberal formulation.

A discourse ethics is, as indicated, determined to break from the ideological presumptions of a liberal model that seeks to defend a presumed already achieved private autonomy. As an account of a mode of interaction between subjects determined to make their needs and their points of view understood, the ethics of discourse puts itself in the service of the 'damaged life'. Supported by an ideology of the self-sufficiency of the private individual, a passive construction of the ideal of tolerance is compatible with the return of all the anti-democratic impulses of a *laissez-faire* society. By contrast, an interpretation of toleration as an active principle invests in discursive arrangements that allow dissident and disadvantaged private subjects a legitimate role in building an account of the generalizable significance of their claims. The point can also be made that a discourse ethics interpretation of the principle of toleration opens this commitment to an expanded account of the meaning of individuality. Against a liberal view that presumes the achieved autonomy of a subject whose needs and capacities are already fully self-understood, the idea of public reason upheld by discourse ethics invests normativity in interactions in which discourse partners elaborate shared understandings to be used as reasons in support of their claims and points of view. In the process of building these shared understandings, participants in discourse must learn to adopt the point of view of the other and hence to adopt a testing orientation towards their own inclinations and motivations. Finally, because the communicative ethics interprets the principle of tolerance as normatively charged procedures of discourse, its commitment to tolerance fosters a practical demand for the democratic reform of the interactions that shape a range of informal cultural and formal politico-legal institutions in liberal democratic societies.

We have seen that Habermas agrees with Mill that the ideal of tolerance needs to be justified in terms of a general principle to which all those excluded from an empirically established consensus might also appeal in their efforts to establish the reasonableness of their claims upon a shared interest. Habermas presents the (U) principle as a formal recognition that the normativity of the modern public sphere embraces the community of all competent speakers. It is in these terms that the discourse ethics attempts to redeem the universalism of classical liberalism's account of the normativity of the principle of tolerance. Here too Habermas supposes that discourse ethics has the advantage. He maintains that, by locating normativity in the rational structure of communication itself, the justification of the universality of the principle of tolerance does not finally need to appeal to an ideology of human nature. A discourse interpretation of ethics does not, it is claimed, presume a particular kind of subjectivity that is supposed to act as a universal standard but advocates a procedure by which different types of subjects interact as its normative point of reference. The discourse ethics is committed to a reconstruction of the grounds upon which culture-bound concrete persons might develop a sense of shared humanity with everyone else in terms that permit 'a *non-leveling* and *non-appropriating* inclusion of the other *in his otherness*'.[26]

Surviving the contextualist critique?

Thomas McCarthy is among the dissenters who insist that Habermas' distinction between the (D) and the (U) principles cannot be sustained and hence that, on at least one important count, the discourse ethics' challenge to conventional liberalism fails. McCarthy points out that the inter-subjectively shared traditions built into the procedural norms governing discursive interaction cannot be stretched so thinly as to be completely free of the values of a common lifeworld. We cannot 'agree on what is just without some measure of agreement on what is good'.[27] For Jean Cohen also '[d]iscourses do not create values and solidarities ex nihilo but draw on already shared commonality and culture, i.e., lifeworld'. The norms generated by participation in a discourse would, she continues, 'thus not be universal, but specific to those who value this form of interaction'.[28] For such critics, a conception of intersubjectively shared traditions, that 'we' which is discovered or reaffirmed in the discursive process, can only appear as the articulation of an already existing common culture. Assent to the idealizing presuppositions implicit in the abstract rules and principles governing the integrity of (U) implies a prior agreement over substantive values. As Agnes Heller points out, participation in discourse already suggests a commitment to certain kinds of culturally laden value ideas and, she concludes, in this sense 'the principle "U" is actually only the principle "D"'. The idea of universal procedure is no less embedded in the Western tradition than is the claim to the validity of certain maxims.'[29] Outhwaite raises a similar concern: '[c]an Habermas justify in universalistic terms a conception of moral reasoning which may not only be class and gender biased but presupposes the specific historical values of European modernity?'[30] It seems that Habermas' attempt to drive a solid wedge between the supposedly universalistic provenance of the principle (U) and the context-specific character of the terrain covered by (D) is guilty of an 'ethnocentric fallacy'.[31]

This line of argument cuts deeply into the ambitions of the discourse ethics. We have seen that Habermas' conception of public reason repudiates liberalism's ideological restriction of its role as mere protector of the rights of a quite particular, self-sovereign private individuality. To him, there can be no qualification on the right of entry into discourse apart from a demonstration by 'competent speakers' of their willingness to redeem their implicit undertaking to argumentatively defend the criticizable validity of claims raised by their utterances. The abstraction of the (U) principle is supposed to describe those procedural norms adequate to the human rights conviction 'that arguments deserve equal consideration regardless of their origin and, hence, also "regardless of who voices them"'.[32] Accordingly, in the critics' protest that principle (U) is redundant Habermas sees a challenge to an undertaking central to the whole theory. At stake is the discourse ethic's intention to offer a universalistic, non-liberal account of the claims of the modern public sphere.

Habermas has framed his response to the supposed redundancy of the principles (U) and (D) partly by an attempt to distance himself from the kinds of concessions that the later Rawls has made to the contextualist argument.[33] As Habermas sees it, Rawls has responded to criticisms of the contrived character of his own early interpretation of the ideal of public reason by cutting back the claims of the theory of justice as a theory of human rights. In *Political Liberalism*, the account of the process of rational will formation no longer owes its rationality directly to the idealized conditions of a communicative practice that makes agreement, in the sense of rationally motivated assent, possible. For Habermas, Rawls has succumbed to the challenges of the contextualists and he now invests, not in a procedural contrivance designed to yield an impartial justice, but in the supposed rational capacity of participants appropriately endowed with aptitudes and dispositions capable of impartial adjudication on matters of the public good.[34] As a consequence, in the later Rawls, 'the concept of person now bears the full explanatory weight in demonstrating the normative content of practical reason ... the theoretical problem of justification is shifted from the characteristics of procedures to the qualities of persons'. Against the example of the later Rawls, who 'now presents his theory of justice merely as a systematic reconstruction of the best normative intuitions of the Western tradition in political thought', Habermas refuses to retreat from the ambitions articulated in the principle (U). He will not, that is, leave open the question 'of whether the reconstructively grounded principle of justice should be regarded as valid only for societies shaped by *our* political-cultural traditions and *for all modern* societies irrespective of their cultural orientation and tradition'.[35]

Yet Habermas' defence of the principle (U) must go further. The critics have not merely challenged the apparent conceptual necessity of the appeal to the principle (U). They have also expressed deep reservations about the tenability of this idea. We have seen that in the first instance, Habermas endeavours to respond to these concerns by pointing to the abstract level upon which the (U) principle is formulated. According to some critics, this formalistic character of the principle, supposed to drain (U) of any dependence on culturally specific norms and values, manages at the same time to empty this principle of all substantial usefulness. Seyla Benhabib argues that the degree of abstraction and formalization of the (U) principle renders this procedural norm too indeterminate to be of use even as an adequate universality test for negative duties.[36] She finds, moreover, that even the level of abstraction involved in the representation of generalizable interests carried by the (D) principle fails to allow any meaningful application of its relevance. With these reservations in mind, Benhabib attempts to introduce an additional principle into the overall framework of discourse ethics. She postulates a criterion under the heading of an ethics of care as an autonomous moral standpoint that complements considerations of justice.[37]

Benhabib concedes that the proceduralism that governs Habermas' search for terms in which the generalizable interests of the self-sovereign polity might be articulated is the only meaningful formulation of the modern democratic ideal that must negotiate the realities of cultural and ethical pluralism. However, she also insists that these procedural norms must be recognized as the bearers of a particular, loaded conception of the aspirations and the capacities of the participants in the discursive process. Specifically, she suggests that the discursive norms reconstructed by Habermas describe the interaction between 'generalized others'. The standpoint of the generalized other 'requires us to view each and every individual as a rational being entitled to the same rights and duties we would want to ascribe to ourselves'.[38] Recognizing only claims made on behalf of this generalized idea of the person, Benhabib fears that the procedural norms specified by the discourse ethics might yield, not an impartial consensus, but a 'common' opinion and will built on the neglect of the profound differences between the communicative actors. She insists, therefore, on the need to include into the proceduralist strategy a recognition of the other as a concrete particularity. As she sees it, the standpoint of the concrete other 'requires us to view each and every rational being as an individual with a concrete history identity and affective–emotional constitution'.[39]

Habermas has pointed out that this kind of critique of the abstractness of the idea of the person recognized in the discourse ethics loses sight of the richness of the theory's communicative and intersubjective presuppositions.[40] Underpinned by processes of ideal role-taking, the discursive interaction is supposed to exhibit a lively and expanding sensitivity to the diverse points of view and to the particularity of the needs of concrete individuals. If we are to build shared grounds of mutual understanding, we need to make the hermeneutic effort of considering matters from the points of view of speaker and hearer, self, and other. We have seen that for liberalism, the procedural norms governing rational discourse seek to contain the points of view of private individuals that might be endured in the name of a shared commitment to personal autonomy but might never claim public, generalizable significance. By contrast, informed by the procedural norm of ideal role-taking, Habermas' reading of the scope of the idea of public reason offers the potentials for self-clarification and, in this sense, enlargement of the particular points of view brought to the discursive process. Benhabib's critique has underestimated, then, the extent to which the discourse ethics breaks with a liberal formulation of the idea of public reason. Unlike liberalism, discourse ethics repudiates the suggestion that the public use of reason is opposed, in principle, to the recognition of the significance of the specific interpretative point of view.[41] For Habermas, while each party may interpret this representation of the generalized interest differently, the 'we' which is reaffirmed or discovered through the processes of argumentation demonstrates the legitimacy of its articulation of intersubjectively shared traditions only so long as it continues to be recognized by all as the best embodiment of their intentions, in a given context, for the time being.[42]

In my view, Habermas' discourse ethics survives certain formulations of the contextualist critique. It can plausibly defend itself against arguments that target the supposed redundancy of the principle (U) with respect to the conceptual requirements of the theory itself. It seems, moreover, that some of the critics tend to neglect the extent to which the proceduralism of the theory permits recognition of concrete particularity in its difference. Yet can the discourse ethics finally evade criticisms that target the merely ideological character of its defence of the universality principle? Can the theory survive, namely, challenges that its appeal to the principle (U) has not only added nothing to its appeal to (D), to its reconstruction of the kinds of significances which *particular* cultures have invested in communicative competencies, but has actually mystified the status of (D), treating it as if it were a principle that could claim universal applicability?

The general terms in which Habermas responds to reservations concerning the universalistic pretensions of the discourse ethics have already been noted. We saw that he conceives the theory as a reconstruction of the significance attached to the trans-culturally relevant fact that we humans acquire and sustain our identity by appropriating traditions, belonging to social groups and taking part in socializing interactions. It is the communicative character of our social formation, the fact that we recognize and constitute ourselves in an on-going dialogic process, that makes a sceptical pluralist affectation of indifference to, or mere aestheticizing appreciation of, the identity claims of the other a 'meaningless option'. Habermas goes on to argue that a recognition of the seeming intractability of our differences with others, an acknowledgement of the apparent untranslatability of our diverse language games, suggests that we already implicitly engaged in a process of building a shared frame of reference in terms of which the incompatibility of the several points of view might be registered.

According to Habermas, this implicit reconstruction of intersubjectively shared traditions capable of admitting the terms of incompatibility finally rests on an acknowledgement that '[c]oncepts such as truth, rationality, and justification play the *same* role in *every* language community, even if they are interpreted differently and applied in accordance with different criteria'.[43] This fact is, Habermas argues,

> sufficient to anchor the same universalistic concepts of morality and justice in different, even competing, forms of life and show that they are compatible with different conceptions of the good – on the assumption that the 'comprehensive doctrines' and 'strong traditions' enter into unrestricted dialogue with one another instead of persisting in their claims to exclusivity in a fundamentalistic manner.[44]

Thus, human difference is lifted out of seeming irreducibility by the discursively achieved recognition of the similar functions played by such abstracted concepts as 'truth', 'rationality', and 'justification' in every language game. In the end, then, the self-justification of (U), the supposed legitimacy of its pretension to a universalistic jurisdiction, refers back to a presumption of the fundamental perviousness of language games. Habermas supposes that the distinctive universalistic scope of the (U) principle is an index to a human capacity to develop a 'bilingually extended identity' in which the languages and rationalities of conflicting language games are fused into a broadened scope of possible understanding.[45]

However, there is a conceptual slide occurring in this argument. Habermas has appealed to the idea of a trans-cultural human capacity for reaching mutual understandings in language as if it means something valuable about how we can structure our relations with others. If (U) is simply an abstraction about the conceptual underpinnings of our uses of language to communicate, then it cannot alone tell us anything useful about good ways of relating to others. As soon as (U) enters the picture as more than a postulate, once it is offered as a value description, it articulates culturally loaded significances. The principle (U) is only interesting in anything more than a theoretical sense because Habermas' discourse ethics is allowing it to migrate into terms that confirm certain cultural choices. It is being implicitly translated in the discourse ethics into terms that confirm choices that a particular cultural tradition can make about its ambiguous potentials. There is, then, a dimension of ideological mystification in Habermas' efforts to draw a distinction between the (U) and the (D) principles. If (U) is really only (D), then the culturally loaded character of (D) is being allowed to disavow its particularity and to assume the status of an idealization presumed compelling to all. It seems that the (U) principle is a normatively charged one, otherwise there would be no point to Habermas' proposal that it must be kept as a placeholder to avoid communicative ethics slipping into the role of advocate to merely parochial cultural choices. However, if (U) is endowed with normative pull, this must be borrowed from certain culturally loaded descriptions of what is good about it, hence from the (D) principle. There seems to be no way out of the ideological confusion between (U) and (D) in Habermas' formulations.

Reviewing the search for normative justification

Discourse ethics invests in the rationalizing dimension of post-conventional communicative interactions. It is interested, namely, in our efforts to make ourselves intelligible to strangers by a process of continual reflection upon, and re-interpretation of, those shared concerns through which private need claims can seek to make themselves understood. We have seen that, in attempting to establish the rationality of his need and identity claims, the private individual also enriches his own self-understanding by engaging in ideal role-taking. In their efforts to arrive at common ground, communicative actors must engage in a testing participation in the lifeworlds inhabited by others. It is in this sense that the rationalizing processes supported by post-conventional communicative interaction do not merely require, but also produce the open, expanded personality.

Habermas is not confident that we can rely on the automatic reproduction of principled commitments to relations based on respect between self-reflecting private subjects. These are expectations that are put under pressure by the hard realism of a world made cynical and need, thereby, to be actively chosen. It is up to the theorist to offer some compelling reasons in their defence via a reinterpretation of the normativity that underpins them. I have argued that there are problems with the terms under which Habermas prosecutes this project of rationally justifying the value commitments upheld by his theory. He is persuaded that it is necessary to determine universal standards against which the normativity of a principled respect for individuality can be formulated. Rejecting any attempt to anchor human rights in a natural order, Habermas argues that the rationality of the interactive relations upheld by a communicative ethics is in principle recognizable to all competent language users. However, even if it is conceded that there is an invariance to the presumptions implicit in the communicative purposes of language, if these conceptual underpinnings are to acquire particular value they must identify themselves within frameworks elaborated by particular communication communities. (U) is interesting only when it makes its appearance as (D).

Habermas' discourse ethics is only able to effectively constitute itself as an attempt to persuade us about the reasonableness of certain ways of interacting within a particular cultural universe. Demonstrating to people the possibilities available to them or showing them 'how it can make goals that they already have more possible' is, Richard Dees points out, all that can be achieved by way of rational justification of a value commitment.[46] I have argued that, on this score, discourse ethics can claim some significant advantages. Its proposal to interpret a commitment to autonomous subjectivity as the ethic that governs a mode of interaction between subjects means that it is responsive to the dissatisfactions of subjects engaged in a struggle to seek recognition for the legitimacy of their self-interpreted needs. Against the presumptions of a conventional liberal ethics that upholds the expectation of autonomous subjectivity as an already acquired attribute that requires protection, a discourse ethics engages with the point of view of the needy self in its quest to participate in setting agendas necessary to the pursuit of its self-determination. A discourse interpretation of ethics can claim, moreover, to reveal attractive meanings to the idea of the autonomous, self-determined personality. Its concept of 'bilingual extension' refers to the heightened self-awareness that accrues to individuals engaged in processes of ideal role-taking as they shift between the positions of speaker and hearer.

Habermas strongly repudiates the suggestion that the reconstructively grounded principle of justice should be regarded as valid only for societies shaped by our political-cultural traditions and not for modern societies irrespective of their cultural orientation and tradition. He thinks that critical theory has to contribute not only to the increased awareness in a given communication community of the unfulfilled potentials dormant in its own explicit value commitments, it also has to be able to contribute to a discussion of standards of rational action that can claim a universal appeal. In a later chapter I will argue that we should not suppose that if discourse theory confines itself to encouraging the critical self-examination of Western political and cultural traditions it necessarily forfeits an interest in, and a capacity for, promoting civilizing expectations across the globe. After all, in a globalizing world it appears vitally important that intercultural exchanges be informed by an acute self-consciousness of all participants about the character and the potentials of their particular cultural horizons. The discourse ethics offers a real contribution to this process.

As Arato and Cohen point out, given the reconstructive ambitions of the discourse ethics, it is true that 'no single model of democratic institutions follows from discourse ethics'.[47] However, it is also the case that its interpretation of liberal democratic normativity requires an institutional level of analysis. Habermas' proceduralist interpretation upholds a mode of interaction governed by the mutual interest of participants in seeking understanding recognition of their need and identity claims. This governing ambition of a communicative ethics is embedded in the concrete contexts, and requires the supporting structure of liberal democratic institutions.

5   A discourse theory of law and democracy

Elaborated throughout the 1990s, the discourse theory of law and democracy extends the project of critically rethinking the capacities of liberal democracies for radical self-reform that was undertaken by the discourse theory of ethics. Habermas' conviction that we have understood our Enlightenment legacies in a partial, one-sided, and distorted fashion does not desert him. Again the critical theorist is given the task of helping us to recover potentials for rationality supposedly implicit in our background cultural knowledges. This time it is not the repressed normativity of an early European bourgeois public sphere nor the counterfactual status of undertakings implicitly raised by competent language users and not even the specifically ethical presumptions of liberal democratic communities that critical theory principally needs to reconstitute. In Habermas' sights this time is the incompletely theorized normativity that is both evident in, and betrayed by, the normal functioning of liberal democratic politico-legal institutions (the law and the Constitutional State). His message is that the major theoretical traditions that had outlined the grounds of the legitimate power of these institutions have not grasped the centrality of the modern public sphere to these expectations and, hence, have underestimated the extent to which critical norms are harboured within the institutionalized arrangements of capitalist democracies as their neglected potentials.

Against the schizophrenia of modern democratic theory, Habermas' major work of the period, titled *Between Facts and Norms: Contributions to a Discourse Theory of Law and Democracy (Between Facts and Norms)* wants to find an approach that 'does not imply an *opposition* between the ideal and the real'.[1] The normative content Habermas set forth for reconstructive purposes 'is partially inscribed in the social facticity of observable political processes'.[2] His reconstructive sociology of democracy chooses its basic concepts in such a way 'that it can identify particles and fragments of an "existing reason" already incorporated in political practices, however distorted these may be'.[3] He is committed to 'performatively refuting the objection that the theory of communicative action is blind to the reality of institutions'.[4] The discourse theory uncovers the critical potentials of misunderstood idealizations embedded in a range of institutions and material processes at work in liberal democratic

societies. The discourse-theoretical approach 'allows a critical relationship
with the self-understanding of familiar political cultures, existing institutions,
and recognized legal systems, with the goal of fully tapping the potentials for
self-transformation stored up within them'.[5] This groundedness of the theory
as a reflection on the misunderstood normativity of liberal democratic institutions is partly to be established by contrasting the comprehensiveness of a
discourse theory reconstruction with the one-sidedness of rival liberal and
republican models of modern democracy. The conceptual weaknesses of these
partial readings of the normativity of liberal democratic institutions is to
be demonstrated by showing that neither alone is able to make good sense of
the complex histories of modern democratic institutions and the range of
functions they are capable of performing. Discourse theory recommends itself
against these partial interpretations of the liberal democratic normativity and
against a fashionable 'normative defeatism' as well.

Contemporary Western societies have lost their self-confidence before a
'terrifying background' that includes the 'conspicuous challenges posed by
ecological limits of economic growth and by increasing disparities in the
living conditions in the Northern and Southern Hemispheres' and in the face
of 'the risks of renewed ethnic, national, and religious wars'.[6] Habermas has
'no illusions' about the problems that our situation poses and the fatalistic
moods it evokes, however, he is convinced that 'moods . . . do not justify the
defeatist surrender of the radical content of democratic ideals'.[7] It is up to
critical theory to clear away the obstacles to our better appreciation of the
self-critical potentials of liberal democratic societies. This project of clarifying
the unrealized choices latent in our ambiguous legacies is even more explicitly
a task of reconstructive analysis. It seeks to 'prove what we already tacitly
assume if we participate in the democratic and constitutional practices that
have fortunately taken hold in our countries. A consciousness that has become
completely cynical is incompatible with such practices'.[8]

Some of Habermas' critics consider that this project of defending the
misunderstood normativity of liberal democratic institutions suggests that
the mature Habermas has become far too reconciled to the degraded realities
and foreshortened vision of empirical liberal democratic nation states. There
are two major strands in this evaluation. For some, Habermas' interest in
potentials for a radical self-reform of capitalist democracies is not critical
enough of capitalist imperatives that erode democratic motivations and
capacities. William Scheuerman, for example, thinks that *Between Facts and
Norms* betrays 'an inadequately critical assessment of "really existing"
capitalist democracy'.[9] For others, Thomas McCarthy amongst them,
Habermas' interest in rebalancing modernizing legacies fails as a radical
agenda primarily because it overlooks the depth of the pluralistic motivations
that have articulated themselves through these complex histories.

The following chapter opens with an account of Habermas' efforts to confront liberal and republican interpretations of liberal democratic normativity
with their lop-sidedness. He argues that neither of these frameworks offers a

sufficiently comprehensive account of the terms in which modern democracies have contrived to rebuild legitimate sociality in the context of the disintegration of comprehensive worldviews and collectively binding ethics. For the discourse theory, the most adequate point of reference for legal authority in contemporary democracies is the subjectless procedures of discursive interaction that are aimed at building rational solidarities between particular subjects. The second part of the chapter will consider Habermas' mature account of the modern public sphere. This is a more complex and concrete version of democratic pathways within liberal democracies than Habermas has ever provided before. He takes on the task of reconstructing the public sphere as a 'single text' composed of a rich interdependency of expectations, processes, and institutional arrangements that cross the spectrum of lifeworld and system relations. The immediate danger for the reproduction of a vital public is posed by that range of threats to the complex and delicate web of interconnections that are its life. The last part of the chapter will review some of the major lines of critique of *Between Facts and Norms*.

Responding to normative confusions

The conviction that the normative foundations of liberal democratic societies are not clearly understood has long preoccupied Habermas. In the work of the early 1990s he lays particular responsibility for the confusions in our thinking about liberal democratic potentials at the door of competing liberal and republican models of democracy. Each in its own way offer a truncated version in which the emphasis on either 'rights' or popular sovereignty monopolizes its vision. In this respect the exemplary Hegelian, it is not Habermas' intention to entirely reject either of these famous models. His defence of the liberal democratic project wants to hold fast to the contemporary truth of each and to fuse them in a coherent synthesis while repudiating only their one-sided distortions of the integral truth of democracy.

The main features of these classic models are well known. The liberal model issues from a defensive understanding of the individual's relation to the state. It is focused on economic society and on the guarantee of the nonpolitical common good of civil privatism.[10] Democratic processes whereby the state is obliged to take into account competing parties, social interests, and values, bridge the gap between citizens and the state. This assumes the form of a process of aggregation and compromise between competing actors and interests. The legitimacy of the system resides in the basic rights of individuals. These secure the fairness of the results through universal and equal suffrage and representation. However, liberalism takes the realistic view that power only emanates from the people to be exercised by the organs of the state, therefore democratic processes and the balance of power between citizens and state more generally are ensured by the constitutional protection of basic individual rights, the rule of law, separation of powers, and statutory control.[11] By contrast, the republican tradition offers an offensive understanding of politics.[12] It provides a normatively charged version of the political that is less about the rational outcome of state decisions and more about rational will-formation. It is this collective deliberation that forms the medium through which the society constitutes itself as a political whole. This deliberation never takes place in a vacuum or on the basis of atomization. From the very start, society is political society that can rely on the substantive support of a culturally established background consensus that is the basis of its ethico-political self-understanding. Upon this foundation, the practice of political self-deliberation allows a collective will to act and the community's self-consciousness to be continually renewed as a reconstituted political totality.

The first movement of Habermas' normative reconstruction of liberal democratic theory is to undermine the polemic that has been prosecuted by many generations of the respective supporters of these classical models. He wants to demonstrate that the struggle between liberal rights and popular sovereignty for the mantle of authentic democrat is illusory because neither has such a comprehensive armoury of credentials to be in a position to confidently grasp the prize. While Habermas has a very forceful theoretical explanation of the one-sidedness of both claims, his work also draws on the tortuous history of the last century to reinforce his arguments.

Between Facts and Norms devotes much attention to the inadequacy of the liberal one-sided reliance on rights.[13] Habermas argues that the ascendency of the welfare state in the post-Second World War era was largely a recognition of the inability of the bourgeois emphasis on formal political rights to deliver the benefits of democracy to the broad masses of citizens in the liberal democratic West.[14] The identification of bourgeois political rights with democracy had faltered on the 'social question' of poverty. Only when the 'social rights' of basic welfare supplemented formal rights could these societies even begin to redeem their claims to be authentically democratic. Yet, these latter rights were clearly not of the pre-political variety that had typically been the classical liberal explanation of their foundational priority.

Because *Between Facts and Norms* is a work on the normative foundations of liberal democratic theory, Habermas has less to say explicitly regarding the historical lessons of the republican tradition. In any case, the theoretical excesses of the Rousseauian 'general will' and its real life imitators in the subsequent history of totalitarian politics are only too well known. While Habermas is keen to preserve the normative force of the republican emphasis on political will formation and solidarity, as a young man he had seen too much of the 'dark times' of the twentieth century at close hand to think of readily identifying these with a single collective subject or an unconstrained political totality. The deep circumspection with which he approaches an attempt to theorize the ideal of the self-directing society in terms adequate to the future of modern democracy is informed by the pointed German national experience of reconstruction after the decade of fascist barbarism.[15]

Between Facts and Norms sees its first great contribution to the contemporary debate on democracy as an attempt to reconstruct in conceptual terms the lessons that the history of modernity itself has taught us: the inadequacy of the liberal and the republican models of democracy and the necessity of arriving at a synthesis of both. Habermas argues that the liberal emphasis on rights can be reconciled with the republican fixation on a popular sovereign will.[16] In fact, he maintains that human rights and popular sovereignty conceptually pre-suppose each other. This is the basis of his understanding of the internal interconnection between public and private autonomy.[17] In other words, the private rights of citizens are not suspended in the air as some sort of gift of God or nature, but are the direct product of the political will of a collective public of citizens whose autonomy is ultimately guaranteed by their individual political rights. This is not a vicious circularity but simply the expression of the cooriginality of both basic rights and popular sovereignty.[18] For classical liberal theory, rights were grounded at the pre-political level of religion or nature. However, in the post-traditional climate of modernity, rights can only anchor their legitimacy in the legal order created by politics. In Habermas' view, it was Rousseau who took the first decisive step to arrive at a more balanced understanding of the relation between rights and sovereignty.[19] Yet this republican insight failed because Rousseau could not explain how his (ascribed) normative general will would be reconciled with the real free choice of individuals. Habermas puts this failure down to the republican mistake of deriving the normative force from the generality of the law rather than from the procedural conditions of will formation itself.

This critical insight is crucial to the construction of Habermas' own procedural synthesis. As I have indicated, he wants to take over the sound elements of both the liberal and republican traditions. In the first instance, this involves the rejection of a singular collective subject or its background cultural consensus. Habermas readily acknowledges his debt to Hannah Arendt and to her idea of a communicative power that emerges from collective action, promises, deliberation, and the political virtue of solidarity.[20] He follows her in viewing this communicative power and its products as possessing a strength and influence that is greater, more rational and normatively powerful than an aggregation of the decisions of atomized individuals. But if this notion points in the right direction, Habermas also wants to see popular sovereignty absorbed into the rule of law, democratic procedures and institutions, and dispersed across the formal and informal public spheres of civil society.[21] Deliberative politics is only one action system, not the centre nor the apex of society. It needs to communicate with other systems and meet them half way. Habermas not only concedes, then, the liberal concern for constitutional guarantees of basic rights, he also allows that only political administration is legally permitted and financially funded to act as the instrument of the public will. Arendt has to be united with Weber.[22] A modern theory of democracy must concern itself not just with the glories of 'public happiness' associated with the narratives of founding constitutions, it has to be just as diligent in its examination of administrative power. It must follow the flow of democratic will formation not just from the finest capillaries of the informal and the grassroots into parliaments. It has also to stick to its trail through formal parliamentary institutions, and carefully scrutinize the transmission belts of ministerial and bureaucratic execution.[23]

The republicans' view of democratic politics emphasizes communicative power. For them, the political process is not just about the aggregation of private opinions. It has an independent rationality of its own that consists in the mediation of opinions, the bundling of interests and the harmonizing of unified perspectives. Despite these insights, republicanism, for Habermas, goes too far in its demand that the individual be totally absorbed in this collective will. Liberalism offers a mediating legal protection of the individual at the level of rights, and its concern with rational political outcomes makes it more sensitive to the needs and efficiency of political administration than is permitted by the republican's one-sided emphasis on political power. A synthesized perspective shows up the role of law in transforming communicative power into administrative power.

Habermas builds his synthetic account of the potentials of the liberal and the republican models of democracy into an analysis of a complex set of interdependencies that govern the relations between informal processes of collective opinion and will formation and the administrative and decision-making functions of the political centre. He refers to this as a 'two track' model of representative democracy. The informal or 'unorganized' public sphere does not appear in the first instance as a set of institutions but as 'a network for communicating information and points of view'.[24] It describes processes whereby problems, formerly encountered privately, are attached to reasons through which their generalizing significance can be recognized. In pursuit of its ambition to facilitate the shift of expressions of private dissatisfactions into the terms of effective claims, the public sphere has then to be 'anchored in the voluntary associations of civil society and embedded in liberal patterns of political culture and socialization'.[25] Habermas' account of the genesis and the reproduction of the informal public sphere describes the democratizing potentials of this process of a communicative or interactive rationality in which legitimacy is generated via processes of argumentation. The legitimacy of claims is to be decided, not on the basis of appeals to authority of tradition or power, but via the use of consensually elaborated principles.

However, more is invested in the procedural norms of the democratic interaction than just the expectation that particular claims might be allowed to demonstrate their reasonableness and their justice. The presumption also that the democratic process can accept the burdens of authority, that it is able 'to get things done', is an expectation that is reflected in operations at the informal, opinion forming end of the public sphere, not just in the decision-making activities of its legal and political centres. Within the informal or unorganized end of the public sphere, problem descriptions need to be 'bundled' to become amenable to the problem-solving activities at the formal, organized end. Streams of communication are 'filtered and synthesized in such a way that they coalesce into bundles of topically specified *public* opinions'.[26] The achievement of the public sphere is, on the one hand, measured in terms of the increased self-understanding and extended mutual understanding discovered by its participants. At the same time, this process of self-clarification finally permits the newly 'bundled' problems to begin to seek patronage as reasonable demands placed on the decision-making bodies of a constitutional democracy.[27]

It seems that Habermas' understanding of the role of the administrative institutions of liberal democracy builds as a synthetic elaboration of features of both the republican and the liberal models. On the one hand the republican tradition is criticized for neglecting the theorization of administrative power and expelling it from the domain of real politics as the 'rule of nobody'. On the other hand, a liberal understanding of administration that is focussed primarily on rational outcomes seems to pacify the citizen and fails to recognize the extent to which the citizen's own self-awareness of issues is a decisive ingredient in meeting real political needs.

Habermas' proceduralist interpretation of the role of the administrative state in democratic processes offers both specific inspiration and more general democratic illumination. In this first respect, it serves as model for democratizing administrative power and for confronting some of the deepest problems that have plagued the welfare state. His main idea is that the 'bluntness' of law and administration as policy instruments in the fraught domains of welfare (described by him as the process of juridification) can be best counteracted by alternative arrangements that attempt to open up democratic forums and enclaves within administrative arrangements wherever possible. This would facilitate clients becoming citizens who articulate their own needs and interests.[28] But this reformist agenda is only one instantiation of Habermas' desire to conceptually spell out the normative meaning of contemporary liberal democracy. The later chapters of *Between Facts and Norms* lay out the way in which money and power present themselves as real obstacles to the complete delivery of the normative content of liberal democratic arrangements. However, Habermas is convinced that the institutional realization of this normative vision is itself a singular historical achievement. This is not simply a laudation of the past. He is also sure that this normative content acts as a vital and powerful counter-factual ideal in resisting colonization and preserving contemporary democratic aspirations.

Immanently critical potentials of liberal democracies

According to Habermas, both the liberal and the republican models inadequately respond to the problems that the disintegration of comprehensive world-views and collectively binding ethics in pluralistic societies raise for an attempt to describe the legitimate exercise of power.[29] For modern liberals, the 'reference point' of legitimacy claims is finally the principle of private right anchored no longer in natural law but in the order created by politics. For the republican, legitimacy sanctioned by law has its point of reference in a description of the political will of a collective public of citizens. By contrast, the discourse theory holds that in liberal democracies the legitimacy of the rule of law depends on its appeal to subjectless procedures of discursive inter-action aimed at building rational solidarities between strangers. We have seen that discourse theory represents itself as a paradigm that has emerged from a reflection on the limits and a selective appropriation of the insights of rival theoretical reflections on liberal democratic normativity. Yet Habermas also claims that his theory offers a conceptual elaboration of learning processes whose results are felt elsewhere, in the complex and ambiguous 'lived' histories of post-war democracies. Reformist practices evident in the functioning of the constitutional state and the legal order suggest that each has learnt in the course of the twentieth century from inadequate, one-sided descriptions of their normativity. For Habermas, the 'internal relation' between the rule of law and democracy has been practically grasped by self-reforming constitutional states and legal institutions within liberal democracies in the wake of the manifest failures of alternative descriptions of the sources of the legitimacy of the law.

The disintegration in post-traditional societies of collectively binding ethics and world-views allows socially integrative functions (not picked up by the steering mechanisms of money and bureaucratic power) to be, partly, taken up by the law and constitutionally organized political systems.[30] In such societies, the law stabilizes behavioural expectations and 'simultaneously secures symmetrical relationships of reciprocal recognition between abstract bearers of individual rights'.[31] *Between Facts and Norms* suggests that the nature of the demands that this role of social integration places on the rule of law finally exposes the inadequacy of one-sided descriptions of law's sources of legitimacy and fosters the practical recognition of its internal relation with democracy.

Habermas maintains that the integrative function performed by the law and by constitutionally organized political systems does not simply rely on coercive mechanisms. This coordinating power legitimates itself by appealing to a universal principle of self-determination. Citizens 'should always be able to understand themselves also as authors of the law to which they are subject as addressees'.[32] However, the 'self' referred to in the idea of self-determination has to be formulated in terms that accommodate the complexity and hetero-geneity of a multicultural and ethically diverse modern citizenry. For a polity in which 'equality' has been appropriated as the effective demand of culturally heterogeneous and ethically diverse populations, only the procedural norms of a discursive interaction aimed at an argumentatively achieved ratio-nal consensus can fulfil the role of the 'self' necessary to sustain the idea of self-determination to which the legitimate authority of a legal and constitu-tional political order might appeal. The politico-legal systems of liberal democracies have been forced to respond to the empirical criticisms of marginalized populations at the exclusionary practices built into their legitimating self-descriptions.[33]

These criticisms have led to reformist practices that are based not on a change in the normative premises of the state and the law but only on the hidden presumptions embedded in 'a more abstract reading of them'.[34] The post-war welfare state compromise was just such a self-reforming response of the constitutional state. Under conditions of organized capitalism dependent on the government's provision of public infrastructure and planning, the idea that the legal order and the constitutional state could draw their legitimacy from their protection of a universally available capacity for self-determination was disclosed as a fiction.[35] It became evident that, as the socialist critique of liberal ideology had long protested, 'the universal right to equal individual liberties could no longer be guaranteed through the negative status of the legal subject'.[36] The constitutional state responded to this legitimacy crisis by introducing the new category of basic rights which recognized 'that legal freedom, that is the legal permission to do as one pleases, is worthless without actual freedom, the real possibility of choosing between the permitted alternatives'.[37]

The newly acquired responsibility of the welfare state in the distribution and protection of basic, not merely formal, rights did not complete the self-reforming tendencies of post-war politico-legal systems in liberal democracies. Describing their legitimacy in terms of their defence of the principle of self-determination, the 'golden age' of the welfare project was to see a contradiction emerging between the goals and the methods of key liberal democratic institutions.[38] The self-described ambition of these institutions was to open up the ideals of individual self-realization and the pursuit of private autonomy via the establishment of forms of life that were structured in an egalitarian way.[39] But evidently the paternalism that clung to the welfare project also compromised the pursuit of this goal that could not be reached via the 'direct route of putting political programs into legal and administrative form'.[40] The contradiction inherent in the welfare state compromise has provided an excuse for winding back these reforms. Yet it can also provoke pressure towards a democratizing re-interpretation of the welfare project in which private individuals seek practical and institutional support for their demand to be recognized as the legitimate interpreters of the rationality of their own need claims.[41]

Reconstructing the public sphere

Habermas by no means predicts that the learning capacities unleashed within liberal democratic societies will engineer a victory for their potentials for rationality. Indeed, the final chapter of *Between Facts and Norms* seems to suggest not much hope that the tensions between the facts and the norms that are necessary to the self-critique of liberal democracies can survive powerful counter-ideologies. Habermas discusses the extent to which a normative defeatism aggressively promoted by market ideologies appears to dominate the political and cultural landscape of the future.[42] The tension between normativity and facticity has all but collapsed and the habitual functioning of the system now appears as 'the *unavoidable* result of structural changes in state and society'.[43] For all that, in a complex society, developmental trends remain ambiguous.

Habermas wants to explore the challenges facing a critical politics aimed at the release of democratic potentials of existing social arrangements and political structures of liberal democracies. He insists that the pathway of double-sided communicative flows between informal problem-interpreting negotiations operating within civil societies and the formal problem-solving functions of a political centre need to be unblocked. The undertaking to overcome system blockages in the potentials for double-sided flows between the opinion forming processes of lifeworld contexts and the decision-making activities of a politico-legal centre is not, in his opinion, a task for a revolutionary politics. It is only a matter of making the most of the potentials of liberal democratic arrange-ments for self-reform. Habermas considers that some of the self-reforms that have already occurred within liberal democratic constitutional and legal systems count as evidence that the internal relation between democracy and the rule of law can be grasped as a practical potential. He is, for example, impressed by the way in which western feminist politics has exploited the self-critical capacities of institutional structures within liberal democracies.[44] Empirical criticisms directed both at ascribed legal definitions of equality and at the paternalism of an undemocratized welfare state project have seen marginalized populations occasionally achieving practical recognition by liberal democratic institutions that those who are affected can best clarify the 'relevant aspects' that define equality and inequality in a given matter.[45]

Habermas aims to bring the project of rescuing the public sphere before us not simply as an idealization disconnected from contemporary realities but as a task that requires a mobilization of communicative currents between social practices and institutional structures that are already in place in liberal democ-racies. It is a project whose appropriateness is already implicitly set out in the terms of the normative self-justifications of really existing liberal democracies. As such, a commitment to rescue the public sphere goes into battle against systemic imperatives within capitalist democracies that contrive to shatter the conditions necessary to sustain communicative flows forward and back between its interdependent layers. It also, as we have seen, offers itself as a critique of those philosophical reflections on the normative underpinnings of liberal democracies that obscure the extent to which the legitimacy of liberal democ-racies finally depends on the reproduction of communicative interactions between the mutually dependent sectors of a complex, decentred public.

The sociological framework of *Between Facts and Norms* reconnects in a striking fashion with the interest of *The Structural Transformation* in mapping the architecture and in analysing the critical potentials of the modern public sphere. The later work does so through the prism of categories and concepts that have been developed in the theory of communicative action. This is a return that sorts out some of the uncertainties about the relations between the private and public that were evident in the first sociological enquiry. *The Theory of Communicative Action* carefully theorized a type of rationalizing interaction that has been all but swamped by a dominant, instrumentalizing construction of modernity's rationality potentials. After this systematic analysis into the complexity of modernity's potentials for rationality, the troubled pre-occupation of *The Structural Transformation* with the relations between private and public domains of action can be moved aside. Since *The Theory of Communicative Action* Habermas more confidently rejects a conception of the public viewed as a sphere that constitutes itself as a typology of concerns whose generalizable, hence 'appropriate', character seems assured. In *Between Facts and Norms* Habermas manages to exploit the systematic analysis of rationalizing modes of interaction elaborated in the communicative action theory to theorize the public sphere as a network of communicative processes that move between an active civil society and the politico-legal centres of liberal democracies. The public sphere now appears as a complex and differentiated network that nevertheless constitutes itself as a 'single text' whose governing purpose is to secure the capacity of private individuals to seek recognition for the reasonableness of their points of view and the justice of their claims upon shared resources.

Key aspects of Habermas' account in *Between Facts and Norms* of the dynamic intersection between lifeworld and system are, then, already familiar to readers of *The Theory of Communicative Action*. Lifeworlds become rationalized as private individuals seek to make sense of a lived experience whose easy coherence has been interrupted by the intervention of system processes. The experience of 'violated interests' and 'threatened identities' provoked by disruptions to contexts of action by system imperatives[46] motivates private subjects to begin to elaborate new reflected upon interpretations from chosen aspects of a shattered lifeworld. Once the arena of private life, the shared intimacy bounded by the face to face encounters between 'relatives, friends, acquaintances and so on',[47] no longer suffices to absorb the efforts of private individuals to make sense of disrupted identities and to respond adequately to the quest for solutions to problems whose collective character has come into focus,[48] automatic interpretive frameworks have to be replaced by reasoned ones.

Yet Habermas is persuaded that some distinctions need to be made here. As long as this reflective process continues to be preoccupied with shoring up the dense particularity of shared concerns, it remains within the horizons of a private sphere. Attempts to elaborate legitimate, mutually agreed upon bases for shared interests, can become the grounds upon which voluntary associations, built around the *defensive* assertion of chosen allegiances, are constructed. The search for common cause can always remain arrested within particular, exclusive, agendas set by 'collectivities, associations, and organizations specialized for specific functions'.[49] Contrived solidarities can only be said to engage with the informal end of a public sphere once they embark on a search to achieve wider recognition for the legitimacy of the rationalized needs, points of view and projects that galvanize them. The spectrum of such affiliations include 'organizations representing clearly defined group interests; through associations...; up to "public-interest groups" (with public concerns, such as the protection of the environment, the testing of products, and the protection of animals) and churches or charitable associations'.[50] These opinion and will forming associations, that are generally designed to generate public influence as problem interpreters, belong to the civil-social structure of the public sphere.[51] With its highly differentiated and cross-linked channels of communication, the informal public sphere forms the real periphery in the process of collective opinion and will formation. Yet in complex differentiated modern societies, opinion-forming associations that specialize in handling particular issues frequently prove unable to adequately meet the needs that they both respond to and amplify.

Habermas agrees with Dewey that the communicative orientations of a political public sphere have a specific trajectory. Its publicity and legitimating functions are structurally distinguished by an interest in finding solutions to problems that must be validated by those who are affected. The purposes of the political public are, then, very different from a merely pragmatic/technicist interest in problem-solving which is unconcerned with testing out the reasonableness of any proposal by appealing to the judgments of those who might be affected. At the same time, the specific purposes of a political public distinguish it from the expressive interests of a literary/aesthetic public. Participants in a political public are drawn to the process by a distinctive investment in establishing the reasonableness, hence justice, of their viewpoints and their need claims. This account of the specific purposes of a political public sphere suggests the framework in terms of which Habermas analyses the interconnected movements between its component parts.

If the bearers of particular problem descriptions are to seek to make legitimate claims upon public resources, they need to make effective use of a range of diverse agenda-setting mechanisms available within the cultural as well as the legal and political institutions of liberal democracies. The mass media, for example, plays a vital role in publicizing and rendering influential selected need and identity claims. It is one of the principal vehicles through which the society-wide significance of particular problem definitions can seek recognition. The law also performs a distinctive function as 'sluice' to communication flows between the informal opinion forming and formal decision-making centres of a complex, two-tiered, public sphere.

Habermas borrows the account of the sluice model of communicative flows in the democratic process from Bernard Peters to characterize the switching mechanisms through which the results of the opinion and will forming functions of an informal public sphere can be delivered up to the decision-making functions of the formal public sphere and then channelled back to seek approval from the affected parties.[52] The ordinary communication processes that serve to interpret needs and to enlarge problem descriptions in an informal public sphere must be channelled into terms appropriate to the exercise of the decision-making functions of the formal public sphere. The legitimation of binding decisions requires that particular need claims articulated by actors in civil society be represented in terms that allow wider, disengaged publics to appreciate their rationality and to acknowledge why they should be met.[53] It seems that the publicity functions of the mass media that amplify the significances of problem descriptions must be supplemented by the translation functions of the 'language of law'. The abstract generalized language of the law places particular problem definitions into terms that can be acted upon by political decision-making centres that must seek to legitimate their rulings in the name of the general interest.

In the political circulatory system, law is the medium through which communicative power is transformed into administrative power. Because politics deals with general problems of integration,

> [i]t must be possible to interpret collectively binding decisions as a realization of rights such that the structures of recognition built into communicative action are transferred, via the medium of the law, from the level of simple interactions to the abstract and anonymous relationships among strangers.[54]

However, the translation functions performed by the law in a decentred modern public do not simply refer to the law as a 'freedom guaranteeing' set of institutions within liberal democracies. They refer also to the internal relation between politics and the coercive power of the law.[55] This resource of the law, its capacity to bring sanctions to bear in support of the rulings of political power, suggests another dimension of co-dependency between the systems aspect of the decentered public sphere and its anchorage in lifeworld processes. The institutions of the law can function to make effective the role of the political centre in protecting the rationalization processes of an active civil society that are a necessary condition for the reproduction of a liberal democratic public sphere. At the most fundamental level, '[f]reedom of assembly and freedom of association, when linked with freedom of speech, define the scope for various forms of association'.[56]

Habermas emphasizes that the sluice-model does not describe the business of politics as it is usually conducted in Western democracies.[57] Under normal conditions, operations in the core arena of the political system frequently proceed according to routines without reference to community-wide processes of collective opinion formation. The capacity for supportive interactions up and down between the informal publics and the formal decision-making publics is frequently blocked by powerful unities engineered between the economic and administrative systems. However, the question remains whether the settled routines of bureaucratized decision-making in accordance with the dictates of established power constellations can be shifted to realize potentials dormant in the system's descriptions of its own legitimacy.[58] Habermas insists that the description of issues identified in the periphery *can* influence the agenda of the decision-making centre in cases in which 'perceptions of problems and problem situations have taken a conflictual turn'.[59] The complex political histories of liberal democracies have suggested that dissenting publics can achieve some effective resonance at the centre for agendas set at the periphery, and will, under some circumstances, be able to ignite a mode of problem-solving that cuts across the routine of bureaucratized decision-making.

Two major potentials of a decentred public sphere must be mobilized if communication flows from the periphery to the centre are to be activated. In the first instance, the peripheral networks of opinion-formation must embody a specific set of capabilities. The informal end of the public sphere must demonstrate 'the capacity to perceive, interpret, and present society-wide problems in a way that is both attention-grabbing and innovative'.[60] Habermas also stresses that these networks must be given sufficient *occasion* to use these capabilities. The political system must, that is, be able to secure the conditions of an active, effective civil society.

Clustered in the associational networks of civil society, the informal public sphere appears as a 'sounding board for problems'.[61] Besides the tasks of perceiving, interpreting and 'signalling' problems, the peripheral networks need to attempt to '*influentially* thematize' them, to 'furnish them with possible solutions and dramatize them in such a way that they are taken up and dealt with by parliamentary complexes'.[62] Civil associations form a part of a differentiated public sphere only if their influence on decision-making processes does not rest simply on a capacity to exploit existing sites of power. Civil associations offer a vital underpinning to a democratic culture as 'social sites' in which the public, generalized significance of points of view and particular claims are argumentatively teased out.[63] Habermas describes the specific function performed by the associational networks in the activation of a democratic culture as a process of filtering and synthesizing streams of communication into 'bundles of topically specified *public* opinions'.[64]

The capacity for 'influential thematization' necessary to move problem descriptions from the periphery of the public sphere to its decision-making centre utilizes latent opportunities available within the social and political structures of liberal democratic states. The later Habermas does not resile from the opinion of *The Structural Transformation* that there is a 'kernel of truth in the theory of the culture industry'.[65] He notes tendencies towards the increasing centralization of the effective channels of communication on both the demand and the supply side of media output.[66] The image of politics presented by the mass media is comprised of issues and contributions that are professionally made up. 'Reporting facts as human-interest stories, mixing information with entertainment, arranging material episodically, and breaking down complex relationships into smaller fragments – all of this comes together to form a syndrome that works to depoliticize public communication.'[67]

However, for the mature Habermas, the critique of the culture industry remained one-sided because it failed to describe such processes within mass media institutions as a systematic betrayal of their normative importance.

Research on the effects of reception has undermined the image of passive consumers as 'cultural dopes'.[68] There is an 'ought' about the function of the media in a modern public sphere that can be, and sometimes is, mobilized. Actually, the conviction that the media could act not simply as an advocate for topically specified public opinions, but also play a pivotal role in extending their rationality potentials underpins the frustrations and disappointments articulated by the critique of the culture industry. Despite everything we still nurse expectations that

> [t]he mass media ought to understand themselves as the mandatary of an enlightened public whose willingness to learn and capacity for criticism they at once presuppose, demand, and reinforce; ... they ought to be receptive to the public's concerns and proposals, take up these issues and contributions impartially, augment criticisms, and confront the political process with articulate demands for legitimation.[69]

Habermas considers that the fluid and decentred structures and ambiguous self-descriptions of liberal democratic institutions make this sort of approach to problem solving a practical potentiality. He supposes that the proof of the pudding is in the eating. Looking back on some of the great issues of the last decade (the spiralling nuclear arms race, the ecological threats involved in an overstrained natural environment, the dramatically progressing impoverishment of the Third World) it seems that '[h]ardly any of these topics were *initially* brought up by exponents of the state apparatus, large organizations, or functional systems'.[70]

In Habermas' 'two-track' view of democratic law-making, formally institutionalized deliberation and decision-making must be open to input from informal public spheres. This means that the political must not become an autonomous system, operating solely according to its own criteria of efficiency and unresponsive to citizen concerns, nor should it become subservient to particular interests that have access to administrative power through unofficial paths of influence that by-pass the democratic process. Conversely, 'the public sphere must not itself be "subverted by power", whether that of large organizations or the mass media'.[71] The political system is intertwined with an autonomous civil society

> through the activities of political parties and elections. This intermeshing is guaranteed by the right of [political] parties to 'collaborate' in the political will-formation of the people, as well as by the citizens' active and passive voting rights and other participatory rights.[72]

Habermas emphasizes the circular character of the connection between an autonomous civil society and the formal political institutions of a democratic public. The latter do not just have to make themselves responsive to the legitimacy claims brought forward by the various publics, they also need to work to actively protect the private basis of the public sphere:[73]

> The constitutional protection of 'privacy' promotes the integrity of private life spheres: rights of personality, freedom of belief and of conscience, freedom of movement...the inviolability of one's residence, and the protection of families circumscribe an untouchable zone of personal integrity and independent judgment.[74]

Habermas thinks that a liberal model of the law and the constitutional state is losing out to a paternalistic construction of the responsibilities of the welfare state. In the early 1990s, the debate was limited to the question of whether it sufficed that the constitutional state guarantee private autonomy through individual liberties or whether the conditions for the genesis of private autonomy should be secured by granting welfare entitlements.[75] As he sees it, both of these paradigms lose sight of the *internal* relationship between private and political autonomy and the 'democratic meaning of a community's self-organization'.[76] Habermas insists that the legitimacy of the political centre derives from its role in securing the conditions of both private and public autonomy for its citizens. It needs, that is, to stabilize the conditions under which the efforts of private individuals to communicate the rationality of their needs could become effective. This is the undertaking for a democratized welfare project.

According to Habermas, a democratized and self-reflective welfare project could break the vicious cycle played out by a paternalistic welfare state that has worked to undermine the conditions of the private autonomy that it is supposed to help secure. Democratizing the welfare project would require that institutional support be extended to help secure the communicative conditions under which a diversity of self-interpreted needs could be bundled up and seek to effectively represent the legitimacy of their claims upon public resources. The centrality of the project of a democratized welfare programme to Habermas' mature conception of the utopian contents of a contemporary critical theory will be reviewed further in later chapters.

Reconciliation with liberal democratic realities?

Earlier I referred to two types of challenges to Habermas' attempt to rebuild critical theory as a reconstruction of the misunderstood normativity of liberal democratic institutions. The first of these considers that this programme is too limited in its ambitions and too 'soft' on capitalist democracies. These are societies that have systematically eroded the capacities that Habermas deems essential to their potentials for democratic self-reform. Main exponents of this line of critique include William Scheuerman and John Sitton.[77] To them, it seems that Habermas has overlooked the extent to which driving imperatives in capitalist democracies have hollowed out the conditions necessary to the realization of their own legitimating idealizations that do not, in any case, supply a sufficiently critical standard against which the rationality of modern social and political arrangements might be judged.

Scheuerman has no major problems with at least one dimension of Habermas' account of the normative standards relevant to the critique of communicative blockages occurring within really existing democratic states. He agrees that modern democratic ambitions are best structured in accordance with a 'two-track' model of deliberative democracy. Indeed, Habermas' central proposition that all manifestations of legitimate political power must finally derive from communicative power, even if indirectly, is not in question. Scheuerman fully appreciates Habermas' analysis of the distinctive functions performed by the informal and the formal publics. The formal political centres of really existing liberal democracies are concerned 'less with developing a sensibility for new problem positions than with justifying the choice of problems and deciding between solutions'.[78] Yet Scheuerman remains deeply unconvinced by the project of *Between Facts and Norms*.

His major accusation is that Habermas' conviction that the transformative ambitions of traditional socialism are no longer a viable horizon for contemporary emancipatory hopes has forfeited too much. In particular, he supposes that Habermas' search for a reformist politics able to rebalance the claims of democratic communicative power against the steering power of money and bureaucracy fails to offer any systematic account of the ways in which conditions necessary to the former are eroded by structural inequalities and material deprivations set in train by the latter. Habermas fails to identify and respond to the destruction of the 'basic capabilities' necessary to the democratic self-reform of capitalist democracies. For Scheuerman, Habermas is insufficiently attentive to the ways that 'avoidable social inequalities undermine the deliberative capacities of the vast majority of humanity'.[79] Habermas 'has nothing adequately *systematic* in character to say about "social asymmetries of power", let alone about how we might go about counteracting them'.[80] Scheuerman believes that to rectify these failings Habermas needs to offer a fuller account of how capitalist domination undermines democratic deliberation and to suggest how 'some alternative to existing capitalism alone can allow deliberative democracy to flourish'.[81]

It is true that Habermas has never been drawn to a totalizing politics devoted to the cause of revolutionary transformation of capitalist democracies. His hopes have always lain with a project of radical democratic reform that seeks

> a new balance between the forces of societal integration so that the social-integrative power of solidarity – the 'communicative force of production' – can prevail over the powers of the other two control resources, i.e., money and administrative power, and therewith successfully assert the practically oriented demands of the lifeworld.[82]

However, this is an agenda that in no way contests the claim that radically unequal life chances distributed by the market systematically undermine the capacities of whole populations to operate as effective participants in democratic processes. After all, this much even the post-war welfare compromises had acknowledged. The Keynesian project had admitted that the market could not be relied upon to universalize the conditions of autonomy and had attempted to intervene, paternalistically, to make good this deficiency. While Habermas endorses the general ambitions of a welfare project that makes public authority responsible for securing the conditions of private autonomy, as has already been noted, he stresses that we need to cease reproducing the contradictory logic that has helped to erode the legitimacy of welfare states. The first point is then that Scheuerman overlooks the extent to which Habermas' attempt to rescue the democratic processes of a modern public offers itself as a critique of, and a response to, the unequal life chances distributed by the logics of capitalism. He makes quite clear his view that '[f]rom the viewpoint of representation and "qualification for citizenship", it is already important to secure the factual preconditions for equal opportunity to exercise formally equal rights'.[83] Habermas believes that the task of securing the preconditions for equal opportunity may, in some contexts, require a basic guaranteed income which would permit the material basis for citizens' self-respect and political autonomy to be 'made independent of the more or less contingent success of the private individual on the labor market'.[84]

Habermas consistently asserts that the radical potentials of the question posed by the welfare project of 'how much strain can the economic system be made to take in directions that might benefit social needs, to which the logic of corporate investment is indifferent'[85] remain substantially untapped. Yet this commitment to the democratization and extension of the welfare project is not far-reaching enough for some of Habermas' critics. Sitton is convinced that there *can* be no negotiation between the alien imperatives of capitalism and democracy. The logic of the former will always trump the practical conditions needed to realize the latter. Sitton stresses that the compromise agenda embraced by Habermas betrays the revolutionary dimensions of a project that aims at realizing the conditions of a properly democratic state. According to him, Habermas fails to grasp that 'the authenticity and effectiveness of the public sphere requires that we recognize that reason without revolution is not possible'.[86]

This is not a point around which Habermas would be prepared to negotiate. His views on the bankruptcy of a Jacobin politics are well known. As he sees it, the history of the twentieth century has demonstrated the real costs of any attempt to eradicate the achieved structural differentiations within modern societies and to install political power as the steering mechanism supposed to orchestrate the diverse functions required in complex modern societies.

Scheuerman's version of the criticism is more moderate than Sitton's. Yet he also thinks that Habermas does not offer a sufficiently radical critique of capitalist democracies. In particular, he is troubled by the seeming lack of galvanizing images in *Between Facts and Norms* of what we might expect of liberal democratic societies reorganized to better reflect the potentials of their own normative foundations. Scheuerman is specifically concerned by the apparent political timidity that speaks through Habermas' proposal that social change responsive to the demands of new needs has to be tempered by an attitude of 'cautious experimentation'. Scheuerman is at a loss because, as he sees it, Habermas fails to provide any illustrations of what might count as an imaginative refunctioning of existing institutional arrangements within liberal democracies.

Scheuerman raises some hard questions about the tasks of critical theory. On the one hand, Habermas clearly agrees with Marx that critical theory is not in the business of 'writing recipes for the cookshops of the future'. Habermas claims only that his theory clarifies the radical character of needs that are concretely manifested by specific developments in the ambiguous processes of liberal democracies. As previously mentioned, Habermas counts the partial success of feminist attempts in getting legal recognition for newly established needs and rights as an illustration of how the interface between the layers of a modern public sphere can be negotiated in the direction of a democratic reform of the welfare project. It is by no means impossible, then, to find illustrations of the imaginative refunctioning of liberal democratic institutions that suggest an exploitation of the potentials of the internal relation between law and democracy. For instance, when in 1992 the High Court of Australia responded to a civil action and granted legal recognition of native title claims to traditional lands, it appeared to clarify the Court's own capacity to function, not simply as protector to already achieved rights, but, as Axel Honneth puts it, as a mechanism for the distribution of depersonalized social respect.[87] Perhaps this is the kind of institutional imagination that Habermas has in mind.

Nonetheless, misgivings about Habermas' ability to supply creative political imagery supposedly necessary to the galvanizing power of engaged theory continue to reverberate in the critical literature. According to Stephen Bronner, while 'Habermas is a brilliant theorist of liberal democracy', the 'time for defensiveness has passed. A certain boldness is becoming increasingly necessary'.[88] Perhaps Bronner would now be prepared to moderate this reaction to *Between Facts and Norms* in the light of the boldness of Habermas' recent proposals for a globalization of the public sphere that encompasses a transnationalization of the welfare project. Even so, the apparent lack of transformative impulses in Habermas' writings is seen by many of his critics to limit the capacity of his theory to respond to the diversity of our emancipatory needs. This is a major topic for the following chapters.

The hidden republican?

Habermas has been in trouble from those who consider that he has abdicated from a supposedly essential task of critical theory: that of supplying mobilizing images of a future that is significantly better than the present. Others maintain that he is too much the republican. Here the view is that Habermas' efforts to reconstruct the centrality of the public sphere to the unrealized normativity of liberal democracies supply us with too much by way of an ascribed vision and fail to adequately acknowledge the profound diversity of motivations and aspirations in a multicultural modernity.

For Thomas McCarthy and James Bohman[89] there is too much of an imposed substantive vision of the 'good society' in Habermas' affirmation of procedural norms committed to building rational solidarities between private actors. McCarthy considers that Habermas artificially brackets the real likelihood that in a multicultural society there will be no agreement about the rationality of forging common projects and that, far from an interest in rational consensus, permanent dissensus might be the order of the day. He thinks that Habermas has underestimated the importance and the depth of the claims of difference within liberal democracies. John Brady also considers that empirically Habermas' theory 'has little to say about how political contestation over questions of cultural, sexual, or ethnic difference shapes the contours of public debate', while normatively the theory 'is unable to attribute any emancipatory potential to...otherness'.[90]

Jodi Dean agrees.[91] To her, Habermas' appeal to the normativity of the public sphere provides an overly limiting construction of the meaning of democratic politics in culturally and ethically divided societies. The commitment to building rational consensus simply assumes certain agreed aspirations and convictions and hence reproduces the failures of a republican model of democracy. Habermas' theory grounds itself in 'a settled ethical conviction' in which discursive partners are committed to achieving 'some form of rational agreement on the correct resolution of an issue under discussion'.[92]

For McCarthy and others, a hidden republicanism lurks in Habermas' presumption of a shared interest in building consensus and, in this sense, the theory remains radically out of step with the multicultural realities of the present. McCarthy finds that a version of liberalism proves, after all, to be the best way of describing the generalizing commitments appropriate to the needs and the diverse goals of modern populations. Others go even further and find that nothing short of a postmodern traversing of all settled identity descriptions offers a mode of articulation adequate to the enthusiasm for the different that has been unleashed within contemporary modernities. For the present I will consider only the moderate formulation of this critique, picking up an assessment of the more radical version in later chapters.

As mentioned, McCarthy insists that the radical diversity in understandings of the good that characterizes the modern world confronts us with the possibility of permanent dissensus. In this situation we can, at best, aim at relations in which compromise with the other is raised as a principled commitment of a civilized co-existence, not just as a strategic consideration aimed at forging mutual advantage. In the face of intractable difference we must settle for an ethic in which difference is accommodated under the description of tolerance, recognition or respect. The arrangements McCarthy has in mind 'would be more a matter of mutual accommodation than of strategic compromise or substantive consensus'.[93] A reconstitution of liberal tolerance seems to offer a way of regulating interactions that bypasses the authoritarian irrelevance of the search for a form of political closure in the face of the openness of the ethico-cultural relations of a multicultural present.

There are several problems with this. Firstly, McCarthy's account of a democratic politics adequate to the radical pluralization of need and interest interpretations in a multicultural present suggests that democratic politics can only sustain a generalizing interest in the rights of all to self-expression and to the pursuit of publicity. However, this project itself presumes certain already constituted competencies and shared interests. As effective bargainers and negotiators, actors in a liberal public sphere are presumed to already possess a clear interpretation of the significance of their needs and problems and are supposedly equipped to defend them as equal partners in rule-governed negotiations. It seems that his attempt to revisit the terms of a liberal public that enjoins forbearance towards self-sustaining determinations of private interests already commits McCarthy to a quite homogenizing construction of the meaning of difference in pluralistic and unequal modern societies.

Defending himself against McCarthy's claim that his proceduralist interpretation of democratic politics rides rough shod over the realities of deep cultural and ethical diversity, Habermas insists that this model actually gives support to the interests of diversity of need interpretations that seek legitimacy in multicultural democracies.[94] Consensus over *particular* goods might remain out of reach in an ethically and culturally diverse world. However, a commitment to the claims of difference is not violated, but rather supported, by a shared affirmation of procedures and processes through which a neglected and marginalized difference might argumentatively defend its legitimacy. Habermas emphasizes that new and overlooked need claims must be able to seek recognition for their legitimacy by participating in interactions aimed at building rational consensus. Self-awareness of difference is also heightened by these discursive processes. For Habermas, the transitory unity that is generated 'in the porous and refracted intersubjectivity of a linguistically mediated consensus not only supports but furthers and accelerates the pluralization of forms of life and the individualization of lifestyles. More discourse means more contradiction and difference'.[95] As we seek to make ourselves understood to others, providing 'yes' and 'no' responses to their hermeneutic efforts, our own sense of particularity is clarified, not sacrificed.

Against the views of McCarthy, Bohman and Dean, Habermas insists that an affirmation of the normativity of discursive procedures aimed at reaching rational consensus is not only benign with respect to the claims of marginalized difference; it even offers the basis upon which the legitimacy of neglected and novel need claims can be recognized. He solidly defends the unprejudiced interpretation that his proceduralist account gives to the meaning of self-determining autonomy. Habermas' defence of the normativity of the interactions of a modern public sphere offers itself as an interpretation of a shared commitment to 'the idea of autonomy according to which human beings act as free subjects only insofar as they obey just those laws they give themselves in accordance with insights they have acquired intersubjectively'.[96] This presumption is defended by Habermas as a 'harmless' dogmatism.[97] It is supposed harmless because it only gives a certain democratic significance to the foundational assumption, shared even by Habermas' critics, of the moral principle of the rights of all to a free, self-determining existence. Habermas recommends this democratizing interpretation of a moral maxim as one that is best able to rescue and to sustain a generalized commitment to autonomous self-determination in a pluralistic and egalitarian age.

Habermas insists that 'autonomy', conceived as the aspiration of private individuals to maximize their ability to live in accordance with chosen ideals, is a value commitment that Enlightenment societies have invested with essentiality. He maintains that there are considerable gains for its egalitarian and pluralistic significance if this aspiration is articulated through discursive procedures that aim at forming reasonable consensus between disparate subjects. Chapter 4 looked at the way that a discourse ethics' interpretation of the ideal of autonomy, conceived, not as an already confirmed private right, but as a shared interest though which private individuals can become aware both of their interdependencies as well as recognizing their real differences, does open up potentials within this cultural ideal that are obscured by its liberal interpretations. However, in my view, even thus reinterpreted, Habermas' claim, that the ideal of self-determining autonomy can simply propose itself as a dogmatism that is harmless, ought not to be conceded. Chapters 7 and 8 will investigate Habermas' neglect of the irreducible significance that Romantic, as well as rationalizing Enlightenment, interpretations of emancipatory hopes have acquired for culturally ambiguous modern societies.

6   Globalizing the public sphere

Final chapters in *Between Facts and Norms* signal Habermas' growing persuasion that processes of economic globalization could undermine the capacities of the nation state as a political centre. He admits that these trends presage conditions that require us to radically rethink the future of democracy. The public sphere will have to outgrow the institutions of politically enfeebled nation states to catch up with galloping economic globalization. A new cosmopolitan agenda will need to be elaborated and an institutional imagination developed that might allow the problem interpreting and solving functions of the modern public sphere to migrate out into structures with a trans-national jurisdiction. Yet in the work of the early 1990s, the task of globalizing the public sphere remains a shadowy thought that only gains substance and clarification in later writings. In a series of major essays published since, Habermas has outlined the urgency of the project of building a global public sphere. He does not underestimate the challenge and does not ignore the adverse signs. The structural violence of a world divided into haves and have-nots, into winners and losers, constitutes a real attack on any hopes for the 'perpetual peace' of a cosmopolitan polity. However, Habermas insists that a global public sphere offers the only way forward and is persuaded that there are reasons to believe that this utopian aspiration is still worth investing in. He puts his faith in our abilities to learn from the turbulent histories of the democratic nation states what needs to be done to forge cosmopolitan ties in a dangerous world. His particular hopes are invested in the contemporary progress of European nation states towards political integration achieved peacefully and multilaterally, by negotiations and without militarism.

The first part of this chapter will consider Habermas' account of the challenges that face the democratic taming of global corporate power. He stresses real continuities, not just differences, in the functions and tasks that the public spheres of the democratic nation states had performed and those that now confront the project of building a global public. Ulrich Beck views what is required of a transnational democratic politics differently. The second part of the chapter will contrast Beck's search for a new normative basis for cosmopolitan democracy with Habermas' efforts to demonstrate the transferability of the normativity that underpinned the democratic welfare states into the global arena. Yet is a dispute over the normative foundations of a global public sphere an argument worth having? One response to the events of 9/11 insists that international terrorism signifies the real hopelessness of a search for the shared grounds, however conceived, able to sustain a global public. Habermas forcefully resists this conclusion. The last part of the chapter will explore his claim that global terrorism has confirmed, not brought into disrepute, the conception of communicative action developed in his theory.

Building a cosmopolitan democratic politics

Habermas stresses that globalization needs to be viewed as a process and not as an end state. It is characterized by the increasing scope and intensity of commercial, communicative, and exchange relations beyond national borders. While these tendencies run in many directions, the dominant one has been economic globalization. A compulsive development of capitalistic modernization has ironically thrown into the face of the twenty-first century an old problem that had seemed to find a solution under the pressure of systemic competition.[1] The goal of post-war welfare states had been to secure the social, technological, and ecological conditions that made the opportunity for equally distributed basic rights possible. This goal has now, apparently, been put under pressure by an economic globalization that is undermining the capacity of the nation state to prosecute its programme. Capital mobility and ecological degradation across porous state borders are just two of the main indices of the nation state's loss of sovereignty in an increasingly interconnected and interdependent world. Capital mobility has been especially telling on the capacity of the state to fund extensive welfare programmes. Fiscal pressures all over the OECD countries have resulted from tax cuts in the attempt to stem capital flight. This has inevitably led to the slimming down of the state and to drastic reductions in welfare expenditure in response to shrinking corporate tax revenues.[2] As 'markets drive out politics', the nation-state 'increasingly loses its capacities to raise taxes and stimulate growth, and with them the ability to secure the essential foundations of its own legitimacy'.[3]

For Habermas, one of the main paradoxes of globalization is the fact that it 'forces the nation state to open itself up internally to the multiplicity of foreign, or new forms of cultural life' while, at the same time 'shrinking the scope of action for political governments'.[4] The paradox of the situation is that, while globalizing tendencies have placed greater demands on democratic politics, forcing it to become less insular and more internationalist in its thinking, they have materially disempowered the old political centres of democratic decision-making. In his essay on 'The Postnational Constellation and the Future of Democracy', Habermas adopts the metaphor of 'opening' and 'closing' to reinforce his point.[5] He argues that European history since the Middle Ages has been characterized by an explosive degree of mobility as traditional forms of legitimation collapsed under the weight of rationalizing imperatives. This process of opening up traditional ways of doing things is, on the one hand, tied to an emancipatory dynamic which sees old authorities interrogated and new possibilities explored. However, the emancipatory implications of the opening up of traditional lifeworlds is only half the story. As much as communities and lifeworlds profit from opening up to their environments, Habermas argues it is also essential that they be able to 'close' this relation. It is vital both for the community and for the individual to absorb new impulses and to loosen ascribed ties of family, locality, social background and tradition so that they can re-organize and then close once more. In fact Habermas comments that the happiest periods of European history have been those when some sort of equilibrium has been maintained between 'opening' and 'closing'. Equilibrium would suggest that newly formed solidarities that permit the self-regulation of the community are forged in terms that embrace and appropriate potentials unleashed by open-ing processes. He suggests that both neo-liberalism and postmodernism ignore the necessity of re-establishing equilibrium between the opening and closing tendencies to the future of modern democracy. They cannot explain how the deficits in steering competencies and legitimation that have emerged at the national level as a result of such 'opening' by economic globalization can be compensated at the supranational level without some form of 'closure' in the sense of political regulation.[6]

Habermas' essay on 'The European Nation-State' stresses the ambiguous legacy of the closure achieved by the modern nation state.[7] He insists that the nation state at one time represented a cogent response to the historical challenge to find a functional equivalent for a disintegrating early modern form of social integration.[8] The nation state had to respond to the pluralism of worldviews that followed the stripping of political authority of its religious grounding in 'divine right'.[9] The secularized state had to derive its legitimation by *politically* mobilizing populations that had been 'unmoored from the corporative social ties of early modern societies'.[10] As it slowly became estab-lished, democratic participation 'generated a new level of legally mediated *solidarity* via the status of citizenship while providing the state with a secular source of legitimation'.[11] Habermas points out that the figure of the citizen, bearer of republican liberty rights, allowed the nation-state to find a way of forging a mode of integration whose abstractness transcended particularistic regional ties to village, family, locality and dynasty. This mode of integration, described as a 'constitutional patriotism', invited allegiance to principles such as popular sovereignty and human rights encountered as constitutional principles upheld by the political institutions of democratic nation states.[12]

Allegiance to a constitution is, for Habermas, the only legitimate political articulation of the identity of the nation in complex and multicultural societies. This is a patriotism towards principled convictions rather than to the orchestrated memories of folk histories. Habermas is certain that this construction of its modern identity is the only way forward for Germany. Shortly before the fall of the Berlin Wall led to the unification of the two German Republics, he wrote:

> [I]f we do not free ourselves from the diffuse notions about the nation-state, if we do not rid ourselves of the pre-political crutches of nationality and community of fate, we will be unable to continue unburdened on the very path that we have long since chosen: the path to a multicultural society, the path to a federal state with wide regional differences and strong federal power, and above all the path to a European state of many nationalities. A national identity which is not based predominantly on republican self-understanding and constitutional patriotism necessarily collides with the universalist rules of mutual coexistence for human beings.[13]

However, Habermas stresses that the histories of the European nation states suggest that a consensual allegiance of citizens to a constitutionally grounded set of institutions could not by itself supply grounds able to integrate a society of strangers. Alone such a legal–political transformation of the basis of integration lacked the motivating and mobilizing force necessary to the staying power and to the ambitions of formerly established republics. This gap was filled by the modern idea of the nation. For

> only a national consciousness, crystallized around the notion of a common ancestry, language, and history, only the consciousness of belonging to 'the same' people, makes subjects into citizens of a single political community – into members who can feel responsible *for one another*.[14]

Volkish ideologies, that bind the nation into a political community able to distinguish between members and non-members, have served to infuse the democratic ideal of collective self-determination with particular content. Habermas' attempt to use the concept of a constitutional patriotism as the basis of a consensual integration in a multicultural society is not simply a hope that new collective identities might be able to galvanize a society of mutually engaged citizens around shared allegiances to legally sanctioned convictions. The point, for him, is to attempt to disentangle this political mode of integration from its historical entwinement with the pre-political crutches of nationality and of a community of fate. A new way of binding citizens into a practical sense of their responsibility for each other needs to be forged.

Robert Fine and Will Smith suppose that Habermas considers that a shared allegiance to formal constitutionally supported principles is all that is required.[15] They deem this inadequate, though, because if we are to live together in a decent fashion we must be willing to make sacrifices in the name of some common good and patriotism to a constitution suggests ties that are too cool, too disengaged, to support such motivations. Actually, Habermas in no way disputes this point. For him, the challenge is to locate the substantive basis in a globalizing present for an engaged and inclusive social solidarity that is able to dispense with the reliance of the old nation states on defensive pre-political loyalties. While he suggests that the coolness of a liberal allegiance to formal principles is not enough, Habermas also supposes that there is an alternative to a communitarian attempt to trace galvanizing solidarities to images of a quasi-natural people. He maintains that a democratized welfare project has a drawing and binding power that is consistent with egalitarian and inclusive aspirations embraced by a modern cosmopolitan polity. This project invites disparate populations to invest in democratic processes and structures that have both a track record and an as yet unfulfilled capacity to respond to the reasonable claims that diverse populations make upon shared resources. This still radically underdeveloped project of a democratized welfare system holds out the attractive hope that democratic citizenship might 'pay off', not simply in terms of liberal individual rights and rights of political participation, but also in terms of the enjoyment of social and cultural rights.[16] The formal character of the pluralistic and egalitarian convictions that underpin the constitutional patriotism relied upon by democratic nation states might be fleshed out and recharged with motivational energies by the concrete achievements of a welfare project that insists that citizens 'must be able to experience *the fair value of their rights* also in the form of social security and the reciprocal recognition of different cultural forms of life'.[17] Habermas makes the point that '[d]emocratic citizenship can only realize its integrative potential – that is, it can only found solidarity between strangers – if it proves itself as a mechanism that actually realizes the material conditions of preferred forms of life'.[18]

For Habermas, it is now urgent that new forms of political closure be developed at the international level that can tame the devastating side effects of aggressive market imperatives across the globe. These are effects that are felt in the division of world-society into winners and losers and also in the diminished capacities of liberal democratic nation-states to execute programmes of self-reform. It is now time to recognize that ' "Keynesianism in one's own country" just won't work anymore'[19] and political institutions on the supra-national level able to deal with the problems unleashed by the globalization of commerce and communication, of economic production and finance need to be developed. Habermas suggests that these emergent political structures do not face tasks different in kind from the difficulties confronted by the nation states in forging legitimate solidarities across diverse and unequal populations. We can learn from the achievements and from the mistakes of the nation-states about how best to mobilize allegiances and set up structures adequate to the project of building a transnational democratic politics. More is required of such a project than the, in any case enormously difficult, task of building democratically constituted political-legal institutions at an international level. As already noted, Habermas insists that the project of globalizing modern democracy requires nothing less than efforts to build a transnationalized welfare project.

The challenge is to try and translate the complex 'two-tracks' of an informal opinion-forming sector of the public sphere and the problem solving function of a formal political and legal centre into terms adequate to the new international arena of the democratic project. Habermas is persuaded that there must be complex forward and backward communicative flows in a multi-tiered democratic structure in which the legitimacy of decisions arrived at by transnational political centres would be secured by their practically demonstrated responsiveness to opinion and will forming processes at work within active civil societies. The whole must be guided by the determination to maximize the effective capacity of diverse and scattered populations to seek recognition for the reasonableness of their claims. Habermas is persuaded that the attempt to forge politically constituted solidarity at a transnational level requires two difficult preconditions. A global public

> must be embedded in the context of a freedom-valuing political culture and
> be supported by a liberal and associational structure of civil society. Socially
> relevant experience from still intact private spheres must flow into such a
> civil society so that they may be processed there for public treatment.[20]

Habermas considers that the movement towards some sort of supra-national institutions of co-operation and regulation is already evident. The development of new economic and trading arrangements like NAFTA, the EU, and ASEAN is an attempt to reduce the number of political actors and to increase the club of those in a position to reach effective arrangements. This is all part of a movement in which the political attempts to catch up with the economic. 'Regimes' have emerged on regional, international, and global levels that partly compensate for the nation state's lost capacities in some functional spheres.[21] The limitation of these developments is that they do not change the overall context of the global economic system itself but only amount to adaptations like defensive trade blocks.[22] As mentioned, in his view, a meaningful, although to this time almost utopian, alternative would be to hand over most of the main regulative functions of the national welfare state to supra-national structures and authorities. The European Union has some potential in this direction. At the moment it stands before the question of whether it can make the jump from a union of economic relations and markets with weak and indirect political regulation to a new federated political structure. This will not simply be the result of constitutional developments. The conditions for such a political entity depend upon the creation of solidarity at the base. Habermas insists that liberal democracy is a juridically mediated form of political integration. It would require that all citizens of the Union be included in the creation of a unified political culture. Solidarity at the base requires democratic processes at the local level to have taken root.[23] This would necessitate a synchronized debate across Europe on its future, fostered by national political parties, with the assistance of education systems promoting foreign languages. The goal would be to establish a polyglot communicative context by interlinking national public spheres and developing both common interests and a European civil society. Habermas is clear that there can be no European federal state worthy of the title of a European democracy

> unless a European-wide, integrated public sphere develops in the ambit of a common political culture: a civil society encompassing interest associations, nongovernmental organizations, citizens' movements etc., and naturally a party system appropriate to a European arena. In short, this entails public communication that transcends the boundaries of the thus far limited public spheres.[24]

At the moment the obstacles seem formidable indeed. All projects to further develop unifying procedures and practices face the reality of vested national interests and asymmetrical inter-dependencies. There is a lack of competent agencies at the international level with the will and the power to agree on the necessary arrangements, procedures, and frameworks for political closure on the opening processes of a globalizing economy.[25] The aim of transnationalizing the welfare project, vital to Habermas' vision of a post-national public sphere, faces real problems. 'Countries that enjoy high social standards fear the danger of a downward adjustment, countries with a relatively weak social safety net fear that the imposition of higher standards will rob them of their cost advantages.'[26] This means that national global actors still prefer to externalize social costs and are generally reluctant to act even in the face of obvious global interests. Nonetheless, while he does not underestimate the task of building an effective public sphere at an international level, Habermas stresses that the difficulties that faced the formation of the democratic nation states were not much less.

The acknowledgement of real obstacles to the project of a globalized public has not dimmed Habermas' enthusiasm for it. Indeed, recent events in world politics have underlined the urgency of his call that the European Union make the most of its capacities to rebuild a democratic project in the international arena. The unilateralism of contemporary US foreign policy has laid down a decisive challenge. Habermas and Jacques Derrida are agreed that

> [a]t the international level and in the framework of the UN, Europe has to throw its weight on the scale to counterbalance the hegemonic unilateralism of the United States. At global economic summits and in the institutions of the WTO, the World Bank and the IMF, it should exert its influence in shaping the design for a coming global democratic policy.[27]

Always convinced that we can learn from the past, Habermas makes the point that the robust national consciousness of the nineteenth century was only gradually produced with the help of mass communications, national historiography, and conscription.[28] His own understanding of globalization is as a process involving not just the increasing scope and intensity of commercial imperatives but the extension also of communicative relations which holds further promise. We are now seeing a changing awareness of planetary interdependence and risk. Whether or not this will lead to a changed consciousness of citizens in a way that brings about cosmopolitan solidarity is impossible to say. Clearly what Habermas has in mind here is not just a fuzzy feeling of shared humanity but an actual preparedness to see policies implemented that successfully redistribute burdens. While he considers that transnational democratic structures cannot elide the problem-solving responsibilities and functions that had been charged to the democratic nation states, Habermas is not a proponent of world government. Any realistic supranational political framework must take into account the autonomy and differences of the existing sovereign national states. This means that a world state is undesirable, even if we aspire to introduce cosmopolitan solidarity as a new mode of social integration. A move in this direction will be possible only when electorates are prepared to reward their political elites for decisions that demonstrate a concern for global governance. At the moment, the chances for this are reduced by the defensive reactions of middle and working class electorates that fear their prospects in a harsher globalized environment. Habermas sees the best hope in the pressures that can be exerted by interest groups, NGOs and civilly active citizens. The future for democracy in our times now rests beyond the nation state and in this new global constellation the best that a national government can do is fight a losing rear guard action trying to hold off the irresistible powers of economic globalization. The only viable and effective solution is to exert more pressure for the creation of supra-national political institutions that are really responsive to democratic constituencies.

Normative underpinnings of a global public

Habermas and his German colleague Ulrich Beck are extremely cautious about any proposals for a political authority with transnational jurisdiction. The next part of the chapter considers their contrasting approaches to the normative basis for a globalized public sphere. Against Habermas' hopes for the transferability of the normativity that underpinned the democratic nation states, Beck insists that we must now look for new normative grounding for a cosmopolitan solidarity.

This dispute over the sources of legitimacy of a global public overlays a certain level of agreement about the character of the processes that are globalizing the contemporary world. Habermas is happy to adopt Beck's language to describe two distinct modernizing phases.[29] Beck identifies the impact of economic globalization in undermining the political authority of the nation state as an aspect of broader processes transforming the imperatives of so-called 'first modernity'.[30] The object of classical sociology, first modernity was driven by rationalizing aspirations bent on mastery of the social and the natural world. 'The collective patterns of life, progress and controllability, full employment and exploitation of nature' were motifs and goals typical of first modernity.[31] Theorists of first modernity never relinquished the ambition of a society rationalized in accordance with its own chosen necessities even as they registered deep pessimism about the chances of taming the self-inflicted threats generated by modernizing developments. The ideal of a sovereign society was embraced as the organizing ambition of the old nation states. 'Second modernity' suggests a new way of reflecting on the dangers unleashed by technological and industrial development. This is an age in which all reference to the co-ordinating 'self' of 'self-sovereignty' has been emptied of substance.[32] For second modernity, the manifest inability of the political centre to subdue modern dynamism in accordance with the rationalizing objectives emanating from elected necessities has eroded the old politics of the nation states. The '"self" (the contour) of industrial modernity gets lost in the modernization process, which shifts its own foundations and coordinates; it is replaced by another self which must be reconstructed, theoretically and politically'.[33] Habermas agrees with Beck that a democratic politics must be 'reinvented' for a globalizing world. However, agreement stops short of any consensus on the character of this new politics and its relationship to the old politics of the democratic nation states. For Beck, we are now looking at a politics that makes openness to the constancy and shared character of risks its new thematic and its exciting challenge. First modernity 'was predominantly a logic of structures, the second modernity is largely a logic of flows'.[34] A politics that is in tune with the collapse of the ideal of closure embraced by first modernity reconciles itself to the limited controllability of the dangers we have created for ourselves.

Habermas agrees with Beck that we can no longer comfortably describe ourselves as inhabitants of a modernity based 'on nation-state societies, where social relations, networks and communities are essentially understood in a territorial sense'.[35] Both recognize that in a globalized environment a politics centred on the state and its institutions can no longer count on its own forces to provide its citizens with adequate protection from the unintended consequences of decisions taken elsewhere. Each considers that risk, an experience of uncontrolled futures in which 'all frontier checkpoints and controls, and ultimately the bulwark of the nation state itself' appear to be washed away, has become thematic to a globalizing world.[36] However, while Habermas maintains that the lessons learnt from the successes and failures of attempts to build democratic politics within modern nation states can guide 'cautious experimentations' with the form of a global democracy, Beck thinks that the old ideal of a self-mastering society that had shaped politics in the democratic nation states is simply out of keeping with the demands facing a new cosmopolitan politics. The disagreement is substantial. Beck considers that the 'legitimating core' of a politics that had aimed at the rationalization of a social world in accordance with agreed upon goals has given way to a politics in which 'avoidance imperatives dominate'.[37]

For Beck, a cosmopolitan democratic politics begins with an appreciation of emancipatory gains in the new contexts of action unleashed by globalizing second modernity. He stresses that a new enabling libertarianism emerges out of the break up of democratic politics centred on nation states. What out-grown idealizations of a self-sovereign democratic polity might herald as a 'loss of consensus', as an 'unpolitical retreat to private life' and a 'new inwardness'[38] can, when seen from the other side, represent the struggle for a new emancipatory dimension of politics. Beck resists any communitarian lament at the loss of settled collective determinations of goods in response to the experience of radical contingency imposed by the risk society. With political freedom placed at its centre, contemporary modernity is not 'an age of decline of values but an age *of* values, in which the hierarchical certainty of ontological difference is displaced by the creative uncertainty of freedom'.[39] Beck insists that a new emancipatory politics must not simply be intimidated by the exposure of cosmopolitan actors to unleashed contingency. This is to be a politics that stresses opportunities, not just dangers, in the restless openings of a cosmopolitan existence.

Beck emphasizes the creative potentials of a life freed from the vocational ethics of first modernity over the debilitating aspects of a constant exposure to risk. In contrast to the engaged, self-denying and one-sided personality of old modernity, the self-responsible and self-enjoying individual of the post-national constellation finds that 'values become more differentiated, and personal autonomy self-evident and inescapable'. He discovers that '*cultural sources have emerged for the joyful and creative taking of risks*'.[40] Beck insists that this is an orientation that is able to support a principled morality. He insists that autonomization and the assumption of self-responsibility do not inevitably breed a callous disinterest in shared fates and are certainly not tied to the reproduction of power relations. New types of individuals playfully engaged in sampling the rich variety of cultural options and attuned to the flexible capacities demanded of them develop a constitutional wariness towards practices of control and discipline. The 'life aesthete' who replaces the vocational personality of first modernity 'does not wish to gain control over the constructed world of his fellow humans'.[41] The only relevant model of inter-subjectivity is one of co-existence with others or 'diplomacy between sovereign rulers'.[42] While it rids itself of the bent of an old politics towards subjugation and mastery, this is not a politics with an introverted agenda. Globalization means that risk, the exposure to the unintended consequences of transactions, is not only shared across a radically unequal world but also imposes a unifying *awareness* of intertwined fates. The distribution of ecological hazards throughout the globe has prompted a civic politics with a global agenda. Beck cites Greenpeace as well as Amnesty International as the prototypes for a new cosmopolitan politics.

A cosmopolitan democracy is to work within a model of co-ordination based upon the contract, on agreements hammered out to the mutual advantage of inhabitants of a shared world.[43] This is not a cynical exercise in which participants refer only to considerations of mutual advantage. It is a morally informed politics, one that is legitimated by a human rights discourse that has, under the pressure of a globalized sense of the reality of the other, been translated from the abstract realm of philosophy into a new empirical sensibility. 'Freedom's children', Beck tells us, 'feel more passionately and morally than people used to do about a range of issues – from our treatment of the environment and animals, to gender, race and human rights around the world'.[44]

Habermas does not dispute Beck's account of the libertarian effects that can attend the challenges of making one's way in a world society in which the diminishing weight of conventions seems to encourage enterprise and innovation. He does not contest the suggestion that a continual interruption into settled lifeworlds can be encountered as a liberation by dwellers in the risk society. He agrees that for some, 'the growing autonomization and individualization of the choice of life projects, all grant a certain charm to the relentless processes of dissolution that characterize organized modernity'.[45] But, in his view, Beck's estimation of the liberatory effect of a life that is disengaged from the, supposedly futile, attempt to tame risks in accordance with rationally agreed upon goals is a real exaggeration. As far as the individual is concerned, a culture of disengagement and self-responsibility has a painful flipside: 'the "flexibilisation" of career paths hides a deregulated labour market and a heightened risk of unemployment; the "individualisation" of life projects conceals a sort of compulsory mobility that is hard to reconcile with durable personal bonds'.[46] Questions also need to be raised about the adequacy of a politics dominated by a conception of the power of withdrawal at the level of transnational relations. Beck considers that a politics that is adequate to the new era of flows must imitate the power that corporate global entities achieve through their always present threat of withdrawal. A coordinated strategy of non-compliance is the trump card in the deck of transnational political power. However, this strategy does seem to set a disappointingly modest agenda for a new cosmopolitan democracy. With the abandonment of the ideal of a global democratic politics normatively grounded in the ideal of rationally controlled futures, so too goes the project of building institutions and structures designed to allow those who are most needy, most at risk, to represent the reasonableness and justice of their claims.

Against Beck's one-sided construction of the instrumentalizing logic that drove the rationalizing agendas of first modernity, Habermas underlines the ambiguity of the ideal of rationally controlled futures that shaped democratic politics in the sovereign nation states. Responding to the painful recognition of the unfreedom delivered by radical contingency, inhabitants of first modernity evolved ways of interacting and created political structures through which diverse populations might seek to secure discursively chosen goods. Habermas' hope is that, in our efforts to negotiate a new episode in the opening processes of modernization, we can carry forward and further develop what has been learnt about democratic modes of closure.

Habermas has problems with the supposed one-sidedness of Beck's diagnosis of the rationalizing project embraced by first modernity and with his unbalanced emphasis on the liberatory potentials of opening processes in second modernity. He takes issue, as well, with Beck's attempt to elaborate new normative underpinnings of a contemporary cosmopolitan politics. Habermas is quick to stress that, for him also, a global democratic politics must seek legitimation as a practical interpretation of tasks suggested by a human rights discourse. However, as Habermas sees it, Beck has not properly acknowledged that a democratic politics refers its legitimacy to a legal, not just to a moral, interpretation of the meaning of human rights. Where Beck sees only a discontinuity between the ideological character of the appeals made by the old political centres to principles of human rights which had 'at best meant nation' and a new cosmopolitan moral sensibility that now purportedly gives a properly universal scope to talk of human rights, Habermas insists on the necessary continuity between the juridical force of the appeal to human rights that had underpinned the democratic polity of the nation state and the effort that is required to find global democratic structures able to confer legally binding meaning on human rights claims in the post-national context. Beck's proposal that a moral interpretation of human rights discourses as an inclusive recognition of others as ends in themselves provides the normative basis for a cosmopolitan democracy, seems to evade the real challenges that face a project aimed at building a cosmopolitan democracy adequate to the force of legal meanings attached to discourses about human rights.

As individual or 'subjective' rights, human rights have, Habermas tells us, 'an inherently juridical nature and are conceptually oriented toward positive enactment by legislative bodies'.[47] This is a point that was already made by Hannah Arendt, who suggested that 'The Declaration of the Rights of Man' at the end of the eighteenth century was the historical turning point to a juridical interpretation of the meaning of a human right.[48] It meant a determination of the constructed character of rights, whose source was now 'Man' not a pre-given moral order set by 'God's command'. Having seized responsibility for rights from God, it was up to us to secure their conditions. In this sense we moderns have become aware of rights as a 'right to have rights' hence as a claim with an essentially politico-juridical nature. Needs are experienced as rights when they offer themselves as legitimate claims upon shared resources. Legal rights, unlike moral rights, must not, Habermas claims, 'remain politically non-binding'.[49]

For Habermas, a cosmopolitan public sphere must be able to refer itself to a legal, not just to a moral, interpretation of human rights understood as justifiable claims made on juridically empowered transnational political centres. Beck's proposed reduction of human rights discourses to a moral language wants to evade the hard but vital question at the centre of Habermas' reflections on the project of building a global public sphere. Habermas hopes to encourage a careful experimentation with forms of decision-making and problem-solving institutions and processes at the international level that might be able to respond to the politically binding dimension of human rights claims. To him, the undertaking to build a global public sphere is sited on a tension inherent in rights both as universal, and as claims on the resources of political communities that are bounded by national borders. The ambiguity cannot be evaded by an appeal to a cosmopolitanism that requires nothing more than fellow feeling. For, as Kant realized, basic rights require

> by virtue of their semantic content, an international, legally administered 'cosmopolitan society'. For actionable rights to issue from the United Nations Declaration of Human Rights, it is not enough simply to have international courts; such courts will first be able to function adequately only when the age of individual sovereign states has come to an end through a United Nations that *can not only pass but also act on and enforce its resolutions*.[50]

Habermas has some hopes that with the use of an institutional imagination and a step-by-step determination to build structures able to support communicative flows between local and trans-national public centres we might be able to carry forward the experiment in global domestic politics that was initiated by the foundation of the United Nations. Despite all the set-backs in the field of international human rights and security policy, the tenuous movement of a European Union towards a transnational democratic authority seems to presage a second chance for the ideal of democratically legitimated political interventions committed to the principle of cosmopolitan justice. Habermas is not overly hopeful. Indeed he is persuaded that 'there is a lack of competent agencies at the international level with the power to agree on the necessary arrangements, procedures and political frameworks'.[51] However, promising signs should not be overlooked either. Habermas maintains that the simultaneity of mass demonstrations that erupted across European centres on 15 February 2003 to the 'sneak attack' of the 'coalition of the willing' on Iraq 'may well, in hindsight, go down in history as a sign of the birth of a European public sphere'.[52] The task of the critical theorist is, as always, to help us to reflect on the nature of the challenge and to make the most of the progressive tendencies at play within an ambiguous present. The optimistic scenario would be one in which supranational agencies 'would empower the United Nations and its regional organizations to institute a new political and economic world order' but this is clouded by 'the troubling question of whether democratic opinion and will formation could ever achieve a binding force that extends beyond the level of the nation-state'.[53]

Terrorism and the limits of a global public

The point was made earlier that Habermas has insisted that global terrorism has confirmed, not brought into disrepute, the whole conception of communicative action developed in his theory.[54] He always supposed that terroristic violence signifies a pathological collapse of the communicative potentials between different cultures. This, of course, is not to say anything as empty as that the events of 9/11 could have been avoided if strangers across the world had been able to understand each other better. The theory of communicative action has never offered itself as a pious hope. It has proposed a systematic account of the practical and discursive conditions under which non-reductive understandings between those who are different might be achieved. For Habermas, the theory of communicative action is well placed to analyse global terrorism as symptomatic of the breakdown of conditions required for effective intercultural communication.

Habermas will have nothing to do with any attempt to rationalize global terrorism. Indeed, he insists that global terrorism, unlike the terrorism of national liberation movements, does not pretend to any secular goals and hence cannot admit any rationalizing purposes. Whereas partisans fight on familiar territory with professed political objectives in order to conquer power, 'global terrorism is new in that the risk cannot be circumscribed with reference to the vulnerability of particular targets determined by unnameable ends'.[55] To this extent Habermas is in agreement with Agnes Heller when she claims that global terrorism manifests the dangerous contempt of fundamentalists for the democratic Enlightenment demand that we make ourselves accountable to the reasonable claims of others.[56] In her view, global terrorism stands as yet another catastrophic outbreak of anti-rationalizing fundamentalism. It renews the scorn of twentieth century totalitarian regimes for human rights and for democracy. Heller draws unexpectedly unequivocal conclusions from this analysis. If global terrorism is just another symptom of a fundamentalist hatred of democracy, the West cannot be held responsible for its recent eruptions: '[i]f the Arab world feels frustrated it was not America that caused the frustration.'[57] For Habermas, on the other hand, while there can be no legitimating explanations, we do need to enquire into the conditions that have fuelled a seemingly boundless resentment of the West and its achievements. The terrorist retreat from interacting communicatively into outbursts of 'righteous' aggression appears to him as a disorder in need of a complex and many-sided interpretation. While it feeds on fundamentalism's panicked response to modernization 'perceived as a threat rather than as an opportunity', terrorism also signals terrible resentment at the savage uprooting of traditional ways of life forced by globalizing markets.[58]

Habermas stresses that the structural violence of capitalism effectively untamed by political democracy sets in train pathological relations across the globe. At home we have become used to 'unconscionable social inequality, degrading discrimination, pauperisation and marginalization'.[59] This systemic brutality does not normally trigger answering aggression because it is situated within certain legitimating ideologies, within a solid base of common background convictions, self-evident cultural truths and reciprocal expectations. From time to time, however, these justifying conventions cease to contain the deep tensions triggered by such brutality. When the consequences of conflicts 'become painful enough, they land in court or at the therapist's office'.[60] A second level of communicative interactions may offer itself, then, as a basis for the co-ordination of action. Across the globe the consequences of unbounded capitalism have been truly catastrophic: 'the deprivation and misery of complete regions and continents come to mind'. This systemic violence cannot wrap itself in a solid base of background conventions, and the release of deep resentment confronts the fact that in international relations 'the curbing power of law plays a comparatively weak role'.[61] In the absence of a 'praxis of daily living together' and a 'solid background of convictions', there is a vacuum of lifeworld conventions able to rationalize abusive power and terrible inequalities. In this case, the fabric of a communicative rationality between cultures cannot be woven from the remains of an interrupted shared lifeworld and requires that 'trust be developed in communicative practices'. This would necessitate, as its two preconditions, the improvement of living conditions, through a sensible relief from oppression and fear and that the institutions of international law uphold respect for human rights.

The expectations of reciprocity and symmetry demanded by effective communicative interactions cannot be met in the context of real material dispossession and exploitation. Effective understanding also requires a hermeneutic effort in which partners in discourse endeavour to take the point of view of the other. Habermas is clear that we cannot simply appeal to the formal principles of liberal democratic freedoms to supply the trust necessary for rational intercultural discourse. He recognizes that a European conception of human rights 'is open to attack by the spokespersons of other cultures not only because the concept of human rights has an individualistic character, but also because autonomy implies a secularized political authority uncoupled from religious or cosmological world views'.[62] Yet Habermas is persuaded that the effort can be made and that we are not forever trapped within the prism of self-referring cultural norms.

Habermas' own account of the possibilities of cross-cultural communication rejects the 'methodological "ethnocentrism"'[63] that informs the 'assimilationist model' of understanding upheld by Richard Rorty. Certainly, it needs to be acknowledged that 'it is always on our own terms that we swear to the solidarity between cultures'.[64] Yet Habermas reminds us that the hermeneutic exertion that is required to build mutual understandings between estranged cultures draws upon competences that are counterfactually presupposed by all effective users of language. As everyday users of language we are constantly presuming the rationality of modes of interaction in which diverse claims seek to elaborate the grounds for their mutual intelligibility. The rationalizing interactions of a liberal democratic public sphere have articulated this universal competency as a particular value commitment. But, because members of *all* cultures know what it means to offer reasons in support of claims and to adopt the roles of speaker and hearer, we can reasonably, if not confidently, embark on the long journey of building the conditions of an understanding recognition between diverse modern cultures. I think that we need to evaluate this argument.

From what we have seen so far, it is clear that the theory of communicative action rests on the presumption that an interest in autonomy is a singular, indivisible motivation. I now want to suggest that the unacknowledged cultural prejudice that shapes this conviction becomes apparent in the one-sidedness of Habermas' construction of terrorism as the pathological consequence of a breakdown in communicative interactions across the globe. The breakdown model suggests that the eruption of violence that is unrationalized by any particular goals amounts to a disorder in an assumed universal investment that we make as users of language in interacting communicatively. However, as noted in an earlier chapter, there is a conceptual slide that occurs in the structure of this argument. An account of the *counterfactual* status of an interest in building the grounds of mutual understanding that is supposedly implicit in the communicative purposes of all language users is being marshalled as the basis of a description of a lapsed *substantive* commitment acknowledged by all. This is a conceptual jump that only appears warranted if we assume that the impact of modernization processes across the globe has universalized an interest in self-determination as a demand interpreted through the rationalizing commitments of Enlightenment. This is a very contestable presumption. Jacques Derrida and Jean Baudrillard, for example, suppose that global terrorism can be partly understood as the violent *resistance* of a particular interpretation of the demand for autonomy to the requirements of communicative rationality, not as a symptom of its breakdown.[65] In general, they stress that the meaning and the motivations of fundamentalism can only be adequately grasped by a framework that concedes that modernization processes have released desires for autonomy that feel themselves irreducible to, and in competition with, the rationalizing demands of democratic Enlightenment. Later chapters will explore further the difficulties that Habermas' construction of modernity's incomplete Enlightenment project faces in attempting to accommodate a rival Romantic interpretation of the meaning of emancipatory hopes.

Habermas considers that interpreting global terrorism as a symptom of the breakdown in the conditions that make reasonable communication between cultures possible has advantages. Only the breakdown model provides a perspective on the pathological character of global violence and is thereby in a position to adequately engage with the ideological 'clash of civilizations' thesis that seeks to naturalize, and hence legitimate, intercultural violence. However, we can describe violence between nations and cultures as a pathology without interpreting this as a breakdown in a supposed fundamental human undertaking to interact communicatively. All that needs to be said is that the irruption of violence signals a breakdown of civilizing, communicative relations that have, as a matter of historical development, also occurred between diverse cultural traditions. Some insights of contemporary anthropology are relevant here. Michelle Moody-Adams suggests that cross-cultural fieldwork indicates that

> it is not only implausible but potentially self-destructive to assume that on matters of any moral significance there might be some antecedently given 'fact of the matter' about the most appropriate way to draw the boundaries between one's way of life and that of the other.[66]

Yet, while she is convinced that intercultural understanding is not helped by the attempt to impose supposedly universal norms, so too Moody-Adams thinks that the evidence goes against the strong relativist assumption of ineluctable moral isolation between cultures. The fact is that sometimes, against all the odds, respectful understandings and sympathetic agreements between very different cultural traditions can be forged.

Clifford Geertz is also persuaded that no philosophical edifice needs to be built around the empirical knowledge of the anthropologist that learning processes between cultures occur.[67] This project is deemed a necessity only because of the misconceptions of the cultural relativist whose 'picture of the world as dotted by indiscriminate cultures, discontinuous blocks of thought and emotion is misleading'. When you look into them 'their solidity dissolves and you are left not with a catalogue of well-defined entries but with a tangle of differences and similarities only half sorted out'.[68] The indeterminacy of cultures in a modern world suggests that we do not need to philosophize on the conditions that make communication between them possible. Geertz makes the point that this is a process that requires us to concentrate our efforts at reflection on building increased *self*-understandings. An interpretation of the attractive potentials of liberal democratic norms can offer itself as a useful contribution to building inter-cultural communication if it is presented 'as a view not from nowhere but from the very special somewhere of a certain sort of Western political experience', as a statement 'about what we, who are heirs of that experience, think we have learned about how a people with differences can live among one another with some degree of comity'.[69] It seems that this learning process has been greatly enriched by Habermas' efforts to provide a systematic and comprehensive interpretation of the unrealized normativity of the liberal democratic nation state.

7   The utopian energies of
a radical reformist

Can contemporary critical theory offer an account of the reasonableness of its utopian inclinations? Habermas has always been persuaded that the survival of critical theory depends upon it. Critical theory needs to be able to establish that hopes for a better future can be anchored in an estimation of frustrated potentials and emancipatory needs loosened by modernization processes. In a social world that is increasingly dominated by the fatalism of neo-liberal ideologies this seems to be a project that is dramatically out of season.

For Habermas, a project aimed at defending the reasonableness of utopian hopes has long been seriously at odds with prevailing moods. Already in the mid 1980s, it seemed to him that our utopian energies had been used up.[1] The 1980s suggested a collapse of faith in a utopianism that had acquired an irrational physiognomy. Careering towards the end of century, humanity faced its own self-produced threats of a spiralling arms race, of the 'uncontrolled spread of nuclear weapons, the structural impoverishment of developing countries, problems of environmental overload, and the nearly catastrophic operations of high technology'.[2] To Habermas, the loss of confidence that characterized the slide towards the twenty-first century appeared not as a gain in realism but as the advance of a debilitating disorientation and as trepidation before the nightmarish results of modernity's own dreams of a self-made future. For Leo Lowenthal also, the 'suspension of the utopian motif' in contemporary cultural life did not signal the advance of a new, mature, scepticism. It represented a retreat into a 'sadness'.[3] This melancholic, bewildered mood appeared as the response of an age that felt itself clogged up with, and threatened by the results of, its dynamic past and unable to choose any of its achievements as the potentials of future development.[4] A new obscurity ensured that the productive forces and 'planning capacities' of a socially, economically, and politically dynamic society would metamorphose into destructive forces, into 'potentials for disruption'.[5] The end of utopia was no welcome news for a generation of critics grieving the loss of the West's capacity to come up with a sceptical interpretation of its own potentials that could offer a guiding sign to critical energies committed to the shaping of a better world.

Two decades ago, Habermas was able to find plenty of good reasons for the apparent exhaustion of utopian energies. Over the years, these seem to have been reinforced and expanded. Alain Touraine holds that today the modernist conviction that our society is 'capable of using its ideas, hopes and conflicts to act upon itself'[6] is under attack from an irresponsible neo-liberalism and remains virtually unsupported by a leftist politics that has also lost all 'belief in the future that might be different' in an 'essential' way from the world of today.[7] For Habermas at the end of the twentieth century, a mood, 'somewhat depressed, somewhat clueless, the whole thing washed over by the throb of technopop'[8] appears to testify to the final defeat of all utopian longings.

In the face of all this, Habermas continues to assert that his critical theory is inspired by remnants of utopianism.[9] He will not give up the search for a way of identifying the reasonableness of utopian hopes. This must be a utopianism that heeds Marx's warnings against mere 'dreams' of a radically transformed future, conceiving itself instead as a 'legitimate medium for depicting alternative life possibilities that are seen as inherent in the historical process itself'.[10] The utopianism that had nourished older versions of critical theory had come to grief because it had relied upon a narrow and one-sided account of modernizing potentials. Habermas undertakes to rescue the utopian credentials of achievements whose significance had been overlooked by a tradition of critical theory shaped by Marxism. He not only considers that we have been looking in the wrong place for our utopian potentials but also that we have misunderstood the character of a utopianism relevant to a historicizing and pluralistic age.

The first part of the following chapter will outline the sense in which Habermas tries to defend his critical theory as a reflection upon our frustrated utopian potentials. His radical reformism expresses no wilful optimism about the future but only insists that we can understand our options better if we contest the limited interpretative framework in terms of which modernizing achievements have been selected and weighed up. To Habermas, the end of the utopianism thesis rested on a one-sided description of the character of modernization processes that neglected the complexity of historically produced needs. Yet the terms of his defence of the utopian credentials of critical theory leave Habermas' own perspective vulnerable. The last part of the chapter will suggest that his diagnosis of the ambiguities of modernization processes is itself too limited. It fails to appreciate the significance of a wider spectrum of descriptions of critical needs that have been produced by modernizing processes. This part of the discussion will weigh up the charge that Habermas' contestation of the end of utopian energies thesis is itself based on a totalizing description of the future-orienting significance of a certain, select interpretation of our emancipatory needs.

Utopianism and the ambivalent potentials of modernity

For Habermas, the end of the eighteenth century saw a fundamentally new time consciousness entering into the description of utopian energies.[11] From that period, 'utopian thought fuses with historical thought' as modern thinkers grasp the new life orienting task of culture in a secularizing age. To an age that starts to see itself as dependent exclusively upon itself, as charged with the task of drawing on itself for its own normativity, the appeal to images supplied by an exemplary past begins to appear as mere ineffectual dreaming.[12] From the twentieth century, 'utopianism' acquired legitimacy as a medium for interpreting potentials of the present as the chosen orientation of a desired future.[13]

A modern attempt to amalgamate utopian and historical thought has typically, Habermas argues, sought its 'solution' in an investment in the productive capacities of social labour which is given the task of giving structure and form to society.[14] This direction of utopian expectations to the sphere of production has nowhere been given a more lasting formulation than in Marx's critique of the dehumanization of alienated labour. This description of the utopian significance of modernity's achievements endowed the formative processes of social labour with the 'capacity to revolutionise the productive forces of society, building an irresistible reservoir of new capacities, skills, needs and aspirations'.[15] For Marx, social labour functions as a vital learning process 'in which subjects become aware of the fact that their capacities and needs go far beyond the possibilities allowed by existing social relations'.[16] The limitations of this attempt to conceive the self-critical potentials of modernity in terms of the ability of human productive capacities to project future possibilities for a collectively better way of life are, for Habermas, dramatically brought home by the traumatic influence of Marx's thinking on some twentieth-century developments. Because he equated the development of productive forces with the cause of social emancipation as such, Marx, Habermas argues, fatefully conflated the dialectics of two aspects of modernizing processes that ought to have been separated.

In Marx's utopia, overcoming alienation meant transcending the antagonism between the openness of productive forces unleashed by capitalism and the closure of its productive relations that saw the individual a casualty rather than a beneficiary of this dynamic system. To Habermas, this account of the dynamism of capitalist productive forces suggests a one-dimensional description of modernization processes. Marx failed to bring to light the significance of a modernizing interaction in which the capacity of private subjects to build rational solidarities has been raised as an explicit value. Rationalization of productive forces at the level of the subsystems of purposive-rational action (technology, economy, bureaucracy), while facilitating a growing mastery of nature from the standpoint of instrumental control, should not be confused with rationalization at the level of frameworks of communicative interactions which removes restrictions on free communication and reflection and encourages socio-political emancipation.[17] Habermas' diagnosis of the double-sided character of modernization processes describes the matching of an evolved self-consciousness in humanity's self-producing capacity by a new awareness of its ability to build interpretive horizons through deliberate, chosen rather than merely traditionally described interactions. For Habermas, this latter account of rationalizing modernization processes describes achievements whose normative potentials we have not yet exhausted.

Marx's interpretation of modernization processes, conceived one-sidedly in terms of the development of humanity's capacities to transform the world in accordance with its own purposes, had two fateful consequences for the history of modern critical theory. In the first place, by committing itself to the role of midwife to the emergent consciousness of the class charged with the responsibility of a non-contradictory realization of this trajectory of modern development, Marx's theory could be appropriated as the ideology of totalitarian states in the twentieth century. As the dislocation between the prescriptive point of view of the theory and the empirical consciousness of the class widened, the utopian commitments of the former became the vehicle of a despairing pessimism. For the later Adorno and Horkheimer, Marx's Enlightenment commitment to the realization of a rational, self-chosen future for a mature humanity evolved into a dogmatic, unreasoned faith in an instrumentalizing reason bent on mastery of the self and the world.

According to Habermas, the exhaustion of contemporary utopian energies signalled by the Frankfurt's School's account of the fateful trajectory of the emancipatory hopes invested in Enlightenment reason, appeared as a response to the faltering of one particular way of describing modernization processes.[18] Modernity's rationalizing potentials are not to be identified with its extension of humanity's capacities for purposeful control over alien nature, they also encompass the continuing claims of an evolved commitment to a mode of interaction aimed at discursively achieved understandings and agreements. For Habermas, modern understanding entails that knowledge and belief are opened up to rational criticism and publicity.[19] Under this description, the ideal of the rational society seeks to elaborate the democratic potentials of a historical epoch for which the meaning of shared contexts loses the unquestioned givenness of traditional authority and becomes more and more subject to the interpretive efforts of participants.

For Habermas, learning from the disastrous consequences of a one-sided appreciation of modernization processes does not require a complete transvaluation of our achievements and potentials. The remnants of the utopianism that inform his revision of a critical theory tradition call for equilibrium between the diverse outcomes and organizing imperatives of modernization. In particular, his works have as their 'vanishing point the demand for conditions that are worthy of human beings, in which an acceptable balance between money, power, and solidarity can come into normal practice'.[20] As Habermas sees it, the reformist account of the ideal of the self-steering society achieved by the welfare compromises of the post-Second World War era suggested an initial, but finally distorted, attempt at the balanced interpretation of modernization processes necessary to modern utopianism. This reformist project appears partly as a result of cruel learning processes forced on us by the zeal of the first decades of the twentieth century.[21] In particular, the welfare compromise 'emerged from the social democratic tradition' to offer the resources of the democratic constitutional state as a corrective to the recklessness of the market that had fed the legitimation problems exploited by European totalitarian movements.[22] There was, however, a fateful continuity here. The reformism of the 'Golden Age' of the post-war welfare compromise failed to interrogate the character of the utopian commitments it had inherited. It clung onto, and tried to make good, the failed promises of universalization of self-realization through social labour. The welfare compromise that grew up alongside the market tried to protect its utopia by promising a paternalistic state bureaucracy willing and able to improve the work conditions of a fully employed population.[23]

By the end of the twentieth century, and partly in response to its own internal contradictions, the welfare project had stalled. As mentioned earlier, Habermas here adopts Claus Offe's diagnosis of the debilitating effects of tensions between the aims and the methods of the post-war welfare state.[24] For Offe, a contradiction between objective and method is inherent in the welfare state project. Its goal is the establishment of forms of life that are 'structured in an egalitarian way and that at the same time open up arenas for individual self-realization and spontaneity'. But evidently this goal cannot be reached 'via the direct route of putting political programmes into legal and administrative form. Generating forms of life exceeds the capacities of the medium of power'.[25] The crisis of the welfare state is in part a consequence of its own contradictory dynamics as the assumption of an increasingly active role by the state threatens to undermine 'traditional value systems like the work ethic on which it itself rests'.[26] At play also is the systemic weakness of the compromise between state power, not itself an autonomous 'source of prosperity', and market forces, which it is both dependent upon and desirous of regulating.[27] 'In such a situation the welfare state is immediately in danger of its social base slipping away.'[28]

In his early writings, Habermas had some hopes that the 'lived' aspect of the crisis in the welfare state might spill over into an enlightening legitimation crisis capable of placing new kinds of demands on the role of the state while at the same time demystifying the power of capital.[29] The active role assumed by the welfare state in attempting to artificially secure the conditions for self-realization through social labour described a new responsiveness of the state to the perceived needs of modern populations. This novel sense of engagement both opened the state to a critique of the legitimacy of the prescribed character of its need interpretations and publicized the incapacity of the market to make good a liberal commitment to a generalized self-realization through labour.[30] The later writings stress that the opportunity for this kind of democratization of the welfare project, which would see it opening up to the self-interpreted needs of a population intolerant of any 'client' status, has not been grasped in any significant way. Today the welfare compromise has all but succumbed to an ideology that constructs its internal dilemmas as the occasion for its virtual defeat, not for its democratizing self-reform.

At the end of the twentieth century, a neo-liberal ideology determined to capitalize on the legitimacy deficits of a struggling welfare compromise insists on the non-viability of this project in an era of accelerating globalization of market forces.[31] Habermas has offered a measured critique of the ideological underpinnings of this description of the significance of globalism. He is, for example, more circumspect than Touraine for whom '[g]lobalism is a *mere* ideological representation or an expression of the despair and anxiety of those who are indeed the victims of new technologies, industrial concentration, financial gambles, and the relocation of certain activities in the new industrial countries'.[32] Habermas is similarly persuaded that the conviction that globalism refers to a world economy that has structurally outrun the political constraints set by national governments is, in some part, an ideological legitimation for the absence of a state-based political will determined to protect the victims of economic modernization. Sheltering behind a neo-liberal fetishization of market imperatives, there is hardly any government in the OECD that has refused 'the usual mix of deregulation, in particular deregulation of labour markets, of lowering taxes, balancing public households and trimming welfare state regulations'.[33] This package is being sold to a public with the argument that the pressures from global competition and international financial markets do not leave any other choice. Yet, for Habermas, the supposition that, at least in its old formulations, the ideal of the self reforming society has been defeated by objective pressures brought to bear in the era of globalism is not to be described as simply a piece of ideological fatalism. It is, he maintains, on the one hand true that the past formulations of this project are radically out of step with the shift in the structure of capitalism from an international to a transnational disposition.[34] However, as we saw in an earlier chapter, Habermas contests as a mere legitimating ideology the fatalistic belief that the project of a self-reforming welfare state cannot be altered in ways that respond better to its own internal dilemmas and allows this commitment to catch up with the new realities of a transnationalizing economy.[35]

If it is to survive, the welfare project must become reflective.[36] It needs, that is, to release itself from the utopia of a labouring society to reinvest the idea of a self-reforming society with a new democratic significance. By seeking to open itself up to contexts and to demands elaborated within the rich network of voluntary associations, movements and channels of communication that form the framework of modern civil society, a democratization of the welfare project could endeavour to harness new motivational energies. A democratizing self-reform of the welfare project would mean the expansion of its agenda from the pursuit of a narrowly conceived programme of reformed conditions of work and employment to a responsiveness to social and ecological rights also. A democratized welfare project would seek to break from the self-contradictoriness of the 'nanny state' to embrace an ideal of autonomy described in terms of the capacity of private individuals to seek recognition for the generalizable significance of their heterogeneous needs. Beyond the redistributive policies of a welfare project informed by the utopia of social labour, the social policy of a democratized welfare programme would seek to recruit sceptical and weary populations to a vision of self-reforming society that embraces 'labour and youth policies, health care, family and educational policies, environmental protection and urban planning'.[37]

Habermas' recent writings stress that, in the context of a globalizing economy, a commitment to the democratization of a welfare state project requires nothing less than the determination to build a transnationalized public sphere. Only this kind of long-term undertaking is adequate to the task of reproducing and developing the ideal of the self-reforming society in terms fit for the realities of a transnationalizing economy. Habermas insists on the need for a new kind of international political closure of an economically unmastered world society.[38] We saw earlier that, for him, this new compromise between economic dynamism and political closure must take effect through transnational institutional arrangements that represent the potentials for rational consensus regarding the preservation of social standards, the satisfaction of rationally justifiable needs and the need to redress extreme social inequities. Only a commitment to building a democratized transnational welfare state can hope to mobilize the legitimacy necessary to its effectiveness and sustainability. This requires systemic responsiveness from transnational political institutions to collective need and problem interpretations that are channelled to them from local sites.

Is this commitment to a democratized and transnational public sphere an optimistic Habermasian fantasy? Actually, Habermas sees optimism and pessimism as 'not really relevant categories'.[39] His residual utopianism anchors itself in the supposition that unrealized liberal democratic ideals continue to have a weak institutional presence and still make claims on us. Habermas' utopianism rests with the persuasion that 'democracy – and the public struggle for its best form – is capable of hacking through the Gordian knots of otherwise insoluble problems'.[40] He is not confident that we will take up the challenge, nor even that we *can* succeed in hacking through. But against the complacent ideologies of our times, Habermas consistently reminds us that we have developed ways of interacting and living with each other that ought not to be sacrificed to an instrumentalizing logic gone wild. And as to the question of success, because we don't know, 'at least we have to try'.[41]

Choosing the future from the present

Habermas argues that the exhaustion of the utopian energies thesis has an ideological dimension. It draws on a description of modernization processes that offers a narrow, distorted framework for weighing up the relevant evidences. He also holds that an anti-modern construction of the meaning of utopian energies can be held partly responsible for a contemporary fatalism. A failure to appreciate the ambivalence that has shaped the evolution of complex, self-reflexive, modernities is complemented and reinforced by a failure to describe utopian motivations as a commitment to the realization of *chosen* potentialities. Habermas traces the ancestry of this anti-modernist construction of the meaning of utopianism to the early formulations of the critical theory tradition.[42] His view is that a thoroughgoing revision in the self-understanding of this tradition is required if critical theory is to equip itself to contest an ideological anti-utopianism.

Because he had equated the development of productive forces with the cause of social emancipation as such, Marx's critique of alienation was haunted by a 'normative deficit' that shaped the course of the critical theory tradition.[43] For Marx, overcoming alienation required forcefully removing those relations that constrained and inhibited the limitless unfolding of modernity's productive potentials. It 'requires a fulfilment, not transfiguration of modern bourgeois society, for it merely carries to its logical conclusion the deification of growth and productivity upon which the logic of capitalism rests'.[44] In this monological construction of dynamic modernity, fate, as Agnes Heller points out, 'creeps in the back door'[45] and utopian thought is released from the burden of seeking to reflect upon alternative contents that might nourish the idea of the self-directing society.

For the Frankfurt School, the defeat of the bearers of its revolutionary possibilities had seen the hopes invested in modernity's dynamic productivity metamorphose into a despairing response at the destructiveness of modernization processes.[46] The later Adorno famously described critical theory's loss of any hope that emancipatory potentials might have lodged themselves within modern public and institutional structures and its growing reliance on the unredeemed promise of art, culture and philosophy as equivalent to 'throwing out a message in a bottle'.[47] Habermas rejects this attempt to preserve the critical status of theory at the expense of its engaged character. He thinks that Adorno adopted a framework that failed to allow the limited emancipatory potentials of the present to come into view. Against the grain of Adorno's retreat from the degraded practical alternatives of the present, Habermas accepts the challenge of reworking the normative commitments that underpin liberal democratic social forms to uncover their radical and as yet unrealized potentials.

A normative deficit, bequeathed by Marx, has shaped the fatalism of a critical theory tradition leaving it helpless in the face of an ideologically driven mood of 'realistic' accommodation. Today, a triumphant neo-liberal ideology, which celebrates the liberatory capacities of the market that is supposed 'to unleash the imagination and the initiative of the individual from the entanglement of all sorts of constraints',[48] is determined to bury Marx's diagnosis of the dire costs of an unregulated market for an alienated humanity. In this context, a critical theory tradition needs to draw on all its resources to contest as a mere ideological distortion the proposition that no vital choices about the directions of our futures are available to us. For Habermas, critical theory needs to attempt to effectively interrupt a neo-liberal project by situating itself as reminder to the democratic interpretations of the need for autonomy of a repressed humanist tradition. It has to be stressed, though, that Habermas does not appear optimistic that demands for a democratized interpretation of the meaning of autonomy can make much headway against the powerful attraction that 'fatefully shifting market forces' seem to exercise for 'young, beaming, dynamic, and well-educated rational choosers' schooled in the 'secular fatalism' of the age.[49]

The 'newness' of neo-liberal doctrines, that enjoin self-responsible private individuals to secure the success of their own futures, refers to their repudiation of the confusing commitments of classical liberalism to principles of human advancement and self-development that had at least offered a potential for a critical perspective on the social effects of the market.[50] Ideology to a generation of ideal-weary pragmatists, neo-liberalism provides a version of liberalism that abandons any commitment to social and political goods that could act as a critical limit on the legitimacy of market activities. Habermas indicates that a neo-liberal determination to treat the past as an irrelevancy ought to be resisted and opportunities for learning seized. In particular, we need to take the learning processes that led to the welfare compromises of the post-War era forward in the hope that we can avoid again being forced to endure the catastrophic consequences of unregulated market dynamism.[51] Critical theory unmasks the distortions of fatalistic ideologies by reflecting on the ambivalence of modernizing trends and so re-opening the task of choosing the future from the potentials of the present. The differentiated analysis provided by Habermas' critical theory 'opens a perspective that does not simply obstruct courage but can make political action more sure of hitting its mark'.[52]

Contesting the exhaustion of the utopian energies thesis does not require critical sociology to seek to 'invent anything'.[53] Habermas does not advocate that indulgence in the 'dream without a method' that Fourier had ridiculed in the speculative utopian thinking of the nineteenth century.[54] 'Nobody', least of all Habermas, 'wants to spin out utopian fantasies' in the current context.[55] He hopes, rather, that a critical and descriptive social science, resistant to the depoliticizing ideologies of the age, can contribute towards the provocation of the project committed to understanding our ambivalent cultural achievements and taking these forward as chosen commitments. Habermas advocates this kind of reflection upon and determination to rescue the neglected normativity of our ambiguous legacies not as a programme aimed at a mere restoration of the past but as a commitment to learn from it and from its mis-formulations. In particular, he thinks that a project aimed at the democratization and trans-nationalization of the welfare project would represent a great advance in our learning processes. As Habermas sees it, the significance of achievements instantiated in 'not only formal guarantees of civil rights but levels of social welfare, education and leisure that are the precondition of effective autonomy and democratic citizenship', remains unrealized and incompletely appreciated.[56] While critical theory does not simply 'make up' the normative claims exercised by these achievements, it seeks to cultivate these potentialities within the various forums and institutions of modern political and civil life. This will never be an easy, neat, or finished task but that is the challenge and perhaps the basis for a new understanding of 'invention'.

The creativity of radical reformism

Habermas thinks that the champions of postmodernism have colluded with legitimating neo-liberal ideologies to proclaim 'an end of politics'.[57] The neo-liberal relies on the spreading conviction that political closure is a thing of the past. The postmodernist also announces the impossibility of building a balance between political closure and modern dynamism.[58] To the latter, the pluralism of a multicultural modernity cannot tolerate the search for homogenizing solidarities necessary to the elaboration of constraining political judgment. For different reasons, postmodernism and neo-liberalism 'ultimately share the vision of lifeworlds of individuals and small groups scattering, like discrete monads, across global, functionally coordinated networks, rather than overlapping in the course of social integration, in larger multi-dimensional political entities'.[59]

However, according to a number of his critics, Habermas' own attempts to defend the necessity of the formation of collectively binding decisions able to guide a desirable course for modern dynamism also fail to strike the right balance. To them, the limited ambitions of his radical reformism itself appear symptomatic of the collapse of forward-looking utopian energies. Jeffrey Alexander, for example, thinks that the 'rationalist bias' of Habermas' standpoint is too bound up with the search for continuities to effectively contest the end of utopian energies thesis. Habermas' diagnosis of the potentialities of the present is 'too mundane, too accepting of realism, the genre that so marks and so distorts the self-understanding of modernity'.[60] Martin Morris also considers himself to be defending the utopianism, the commitment to 'facilitate alternative modes of being and communication to those forced upon us by the reified world', essential to critical theory against the search for continuities that preoccupies an overly rationalistic Habermas.[61] However, the radical reformist has his supporters too. Leo Lowenthal has denounced an attempt to deride Habermas' search for a rational basis for utopian hopes as the 'ballast' of a 'speculative-utopianism'.[62] After all, 'one cannot live only on utopian hopes based in never-never land, whose realisation seems scarcely within the realm of the possible'.[63] Maria Markus is similarly convinced that the preservation of utopian energies must be tied to the ideal of the self reforming society for, she points out, if a utopian horizon 'is removed too far from the actuality of a given society, its mobilising action-orienting effect might easily be lost'.[64]

Chapter 5 looked at some constructions of Habermas' 'rationalist bias' that objected to a lack of 'boldness' in his construction of the self-reforming capacities of liberal democratic societies. These were views that supposed that Habermas' commitment to a project for a reformed compromise between democracy and capitalism was too 'soft' on the latter, too naïve about the essential antipathy of its imperatives to conditions deemed necessary to a substantial democracy. Habermas' supposed rationalist predilections have come in for other types of criticism as well. Some of his critics suppose that Habermas' critical theory is too unresponsive to the *range* of emancipatory motivations that have acquired significance in an ambiguous modernity. On this line of argument, Habermas' attempt to tie the utopianism of critical theory to a search for a regulative ideal anchored in the neglected rationality potentials of modernization processes fails to fully appreciate the significance of processes of differentiation and pluralization that characterize a multicultural epoch.[65]

Martin Beck Matustik's political-philosophical biography of Habermas invites us to consider his *oeuvre* as an attempt to balance two distinct claims that the politics of post-war Germany made on the allegiances of the progressive intellectual. For the survivor of the Nazi catastrophe, the question, '[w]hich of our traditions shall we continue and which shall we jettison?'[66] insists upon being answered. The trajectory of radical politics in late twentieth century Germany was to burden Habermas with the need to respond to an additional set of questions. The impatient hopes of radical student politics in the late 1960s invited the critical theorist to join in the attempt to describe future life forms adequate to the emancipatory needs of evolving and plural identity descriptions. Matustik suggests that Habermas' politico-theoretical *oeuvre* can be usefully interpreted as an attempt to overcome the seeming tensions between these two tasks. His work is to be read as a specific integration of the 'democratic needs of 1945 and the revolutionary core of 1968'.[67] The former drew its inspirations from a sceptical reflection upon, and a questioning appropriation of, past achievements; the latter was inspired by the impatient, creative urges of newly self-conscious identities keen to overthrow continuities in the search of the 'qualitatively new'.[68]

Matustik argues that Habermas' suggestion that a radical politics must integrate both of these emancipatory motivations has proven to be out of step with the radical impulses of a contemporary politics. In particular, he thinks that Habermas' proposed integration of a sceptical appropriation of traditions of the democratic nation states with an interest in the discovery of life-forms adequate to new kinds of radical needs and identity claims falls short of the urgency of the transformative hopes that have been pushed to the forefront by recent social movements. Matustik's argument touches on a nerve because the new progressive movements and the voluntary associations of an active civil society are upheld by Habermas as a lynchpin of the project of democratizing the welfare project and hence are major bearers of the utopian motivations his theory offers to clarify.[69]

Because he skewed the balance of claims towards the transformative impulses of the 1968 generation of radicals, Matustik suggests that Herbert Marcuse offered an integrated perspective on the interests that build our utopian energies that would better 'deliver *us* to a genuine vanishing point of *our* post-1989 hope for liberation'.[70] Joel Whitebook agrees. He argues that Habermas' interest in a critical retrieval of the past, informed by an interpretation of present needs, represents a 'de-utopianization' of critical theory that imperils its capacity to describe the pathologies of modernization processes.[71] Martin Morris also feels that, by emphasizing the necessary *unreasonableness* of transformative utopian longings, Marcuse has reconstructed the influences on contemporary utopianism in more illuminating and effective terms than those achieved by Habermas' sober interest in building chosen continuities.[72]

In my view, neither Matustik's critique, nor Habermas' own framework, offer fully adequate ways of looking at the complexity of contemporary critical and emancipatory needs. If, as Matustik says, Habermas is out of step with the terms in which the new social movements interpret their radical needs, this is not because he gets the balance between the critical, sceptical impulses and creative transformative ones that inform contemporary utopian energies wrong. I want to argue that it is the project of integration itself that needs to be reviewed. Habermas' synthesizing ambitions seem to blind him to the importance of maintaining a functional balance between significant tensions in the motivational sources of contemporary utopian energies. In the first part of the chapter we saw that Habermas contests a conviction that utopianism is now defeated. He argues that in an ambiguous modernity, the choice of cultural potentials is always there to be made, even if we should prove finally unable to carry the burden. Yet it appears that Habermas himself suggests an overly restrictive interpretation of the radical needs that might offer themselves as our emancipatory potentials. Habermas' efforts to integrate the significance of a sceptical appropriation of the achievements of democratic Enlightenment with transformative longings impatient for creative self-expression fail to acknowledge the importance of ongoing negotiations between two distinct, and irreducible, interpretations of emancipatory hopes that are the outcome of two axes of cultural modernization. The line of argument that is broached here will be developed further in the chapter that follows.

* * *

Several commentators have endorsed Matustik's view that Habermas' reconstruction of the character of our utopian interests gets the emphasis wrong. Even some quite sympathetic critics think that Habermas fails to demonstrate that a sceptical appropriation of our liberal democratic traditions can accommodate the creative, transformative impulses that underpin utopian hopes. Seyla Benhabib raises doubts about the emancipatory power of a commitment to communicative rationality that 'seems like...a natural outcome of the present'.[73] For her, the question here is: 'does such a demand for the fulfilment of modern reason project the image of a future we would like to make our own?'[74] I have already mentioned that Whitebook has similar misgivings. According to him, Habermas' communicative turn tries to deny that capacity for dreaming which is essential to the transformative ambitions of utopian longings.[75] However, Habermas does actually attempt to recruit transformative longings to his account of what the self-reform of liberal democracies might achieve.

It might not always appear so. Indeed it would seem that Habermas himself has admitted the limited galvanizing power of a critical theory that adopts the cause of the democratic self-reform of society. His essay from the early 1970s that weighs the animating capacity of immanently critical theory against the provocative power of Walter Benjamin's redemptive criticism has continued to provoke controversy. Here Habermas voices deep reservations about any idea of progress that informs 'a joyless reformism whose sensorium has long since been stunted as regards the difference between an improved reproduction of life and a fulfilled life'.[76] Whitebook assumes that Habermas is talking in a totally general way about the limited appeal of reformist demands that inform an immanently critical standpoint on unfulfilled liberal democratic potentials.[77] He thinks that Habermas is reflecting upon the 'disturbing possibility' of a meaningless emancipation opened up by even his *own* reformist ambitions. It seems to me that Habermas is only saying that *if* it lacks nourishment from the urgency of particular longings for a trans-formed future adequate to the radical needs of the present, it is possible that the ideal of the self-reforming society could produce a liberated humanity that encounters 'itself within an expanded space of discursive formation of will and yet be robbed of the light in which it is capable of interpreting its life as something good'.[78] It seems reasonable to suppose that Habermas wants to firmly distance the radicalism of *his* sceptical reforming ambitions from a reformism that is too timid to let go of a past that remains essentially uninterrogated by the concrete and critical needs of the present.

A depiction of 'mundane' Habermas is not entirely fair to his account of the utopian longings necessary to the task of breaking through the 'Gordian knots' of our seeming insuperable problems. First, the critique does not acknowledge that a defence of the neglected and misinterpreted rationality potentials of democratic Enlightenment might well appear as a real inter-ruption of the course of development in really existing capitalist democracies. Martin Krygier is sure that the regulative norms of democratic procedures cannot supply a positive value commitment able to stir us on to the task of building significantly better ways of life. 'Civility', he writes, 'is not one of those ideas that quicken the pulse, ... [it] is not to die for'.[79] Krieger's point, that our appreciation of the real importance, and even the meaning, of general civic ideals, is conditioned by the concrete circumstances in which we encounter them, needs to be conceded. Yet, as Habermas' generation of survivors of fascist Germany might well confirm, this consideration does not necessarily diminish the capacity of these formal principles to inspire, precisely *under the description* of general ideals. Second, the charge that Habermas' reforming interest is governed by an overly cautious, backward-looking, preoccupation with sustaining already secured achievements overlooks the extent to which he supposes that a *critical re-appropriation* of historical potentials can be energized and guided by the contents of transformative longings whose creative vigour it tries to assimilate. Habermas consistently places his hopes in the ability of humans to learn from the disasters of the past.[80] For him, it seems that there is a kind of joy to be had from the attainment of a reflexive distance on, and a critical, discriminating re-appropriation of, the unrealized potentials of our own democratic traditions. Their sceptical rein-terpretation is worth the effort if it signals our determination to free ourselves from the continuum of catastrophes that is certain to be the legacy of a blind, unthinking, relation with the past. Critical and reflective interests in responding to the question '[w]hich of our traditions shall we continue and which shall we jettison?'[81] can be infused with utopian urgency by a keenness to build futures that do not repeat the terrible mistakes of the past. It seems, then, that Habermas *does* look to the chances for a mutually enriching integration between distinct types of radical needs deemed necessary to the reproduction of utopian commitments. For him, the task of rebuilding a con-temporary utopianism requires a balanced appreciation of the contributing influence of two sets of motivations. He describes the yearnings of new needs for a release from the inhibitions of the past as a tool necessary to a sceptical inquiry into the worth of our cultural inheritances.

This determination to include transformative energies in a balanced description of the project of a revived utopianism has revealed itself in the terms of Habermas' appreciation of the agendas of radical student movements in the post-1968 period. In these impatient longings for a release from a con-fining and materialistic present, he has discovered a pool of expectations able to contribute positively to a suspicious and creative appropriation of the potentials of German democratic institutions and structures. In particular, the transformative agendas of the young radicals offer a corrective to tempta-tions in post-1989 Germany to seek an 'easy' relationship to the past.[82] Habermas supposes that the utopianism of his own post-war generation has been limited to a wary attempt to redeem and critically re-appropriate liberal democratic principles that had been shattered in Nazi Germany.[83] These ide-alizing investments in the regulative norms of democratic procedures need to recognize an important ally in the motivations of a new generation that is calling for a release from conventional descriptions of identities and priorities of life. Habermas advises that the meeting place for these two sets of critical needs could be found in their shared rejection of any complacent appropria-tion of the significance of the German past. The urgency of this struggle has by no means diminished in the post-1989 period. On the contrary, today the critical energies of transformative hopes are urgently needed to obstruct the passage of the two 'Big Lies' that plague modern German history:

> the post war lie of being always already democrats and the Post-Wall Lie of becoming once again a normal nation. The two Lies, motivated by an inability to speak truth about the catastrophic past express social

pathology. Their existential usefulness to democracy consists in fortifying self- and other-deceptive, willed ignorance among its democratic practitioners.[84]

Habermas insists that it is not up to the critical theorist to tell us what in the past is worth taking forward. The theorist is limited to an interpretation of the implications of certain kinds of choices we make. Nothing, Habermas says, makes him 'more nervous' than the suggestion that critical theory should propose an ideal of the rational society towards which we are to proceed.[85] His critical theory wants to install communicatively acting subjects in the role of legitimate interpreters of their own needs and aspirations, hence as vital participants in an on-going determination of the present interests from whose point of view the past is creatively appropriated. However, for some of his critics, Habermas offers a totalizing construction of the significance of emancipatory needs that seems to be at odds with the reconstructive purposes of this theory.[86] While his critical theory might be happy to absorb the vitality of transformative impulses into its framework, the point remains that, for Habermas, only such aspirations as are prepared to offer themselves as claims willing to submit to the rationalizing procedures required to establish their justice can be admitted as having critical significances.[87] Iris Young, for example, thinks that the tendency of Habermas' theory to 'restrict democratic discussion to argument carries implicit cultural biases that can lead to exclusions in practice'.[88] The radicalness of needs impatient at the demand that they make themselves accountable to generalizable norms that can be advanced as supporting reasons appears to be consigned to the ineffectual stuff of Romantic dreams.

Matustik is particularly worried that Habermas' totalizing framework only responds to certain constructions of emancipatory needs and so inevitably mis-recognizes, and hence alienates, some of the vital cultural tributaries that have swelled critical potentials in liberal democracies. He thinks that Habermas has failed to speak to the new social movements in terms that correspond to their *own* understanding of the balance of influences on, and the necessary route for the development of, their utopian energies.[89] Habermas' appreciation of these energies constitutes them as an immature set of motivations that must finally show themselves 'willing to become pacified by democratic procedures, law and civil order'.[90] The danger in this interest in a subduing appropriation is that motivations that draw their critical impulses from a profound suspicion at the 'managing' effects of all consensual understandings will consider their main aspirations have been misunderstood and repulsed.

The point certainly needs to be made, though, that a politics that is preoccupied with testing the limits of conventional identity descriptions, with an exploration of untried images of cultural difference and ways of living, needs to be finally able to recognize its dependency on the pluralistic and egalitarian commitments of democratic institutions. However, this is not to be confused with the stronger conviction that the *meaning* and *significance* of such aspirations can be counted as simply an immature construction of the supposed essentially rationalizing purposes of a democratic Enlightenment interpretation of emancipatory motivations. Jeffrey Alexander has remarked that there is no reason to think that a politics that is fuelled by an interest in testing out and experimenting with identity descriptions could not cling to the separateness of its own agenda while also recognizing its dependence on institutionally sustained pluralistic and egalitarian principles. While the vibrancy of movements concerned with, for example, race, ethnicity and gender draws substantially on the transformative needs of evolving identity descriptions, Alexander nevertheless thinks *'it would also be strange* if the energies of the sphere-specific idealising movements . . . did not inform, and were not periodically sustained by, some reference to a broader and more unifying ideal'.[91]

Habermas seems to consider that a cultural resistance that is inspired by determination to break through the 'managing' effects of conventional identity descriptions and ways of doing things provides a mere 'training ground'[92] for a politics that is committed to the creative re-appropriation of liberal democratic normativity. However, he also offers his critical theory just as an illumination of the 'alternative life possibilities . . . seen to be inherent in the present'. The problem is that the totalizing framework that is proposed by his theory seems to undermine its capacity to adequately negotiate deep tensions in the terms in which alternative life possibilities of the present are conceived. Actually, Habermas does indicate good reasons why a reforming interest in the *sceptical* appropriation of a liberal democratic normativity might need to draw upon the critical and creative energies supplied by transformative hopes that are intolerant of any easy continuities between past, present and future. He also indicates that a reliance on liberal democratic principles that enjoin values of tolerance, pluralism and respect cannot be avoided by an identity politics that seeks to reshape conventional expectations. It seems, then, that Habermas does suggest some convincing reasons why distinct formulations of emancipatory needs should take each other into account. Yet these reasons remain inadequately exploited *as* reasons that are capable of informing the developmental path adopted by each as long as one interpretation of our critical aspirations is represented as simply an episode within the rationalizing trajectories of developed investment in the ideal of a self-determining life.

Kolakowski makes the point that if our utopian energies are to be revitalized we need to encourage a productive interchange between two relatively distinct types of motivations. As he sees it, open and decent modern societies need both 'diggers', utopians who dream of a world of unfettered self-realization, *and* 'healers', sceptics interested in a reflective appropriation of chosen continuities. It is these latter who attempt to: '. . . keep us vigilant . . . not to let us be carried away by wishful thinking'.[93] Unlike Habermas, Kolakowski does not encourage us to try and harmonize these diverse impulses within modern utopian thinking. He points out that we need to bear their differences in mind and to seek, not the subordination of one to the other, but an attitude mindful of their tensions and of their complementary commitments. As Kolakowski says: 'We need them both.'

The normative investment in interactions aimed at the formation of rational solidarities that underpins Habermas' critical theory has long been under pressure from his postmodern critics. Chapter 8 will explore this aspect of Habermas' dispute with these critics. It will suggest that the stand off that marks this relationship is a product of the attempts by each side to invest distinct, but complementary, emancipatory hopes with totalizing significance.

8 Romantic and Enlightenment legacies

The postmodern critics

Habermas has always supposed that his description of modernity's 'unfinished project' of democratic Enlightenment indicates a real appreciation of the diversity of modernizing processes against the one-sidedness of the dialectic of Enlightenment thesis. He has wanted to expand our comprehension of the complexity of the Enlightenment's rationalizing potentials and to promote the normativity of the interactive rationality that underpins the legitimacy of democratic power against the hegemonic tendencies of an instrumentalizing reason. However, some of Habermas' critics maintain that this attempt to widen the interpretation of its rationality potentials still fails to capture the extent of the impact of the Enlightenment. Johann Arnason, for instance, considers that an expanded account of its rationalizing trajectories is too narrow a frame within which to appreciate Enlightenment's full significance.[1] Habermas, Arnason maintains, has overlooked the on-going cultural tensions released by the legacies of Enlightenment reason that not only conflict with its original self-interpretations, but also challenge its capacity to set itself up as modernity's incomplete project. For Arnason, the Romantic structures of consciousness that are also a part of our cultural inheritances constitute such a response. A Romantic consciousness signals a determination to interrupt, not complete, the rationalizing project of modernity. It craves recognition for the beautiful uniqueness of each subject and discovers an intolerable authoritarianism in the Enlightenment's insatiable demand for reasons.

This critique of totalizing images of modernity's Enlightenment project strikes a chord that is not unfamiliar. Isaiah Berlin also wanted to remind us of on-going tensions between the rationalizing imperatives of the Enlightenment and its Romantic critics.[2] He insisted that we are 'children of both worlds'.[3] On the one hand, modern consciousness is organized by an Enlightenment interpretation of Western rationalism that affirms the capacity of human reason to finally discover what the world is like:

> what things are, what they have been, what they will be, what the laws are that govern them, what man is, what the relation of man is to things, and therefore what man needs, what he desires, and also how to obtain it.[4]

Yet we are also 'products of certain doubts', heirs to a Romantic undermining of all confidence in the notion that 'in matters of value, politics, morals, aesthetics there are such things as objective criteria that can operate between human beings'.[5] With its love for the free untrammeled will and its attempts to 'blow up' the very notion of a stable structure of anything, Romanticism also plays a vital part in establishing the tensions that structure a modern mentality.[6]

The real divergence of Enlightenment and Romantic legacies is generally acknowledged.[7] However, the appropriate role of the theorist in weighing up and responding to the strained relations between the rationalizing commitments and the Romantic ideals of a schizophrenic modernity remains a deeply controversial topic. Arnason refers to modernity as a 'field of tensions'.[8] This account tends to relieve the theorist from the task of supplying a synthesizing framework. It does not suggest, though, that the critics must thereby forfeit the role of critic. Rather, as interpreters of modernity's 'field of tensions', theorists are called upon to reflect on and clarify distinct cultural legacies and to alert us to their mutual interdependencies.[9] We have seen that, by contrast, Habermas' account of modernity's incomplete project of Enlightenment ascribes an integrative task to the theorist.[10] In this synthesizing approach, critical theory is to offer itself as an advocate for neglected democratic Enlightenment potentials and to seek to establish the conditions under which a Romantic consciousness might be recruited to the revitalization of this project.

Habermas consistently repudiates a one-sided appreciation of Enlightenment legacies and tries to uncover the neglected promise of a double-sided process of cultural modernization. He emphasizes that Enlightenment rationality does not prove its worth merely by appealing to the efficiencies and the emancipatory effects of instrumentalizing descriptions of subjects' relations to their world. An Enlightenment commitment to the principle of public reason, understood as the mechanism of an achieved consensus between private individuals, offers a specific interpretation of the meaning of human freedom. An interactive rationality can be seen to foster the expansion of capacities for self-reflection, a commitment to democratic decision-making and to individualistic patterns of identity formation. As Habermas sees it, the significance of Romantic tendencies unleashed by modernization processes lie in the energies they can contribute to democratic Enlightenment achievements that are, at the same time, called upon to subdue and tame these anti-rationalizing impulses.[11]

Part of the purpose of this chapter is to critically assess the totalizing impulses in Habermas' construction of the task of critical theory as a sponsor for modernity's 'incomplete project'. However, arguments against a synthesizing perspective on distinctive Enlightenment and Romantic inheritances cut both ways. Asserting themselves as the repository of contemporary Romantic hopes, some versions of postmodernism also fail to accept the limits of the frameworks through which they interpret processes of cultural modernization. The first part of the chapter will focus on the incoherencies that result from attempts to describe democratic ideals in terms borrowed from anti-rationalistic, Romantic interpretations of modern cultural legacies and potentials. Turning the focus around, the last part of the chapter will evaluate Habermas' efforts to assimilate Romantic motivations into his description of the emancipatory potentials of democratic Enlightenment. I will argue that, while Habermas' theory can survive well some versions of a post-modern critique of the supposed *essentially* repressive impulses of his investment in the ideal of rational solidities, the postmoderns have also suggested an interpretation of the longing for emancipation from whose point of view the rationalizing demands of Enlightenment can only appear as an intolerable constraint. It seems that the framework through which Habermas has interpreted the ambiguous potentials of modernization processes needs to be widened and the description of the role of the theorist modified to take into account the complexity of the relations between distinct versions of the need for emancipation that have been set in motion by the historical Enlightenment.

Romanticizing democracy: Carl Schmitt and beyond

Nobody, it seems, has constructed the question of the relative influence of Enlightenment and Romantic legacies on the formation of modern democratic ideals more strikingly than Carl Schmitt. The Grand Jurist for the Third Reich insisted that liberal democratic politics is itself the incoherent product of an attempt to marry incompatible Enlightenment and Romantic allegiances. For him, the *semblance* of rationalistic aspirations harboured by the liberal democratic polity turns out to be no more than a Romantic betrayal of the political.[12] The contemporary cultural critic F. R. Ankersmit endorses this account of 'the essentially Romantic character of democracy'.[13] The postmodern aestheticization of the political that is advocated by him, Dana Villa[14] and others owes much of its inspiration to themes elaborated in the work of Jean-Francois Lyotard.[15] These recent attempts to describe the indebtedness of modern democratic politics to Romantic influences largely accept Schmitt's characterization of the democratic process yet, by giving an alternative interpretation of the *goals* of liberal democratic politics, they have evaluated the supposed Romanticism of modern democracy in quite different terms. The following discussion will examine the success of their efforts to evade the implications of Schmitt's account of the Romanticism of modern democratic ideals.

   Schmitt maintained that liberal democratic politics offers a hopelessly muddled interpretation of its own legitimacy; an incoherence that can be traced back to its confused appeal to the idea of public reason. Schmitt did not argue that we should try to redeem this distorted ideal that had been betrayed in the flawed institutions and corrupted practices of liberal democratic societies. He sought not to reclaim the concept of public reason but to 'strike at the root' of its metaphysical pretensions.[16] In modern liberalism, the idea of public discussion, upheld by the historical Enlightenment as an ingredient essential to practical strategies aimed at unmasking the metaphysical pretensions of the age, is redescribed in absolute metaphysical terms as the way of truth.[17] The fallacy of liberal democracy's metaphysical attachment to the ideal of public reason rests on the unrecognized incompatibility of the distinctive norms that govern liberalism and democracy. Democracy, Schmitt insisted, refers to the ideal of the self-sovereign society while liberalism's principled commitment to pluralism renders incoherent any appeal to the 'self' needed to make sense of this ideal. For Schmitt, the political, described as 'the basic characteristic of human life', requires the constitution of a people as a 'fighting collectivity' able to recognize and prepared to defend their kind of existence against the threat of the enemy.[18] Celebrating the ideal of a plurality of diverse wills, liberalism appears, then, as an anti-politics. Its conception of public reason could never be relied upon to bridge the gulf that stretches between the heterogeneous self-interested wills of the bourgeois mass and the identification of a general will that could guide a democratic polity. In the context of a socially and culturally heterogeneous modernity, the exercise of public reason produces nothing more than perpetual discussion. Its 'achievement' is to confer self-importance on the endless and futile conversation of a self-absorbed and distracted mass. The vain hope that the self-interested and privatistic motivations of the masses could offer fertile ground for the achievement of rational consensus simply masks liberalism's actual allegiance to a decadent Romantic preoccupation with the mere contemplation of differences.[19] Under a liberal democratic description, politics becomes aestheticized and nothing gets done. All substantial differences, all contestations around a preferred way of life, are described as a creative tension between diverse points of view. When confronted by a conflict in the real world, the liberal democrat aestheticizes the moment and a real opposition is 'paraphrased into an emotive dissonance ... [t]his paraphrase is then subjected to the creative play of the imagination with the result that dissonance is reconciled'.[20] This appreciation of the interplay of differences carried over into a delight in *Wortspiel*: word-games in which postures and opinions are trialed, paraded and discarded.[21]

Habermas repudiates Schmitt's efforts as an attempt to dress up an ideologically inspired attack on the ideal of public reason as a critique of the incoherence of a contemporary attempt to team up this Enlightenment ideal with incompatible Romantic motivations.[22] Habermas insists that, interpreted as a discursive procedure, the Enlightenment principle of public reason offers itself as a fully coherent description of the 'self' in the ideal 'self-sovereign society' in conditions of ethical and cultural pluralism. No longer able to represent itself as a description of an objectively meaningful world, contemporary reason retreats into an account of the procedural norms governing consensus-building interactions between private individuals. In this context, the ideal of the self-sovereign society refers to the normativity of those communicative interactions through which private individuals in dynamic modernity seek to produce rational solidarities.

Habermas invites a contemporary loss of faith in the concept of public reason to look into the mirror of Schmitt's decisionism to remind itself of the intolerable price of a retreat into irrationalism.[23] Despising the very idea of 'government by discussion', for Schmitt, the defence of democracy requires a sovereign prepared to act to bring about the friend-enemy relations necessary to its prosecution. Given the sociological and psychological heterogeneity of the masses, the 'general will' necessary to democratic self-sovereignty must be fabricated from the mythologies of the *Volk*. Habermas warns that only by investing in the procedural principles of public reason can we theorize and defend a commitment towards reaching 'an understanding over political questions without resorting to violence'.[24] A contemporary challenge to the normativity of 'public reason' fancies itself able to reply to Habermas' fears. Recent formulations of this critique typically put demands on the adequacy of a modern interpretation of democracy that are quite different from Schmitt's. They claim that a revised interpretation of the goal of democratic politics can release a contemporary attack on the ideal of public reason from the perils of decisionism.[25]

Schmitt's attack on the ideal of public reason alleged that this concept is unable to offer a coherent account of the ideal of the self-sovereign society and, because he supposed that an attempt to theorize the idea of self-sovereignty is central to an account of democratic politics, the concept of public reason must be rejected as a failed interpretation of its meaning. Influenced by a postmodern 'incredulity toward metanarratives',[26] some recent commentators agree that there *can* be no formulation of the ideal self-sovereign society that is compatible with modern pluralism. For them, the ideal of self-sovereignty cannot be saved by appealing to a proceduralist interpretation of the public use of reason. We saw in an earlier chapter that Thomas McCarthy and James Bohman doubt the adequacy of an appeal to the principle of consensus-building through the exercise of public reason as a way of describing the normativity of democratic interactions in a multicultural modernity.[27] McCarthy describes consensus-building as an incoherent ambition in a culturally and ethically diverse world, for 'many intractable ethical-political disputes cannot be settled by such means'.[28] Ankersmit goes further than this. He boldly embraces the implications of a full-blown version of a critique of public reason for an interpretation of the modern democratic ideal. Ankersmit insists that the radical character of postmodern suspicions about the ideal of public reason ties it to an alternative Romantic account of the meaning of modern democracy. Where Schmitt went wrong was not in proposing the essentially Romantic credentials of democratic politics but in his *contempt* for this reassertion of the Romantic attitude.[29] Schmitt despised the Romanticism of the democratic temper because he misinterpreted the telos of the democratic process.

Ankersmit supposes that there can only ever be a repressive response to the search for the 'self' of the 'self sovereign society' and he goes on to insist that Romantic preoccupations only appear to offer a confused interpretation of democracy when assessed, inappropriately, from the standpoint of a misguided identification of the meaning of democracy with the ideal of a self-sovereign polity. While Ankersmit shares certain of Schmitt's key convictions, he wants to overturn the scale of values that inform the latter's portrait of the Romantic temper of liberal democracy. Ankersmit agrees that the ideal of the self-sovereign society requires an attempt to locate secure foundations capable of anchoring judgments about right and wrong, just and unjust, that must cut across the recognition of a legitimate diversity of view points.[30] However, Ankersmit responds to this seeming dilemma not by advocating the decisionistic power of sovereign authority but by repudiating the supposed *necessity* of the ideal of self-sovereignty to the meaning of modern democracy. The democratic ideal is not tied to a principle of self-sovereignty, it only affirms a mode of inter-subjectivity that permits the unleashing of the creative potentials of each participant in the interaction. As Ankersmit sees it, 'the curious lack of principles observed by Schmitt pertains to the essence of democracy and ... it is exactly in this chaos devoid of principles that the unparalleled creative political power of democracy is to be found'.[31] The contemplative appreciation of the play of differences, dismissed by Schmitt as a futile Romanticism, actually refers to the creative power of democratic interactions.[32] According to Schmitt, the 'rootlessness' or 'undecidability' of the canvassing of views in a liberal democratic polity, the inability to seek anchorage in the appeal to any legitimate authority, finds expression in the banality of the 'endless conversation' that stamps the anti-politics of liberal democratic societies. Ankersmit, by contrast, insists that this undecidability lays the grounds for the peculiar fruitfulness of the modern democratic relation. For him, the mutual understanding of others in all their strange individuality must be affirmed as the only interpretation of the meaning of democracy that is tolerable for a heterogeneous public. Undecidability and the lack of shared principles offer the space necessary for the creative achievement of recognition between those who are different.

Faced by the constraints of radical cultural and ethical pluralism, the democratic ideal can no longer interpret itself as a description of principles and convictions held in common. It can now only serve as a description of the essentially imaginative act through which understanding between strangers is achieved. In democratic interactions, the subjective point of view attempts to make itself understood and to clarify its own self-understanding by discovering fragments of shared meanings within the perspective of the other. The lack of definition, the inability of the subjective point of view in the liberal democratic interaction to fully locate itself within the terms of a foundational principle, makes possible that non-repressive recognition of the standpoint of the other that is, for Ankersmit, the goal of the democratic interchange. This 'intertextuality of political positions', the fact that political positions can only articulate themselves in and by means of each other, 'is more than a simple expression of the desire for consensus. It expresses the acknowledgement that the realization of one's own position is partly also the realization of the other's position and vice versa'.[33]

An attempt to defend the centrality of public reason to the normativity of modern democratic principles needs to respond to two aspects of this argument. First, the insistence that the democratic relation can be coherently interpreted without reference to the idea of the self-sovereign society requires a reply. Second, the claim that any formulation of the ideal of public reason can only compromise a recognition of the multiplicity of diverse claims and points of view in a heterogeneous modernity also should be addressed.

For Ankersmit, democratic interactions mimic the repudiation of all extrinsic purposes and goal orientations that are typical of the specificity of aesthetic communication. 'Democracy' refers to creative interactions in which shared understandings are forged across the spaces that separate diverse points of view. However, it seems that, by limiting the interest of the democratic relation to a sympathetic disclosure of differences, Ankersmit is unable to theorize commitments implicit in his own postmodern perspective. After all, his repudiation of Schmitt's decisionism is informed by a clear interest in defending the claims of *vulnerable* particularity. He rejects both the appeal to decisionistic power and the appeal to the procedures of public reason on the grounds that neither responds properly to the unmet needs of marginalized subjects in pluralistic societies. This critique speaks of Ankersmit's postmodern interest in the search for egalitarian justice; it voices his very unSchmittian, persuasion that all points of view ought to get a fair hearing. However, it appears that Ankersmit's aestheticized reading of the meaning of the democratic interaction is unable to reconstruct the conditions under which the legitimacy of unmet claims might be acknowledged.

There might appear to be a way out here. A rejection of the centrality of the principle of the public use of reason to the democratic ideal can try and avoid decisionistic implications of its posture by interpreting its defence of the principle of diversity as the non-conflictual, expressive play of differences between self-sustaining subjectivities. In this case there could be no call upon the decision-making, problem solving functions that, in their different ways, both the ideal of a rational consensus and the appeal to decisionistic authority attempt to legitimate. However, this would not work for Ankersmit. As already noted, his repudiation of decisionism is inspired by a principled commitment to defending the claims of vulnerable, mis-represented and marginalized subjectivities. Decisions on equity and fairness have to be made and the question of the grounds of their legitimacy cannot be side stepped. It seems that, when it is tied to a postmodern critique of an authoritarian neglect of the claims of marginalized and needy subjectivities, an account of the merely aesthetic, expressive character of a democratic interest in plural identities cannot do the job.

Democracy as reasonable consensus

According to Habermas, it was Nietzsche who fathered the postmodern attempt to defend the claims of unique subjectivity against the 'leveling' attitude of a rationalizing Enlightenment.[34] Nietzsche discovered that behind the supposedly universal claims raised by Enlightenment reason lay hidden the 'ebb and flow' of an anonymous process of subjugation to a 'transubjective' will to power.[35] Habermas suggests that the radical character of Nietzsche's attack on reason rendered his commitment to the idea of an authentic will to power, understood as the 'power to create meaning', an empty gesture. If reason was described as a distorted will to power that insinuated itself through each attempt to suggest the intersubjective character of all evaluative claims, if it was identified with the *shared* character of cognitive, purposive and moral judgments, then the meaning-producing ambitions of an authentic will to power became blocked.[36] Because 'reason' was allowed to monopolize the interpretation of (and to contaminate the commitment to) the ideal of shared meanings with its repressive, leveling attitudes, the creative will to power could not seek recognition for its significance. The authentic will to power could only protect its purity by reconciling itself to its inability to create meanings.

Habermas insists that the aporetic character of Nietzsche's argument has been inherited by a postmodern deep scepticism towards the repressive, unifying imperatives that lurk behind the cloak of legitimacy supplied by the appeal to reason.[37] In an essay titled 'The Other of Justice: Habermas and the Ethical Challenge of Postmodernism', Axel Honneth refines and extends the terms of Habermas' critique of the conceptual *cul de sac* that emerges from the radicalism of a postmodern attack on reason.[38] Honneth stresses that, under certain descriptions of its motivations and conceptual interests, postmodernism is unable to sustain its own description of the necessary antagonism between particularistic claims and universalizing norms. Honneth wants to show that Lyotard's attack on reason cannot be reconciled with motivations that are also fundamental to his postmodernism. In sharp contrast to anti-democratic Nietzsche, Lyotard's critique of repressive reason is inspired by an egalitarian interpretation of the 'injustice' of totalizing perspectives that contain and repress the self-expression of the heterogeneous and the unique.[39] Honneth points out that Lyotard's principled interest in extending recognition to claims raised by marginalized points of view or ostracized language games must, in the end, appeal to (supposedly repulsive) universalizing norms of reason. In Honneth's view, without moral universalism 'one cannot at all understand what having to defend the particularity of the suppressed language game against the dominant agreement is supposed to mean'.[40] Once a Romantic longing for a free expression of concrete uniqueness untrammeled by the demand for reasons is teamed up with a call for justice interpreted as a principled commitment to the idea of an equality of life chances, a construction of the fundamentally antagonistic relation between universalizing norms and particularistic claims begins to unravel.

Habermas supposes that liberalism has also failed to grasp the fundamental dialectical relation between the particular and the universal point of view. He insists that, in its determination to defend private right, liberalism has over-burdened formal, universalizing categories. On the one hand, and in a limited sense, liberalism has been right to insist that, in a world divided by potentially conflictual cultural and ethical difference, particularity has to appeal to increasingly abstracted norms as the grounds upon which it can seek recognition for the justice of its claims. In the context of the growing fragmentation and differentiation of a multicultural world, the scope of recognition finally must shrink back to the level of common assent to idealizing presuppositions implicit in the general rules and principles that govern the integrity of discourse. Particularity becomes more and more dependent on abstract universality as the concreteness of a world in common slips ever further out of reach. 'The more abstract the agreements become, the more diverse the disagreements with which we can *nonviolently* live.'[41] Yet, while frustrated particularity has increasingly turned to abstract categories to establish the legitimacy of its claims, as long as generalizing norms are seen to embody the principle of impartiality, the idea of unity, Habermas insists, will 'still be treated as the enemy of individualism, not as what makes it possible'. The unity of reason will continue to be 'treated as repression, not as the source of the diversity of its voices'.[42] The 'impartiality' and disinterestedness supposed essential to the generalizing point of view of reason have seemed to deny frustrated particularity any opportunity to offer its distinctive claims as a reappropriation of those norms and categories through which it can seek recognition.

The discourse ethics account of the interdependency of universal value commitments and particular claims for autonomy proposes a middle course between a liberal and a postmodern interpretation of the relationship. Habermas rejects as a futile gesture a postmodern conviction that the struggle for recognition waged by marginalized difference can repudiate the demand that it seek to justify the legitimacy of its claims. He also distances himself from the one-sidedness of a liberal interpretation that effectively denies to concrete particularity any appropriate role in interpreting those norms by means of which the rationality and the justice of its claims are to be assessed. According to Habermas, liberalism's commitment to the principle of impartial disinterest has offered itself as a strategy designed to 'contain' the problem of a pluralism of perspectives. Whereas

> Rawls imposes a common perspective on the parties in the original position through informational constraints and thereby neeutralizes the multiplicity of particular interpretative perspectives from the outset (. . .) discourse ethics views the moral point of view as embodied in an intersubjective practice of argumentation which enjoins those involved to an idealizing enlargement of their interpretive perspectives.[43]

We saw in Chapter 4 that, according to discourse ethics, 'public reason' describes a mode of interaction that is governed by a commitment to respond to the rationality of individual claims rather than by a disinterested impartiality about them. Articulated through procedural norms that require reciprocity and symmetry between discursive partners, this commitment is formulated in terms that seek to avoid all prejudgments on what capacities are required to make the reasonableness of claims understood. For Habermas, a responsiveness to novel claims and modes of self-expression is built into the complexity of the theory's communicative and intersubjective presuppositions.[44] Each discursive participant is recognized as a legitimate interpreter of the distortions, or success, of a communicative act governed by the goal of building mutual understanding. It is, then, necessary to remain vigilant about the exclusionary implications of the manner in which 'good reasons' come to be identified within the political and legal institutions of democracy.[45] Settled formulations of what counts as convincing arguments inevitably appear as the result of the struggles for recognition that have been waged by particular subjects armed with their own peculiar needs and aspirations. Yet Habermas insists that grounds for the critique of the empirical standards upheld by really existing liberal democratic institutions can be extracted from idealized expectations about the rationality of deliberative processes that are also embedded in this facticity.

Can this defence of the responsiveness of the norms of public reason to the claims of concrete particularity expect to quell fears that have motivated a postmodern antipathy towards universalisms? Some of Habermas' critics remain unpersuaded. They point out that a longing for emancipation that is conceived as a desire for the uninhibited expression of a novel self can only encounter the expectations of accountability built into the norms of public reason as an alienating demand. Lyotard's determination to 'wage war on totality' and to 'save the honour of the name' is undiminished when confronted by Habermas' proposal that concrete particularity might argumentatively establish the reasonableness of the marginalized point of view. He remains deeply suspicious of the 'kind of unity' this 'reputable thinker' has in mind.[46] For Lyotard, the assumption that 'it is possible for all speakers to come to agreement on which rules or metaprescriptions are universally valid for language games' seeks to reduce their irreducible heterogeneity.[47] Villa backs up a critique of the 'outmoded and suspect' character of public reason as a value. He endorses Lyotard's interest in a 'pagan' politics that tries to break with all attempts to ground action and practical decision in a theoretical discourse of legitimacy.[48] Stephen White also expresses the 'deepest reservations' about Habermas' pretensions to be able to settle 'the problem of otherness' adequately within his framework.[49] To such commentators, the demand for reasons only appears benign given the presumption of a certain type of subjectivity schooled in particular kinds of motivations and bearer of certain types of interests.

Critiques of the normativity that Habermas invests in the ideal of public reason go further than a mere reminder that existing descriptions of 'reasonableness' might block the recognition of new and disruptive claims. For some postmodernists, at stake also are the longings for free self expression that would regard the call for the elaboration of shared understandings able to act as reasons as an intolerable constraint.[50] Lyotard resorts to Kant's description of the sublime to evoke the exhilarating sense of release experienced by a self as it strives to shake free the demands of common purposes.[51] Refusing to countenance that the importance of its self-expression might be construed as a mere contribution towards building the grounds of a shared intelligibility, the subject caught in the experience of the sublime insists that the mind be allowed to 'busy itself with ideas that involve higher purposiveness'.[52] Lyotard protests that his appropriation of the Kantian 'sublime' has been too readily dismissed by those who see in this sympathy for the demands of a self radically dissatisfied with the everyday a recipe for a willful politics of self-assertion, of terror even. Lyotard insists that he has used this category only as a reminder that, in their expression of a desire for transcendence from the mundane, these 'pagan' motivations are also part of the modern 'cultivated' impulses that influence the agendas of contemporary cultural life.[53]

Habermas points out that, unlike liberalism, his discourse reconstruction of the norms of the public sphere is marked, not by a disinterest in the points of view of concrete individuals, but by a concern to elaborate the conditions under which the rationality of their claims can be recognized. Even so, it seems that the theory cannot respond to some culturally significant experiences of self-interpreted difference. According to some of Habermas' critics, his investment in the normativity of the public sphere places discriminatory expectations on subjects who have been shaped by non-argumentative ways of representing their needs, interests and identities. Moreover, upholding the rationalizing procedures of the public sphere as the discursive channel to be negotiated seems to confront some types of emancipatory needs as an intolerable constraint. Villa speaks out for those whose sense of uniqueness demands a politics 'engaged in the endless subversion of codes'.[54]

Villa is clearly right when he points out that Habermas' description of public reason offers a limiting account of the spectrum of motivations and interests that are relevant to the democratic interchange. While no prejudgments on the generalizable significance of particular issues are to be admitted, a willingness to argumentatively justify the wider relevance of one's needs and legitimacy of one's claims on public resources is required of effective participants in Habermas' version of the public sphere. This reconstruction of its normativity does suggest a restrictive account of motivations and interests deemed necessary to participants in the democratic relation. We still need to be precise, though, about the sense in which this limited account of the interests and motivations that could be accommodated by it represents a *problem* for an interpretation of the normativity of the democratic ideal. Let us, for a moment put the onus on the critics. Advocates of an aestheticizing interpretation of the democratic ideal should be able to persuade us that we lose nothing we value about this ideal by thus opening its scope.

Habermas does acknowledge the distinctive contribution that an aesthetic/expressive mode of communication can make to an enrichment of contents recognized as relevant to the democratic process.[55] According to him, its peculiar interest in shaping new forms of representation adequate to emergent modes of consciousness, to new needs and novel issues has seen a modernist aesthetic occupying an important role as tributary to the revitalization of a democratic culture. However, Habermas sees the aesthetic interest in the light of a 'signal function' that can never be completely identified with a democratic interest in the communication of needs and particularistic points of view.[56] For him, the aesthetic mode of communication cannot propose itself as an interpretation of the democratic ideal because it is unable to account for functions that are central to the specificity of a democracy as a social and as a political form. Habermas always insists that an aesthetic interest in elaborating the conditions under which concrete particularity can achieve recognition for its uncompromised singularity cannot help to specify the conditions under which particular subjects might establish the legitimacy of their claims upon public resources.

A postmodern attempt to describe the meaning and the goals of the democratic process in terms borrowed from the communicative power of the work of art seems to be trapped by a tension between its objectives and its conceptual tools. To the extent that a postmodern investment in the communicative power of the aesthetic offers itself as a response to the frustrations of marginalized and mis-recognized points of view, a politicized postmodernism appears implicated in the interests of egalitarian justice. Honneth points out that, for Lyotard, and we can say also for Villa and White, the postmodern is interested in achieving 'moral protection' for the 'ignored element of the heterogeneous and the unique'.[57] This kind of politicized postmodernism is called into being by its responsiveness to the needs of subjects whose claims have been marginalized and overlooked. And yet, embracing an agonistic construction of the democratic process, postmodernism seems to disavow the necessity of providing any account of a process whereby the legitimacy of both already recognized and novel claims might be determined.

Arguing along similar lines, Richard Wolin supposes that Lyotard's brand of postmodernism is guilty of a 'performative contradiction'.[58] While Lyotard insists that the idea of an uncoerced rational accord is a fantasy, for '[u]nderlying the veneer of mutual agreement lurks force', Wolin wonders 'how Lyotard expects to convince readers of the rectitude of his position if not via recourse to time-honored discursive means; the marshalling of supporting evidence and force of the better argument'. He concludes that 'ultimately there is something deeply unsatisfying about the attempt by Lyotard and his fellow poststructuralists to replace the precepts of argumentation with rhetoric, aesthetics, or agonistics'.[59]

A postmodern determination to rid the democratic ideal of any reference to procedures that are aimed at building a rational consensus faces some unattractive options. It can cling onto an expressive/aesthetic interpretation of the purposes of the democratic relation only if it gives up its commitment to the defence of the neglected claims of marginalized and vulnerable subjects. If an account of the democratic process is not required to legitimate the power to make decisions able to respond to the plight of the disadvantaged and oppressed, then postmodernism can, of course, do without endorsing the ideal of consensus building through the public use of reason. Schmitt also made it quite clear that modern democracy can be interpreted in terms that dispense both with an appeal to the public use of reason and to the pluralistic, egalitarian commitments that it is supposed to articulate. If 'public reason' is to lose its place in a description of the democratic project then the trade off seems to be either a conception of legitimate decision-making that excludes the participation of those who are affected or the sacrifice of any conception of legitimate power at all.

However, Lyotard is right to remind us that modern cultivated impulses also include a 'pagan' desire to give expression to the concrete and the unrepeatable. Indeed, it appears that the postmoderns give voice to emancipatory hopes that put to the test Habermas' claim that insisting on the universality of a rationalizing Enlightenment interpretation of autonomy represents an only 'harmless' dogmatism.[60] Habermas stresses that, in post-Enlightenment societies, the value of autonomy suggests that human beings 'act as free subjects only insofar as they obey just those laws they give themselves in accordance with insights they have acquired intersubjectively'. This is supposed dogmatic in only a harmless sense because '*for us*, who have developed our identity in such a form of life, it cannot be circumvented'.[61] Habermas' critical theory proposes and elaborates the procedures of a discursive rationality as a mere extension and clarification of commitments already embraced by subjects for whom emancipation is supposed to mean practical entitlements to participate in fashioning their own futures. However, as the Romantic currents of postmodernism remind us, an ambiguous modernity has also produced longings for freedom that contest the regimes of self-rule. A thirst for experimentation with the play of cultural possibilities that modernization had dislodged from anchoring traditions (also a 'form of life' that is familiar to 'us') will sometimes encounter as an alienating dogmatism the rationalizing demands that attend a modern commitment to a self-determining autonomy.

Wolin appears quite intolerant of all alternatives to a rationalizing Enlightenment reading of modern emancipatory hopes. He is persuaded that 'postmodernists rely unwittingly on arguments and positions developed by proponents of Counter-Enlightenment' and that their trademark 'identity politics' is locked within a culture of narcissism that usurps the traditional left-wing concern with social justice'.[62] He takes it that the only construction of autonomy that remains for a posture that repudiates the quest for reasonable consensus central to the legitimating function of the democratic relation is the self-assertion of blind, hence authoritarian, identity claims. However, it seems useful to introduce some discriminations here. The performative contradictions in postmodern theories, that identify an essentially coercive imperative in rationalizing procedures but are unable to explain how else the legitimacy of frustrated and marginalized need claims can be determined, suggests that an easy identification with the politics of counter-Enlightenment that simply turns its back on ideals of universal justice, is not typically at play. The performative contradiction, noted by Wolin, seems to signal something else. Perhaps it is indicative of the complexity of post-modernism as a cultural form sited on the cusp of the tensions between Romantic and Enlightenment legacies. We return to this point in Chapter 9.

First, though, we need to turn from a discussion of the aporetic consequences of attempts to articulate ideals that have been shaped by democratic Enlightenment legacies through the anti-rationalizing categories supplied by Romanticism to consider problems that attend the attempt to recruit distinctive Romantic interpretations of emancipatory hopes to a project aimed at completing the unfinished project of democratic Enlightenment.

Negotiating tensions between Romanticism and Enlightenment

We have already noted that Habermas' advocacy of the neglected potentials of ambivalent Enlightenment legacies does acknowledge the contribution of unreconciled Romantic longings. He supposes that the transformative character of such hopes can ignite our critical energies and can encourage our impatience to rid ourselves of the grip of slavish continuities between present and past. Yet Habermas also insists that an impulsive, transformative zeal needs to be tempered by a capacity for critical judgment that provides a discriminating assessment of those unrealized potentials that are *worth* carrying forward. His hopes go with our capacities to learn from the past and with our ability to establish a reflective, discriminating solidarity with chosen aspects of inherited legacies.[63] The transformative hopes of the unreconciled need to be harnessed to a project aimed at the critical appropriation of the unrealized promise of democratic Enlightenment. Its energies supply helpful motivations to our reflections on past mistakes and inspire our determination to prevent their recurrence.[64] On this account, the hope that we may take forward the unrealized potentials of Enlightenment legacies attempts to exploit Romantic longings but must finally attempt to subdue this rival utopia whose untamed impulses it sometimes construes as a threat.

A strategy aimed at containing the rival utopianism of Romantic hopes within the sobering influence of rationalizing Enlightenment is a familiar one. Perhaps a recent study of the ill-fated consequences of liberalism's history of refusal to enter into dialogue with intractable Romantic longings offers a useful warning of the dangers implicit in any strategy that aims at simply containing these impulses via an encircling construction of modernity's Enlightenment project. Michael Halberstam's *Totalitarianism and the Modern Conception of Politics* investigates the costs of liberalism's refusal to concede anything more than private significances to Romantic motivations.[65] He suggests that the rationalizing commitments of liberalism struggled to close off any intercourse with disruptive Romantic impulses interpreted as 'dark particularist imperatives' determined to 'do away with any universal conception of right and culturally independent perspective from which to assess the merits of a given political regime'.[66] Halberstam suggests that in this attempt to relegate Romantic impulses to a publicly irrelevant private sphere lie the seeds of liberalism's political failures throughout the course of the twentieth century. Repulsed by liberal creeds that will not heed its trepidation about the social consequences of the rule of reason, a Romantic longing for recognition of a particularity unsullied by the search for common purposes turns to anti-liberal political ideologies for protection. Totalitarianism wins over the Romantic by its promise to 'give substance to the life of the individual'.[67] It sympathetically responds to a public grown weary of a politics that recognizes only the abstract individuality of a citizenry bound by formal rights. Some years ago Norbert Elias diagnosed the sense in which terrorism is connected to an exploitation of a Romantic defiance of the demand for rational accountability. He pointed out that a Romantic loathing for a 'stale abominable world' can feed a politics of the radical gesture whose transformative aim may get no further than a desire to annihilate and destroy.[68]

Charles Lamore is also deeply concerned about the consequences of entrenched patterns of alienation between Romantic and Enlightenment allegiances. He does not, in the first instance, hold the advocates of democratic Enlightenment responsible for this dangerous environment. He is convinced that the 'mistake' has been the responsibility of a heady Romanticism.[69] A liberal democratic tradition has not been able to respond to the specificity of Romantic interests because of a 'striking deficiency in Romantic political thought'.[70] With its tendency to see the state as 'either everything or nothing', total support to self-asserting ambitions or their feared enemy, Romanticism has neglected the extent to which 'political association has a specific function, essential but delimited'.[71] Romanticism has, namely, failed to appreciate that the commitment to abstract freedom carried by liberal democratic traditions also promises a framework necessary to the protection of the longings of concrete particularity.[72] Wolin thinks that the 'mistake' has been carried forward by a postmodern antipathy towards the idea of public reason enshrined in a modern democratic political culture.

> Postmodernists equate democracy with 'soft totalitarianism'. They argue that by privileging public reason and the common good, liberal democracy effectively suppresses otherness and difference. Of course, one could very easily make the converse argument: historically speaking, democracy and the rule of law have proved the best guarantors of cultural diversity and political pluralism.[73]

An insight into the mutual interdependence of Romantic longings for the free expression of unrepeatable particularity and a democratic Enlightenment interest in the rational arbitration between contesting claims does not only require that a Romantic self-consciousness of a supporting political culture become more developed. Lamore insists that the champions of the public use of reason also need to loosen themselves from reified formulations of their value commitments. Adherents of a democratic Enlightenment tradition must be prepared for the shock impact that the demands of novel hopes and ambitions can have on settled descriptions of the kinds of needs that might seek public recognition of their justice.

The potential hazards of ongoing alienation between democratic Enlightenment and Romantic impulses cut both ways. On the one hand, a frozen construction of the rationality of democratic procedures threatens to cut itself off from a vital source of utopian energies needed to invigorate it. At the same time, repulsed by the seeming neglect of a rationalizing political culture, Romantic urges can threaten to enter into a cycle of self-destruction setting off dangerous chain reactions. It seems that critical theory needs to develop a framework that permits recognition of the distinctiveness of Romantic and democratic Enlightenment urges as two separate cultural forms. Gyorgy Markus's description of the 'paradoxical unity' between Romanticism and Enlightenment as two great ideological tendencies of modernity seems to offer such a paradigm.

Markus theorizes the tensions between Enlightenment and Romanticism as two opposing interpretations of challenges that confront the task of cultural modernization. Romanticism and Enlightenment stand as 'two great and quite cosmopolitan ideological tendencies, representing opposed orientations concerning the meaning and role of culture and fighting each other over the direction of development'.[74] Central to this account of the tensions between Romanticism and Enlightenment is a description of a shared interest in responding to the task of elaborating the life-orienting role of culture in the context of secularization.

In the context of the disabling of religion as a coherent ideatory-symbolic system able to regulate the conduct of individuals, Enlightenment and Romanticism emerged with the common intention to 'regain for culture this life-orienting role'. However, they have distinct, even fundamentally opposed, ideas of 'what the realisation of such an end would mean and what are the actual cultural powers that may be capable of its realisation'.[75] An Enlightenment tradition has interpreted the task through its distinctive commitment to the realization of a 'truly *democratic public* whose autonomous members would regain control over their life and could participate equally in decisions concerning the common affairs of their society'.[76] Romanticism has interpreted differently the means by which culture could respond to the task of cultural modernization. Its project is aimed at the 'willed recreation of that lost organic community which was sustained by the living force of shared tradition, ungroundable in its uniqueness and able to confer meaning upon life'.[77]

A longing to recreate the 'beautiful' effortless solidarities of organic community and a determination to give substance to the life of unique, unrepeatable, individuality is irreducible to a commitment to the creation of achieved solidarities between strangers bound only by their shared capacities for reason. Yet the tension between these two rival interpretations of the life-orienting role of modern culture allows each to offer itself as a corrective to a dogmatic interpretation of the significance and the meaning of the other. Because Romanticism and Enlightenment form the 'paradoxical unity' of competing interpretations of the orienting role of culture, each is capable of making the other accountable to, at times even a beneficiary of, its alternative vision of modernity's open-ended prospects. Enlightenment rationality has something to offer frustrated Romantic hopes for '[t]his universalising radicalism offered ideas . . . that made it possible to represent the grievances of particular groups in the public arena as instances of some general malaise, a matter of common concern'.[78] Equally too, Romanticism's pained response to the atomization of isolated individuals and their transformation into 'mere objects of the impersonal machinery called "progress" '[79] could promote needed circumspection in the pursuit of Enlightenment's 'cause'.

This account of the 'paradoxical unity' between Romantic and Enlightenment traditions suggests a role for the critical theorist that is quite different from Habermas' conception of their synthesizing task. As interpreter to a 'paradoxical unity' within modernizing cultures, the critical theorist appears reconciled to the ongoing tensions between Enlightenment and Romanticism. In this framework critical theory accepts the task of reflecting upon and attempting to clarify the significance of hopes articulated by each of these cultural legacies and offers warnings of the dangers should either simply dogmatically assert its claims as the rightful interpreter of modernity's supposed unitary 'project'. The critical theorist can suggest, moreover, terms in which the distinctive goals of each legacy could be promoted by a suspicious and creative appropriation of aspects of opposing tendencies. Because the theorist of modernity's 'paradoxical unity' is armed with insight into the dual character of distinct negotiations of the shared problem of interpreting the life-orienting role of culture in pluralistic and secular modern societies, he can seek to propose the terms of productive interchanges between these cultural inheritances.

Descriptions of modernity both as a 'field of tensions' and as a 'paradoxical unity' permit the theorist to assume a key role as interpreter of the complex interdependencies and mutual limiting commitments of Romantic and Enlightenment legacies. By contrast, Habermas' 'incomplete project' metaphor positions the theorist, not only as an advocate to the 'cause' of a particular axis of cultural development, but also as interpreter of its claimed capacity to comprehensively account for the range of our emancipatory hopes. This posture finds its pair in an uncompromising postmodern repudiation of the normativity of a public use of reason as the most appropriate way in which to interpret the need for self-determining autonomy in an egalitarian and pluralistic age. The danger of such totalizing frameworks is that mutually alienated critical motivations will continue to present themselves in the light of powerful risks that seem to vindicate a spiral of answering dogmatic self-assertions. The history of feminism's ambivalent relationship to Habermas' efforts to interpret critical impulses through the legacies of democratic Enlightenment seems to bear out this thesis of the lost opportunities for a productive dialogue between interpretations of emanciptory hopes that recognize both their irreducible distinctiveness and their mutual dependencies.

9 Distorted communications

Habermas and feminism

For a long time Habermas' social philosophy and contemporary feminism evolved in mutual indifference. When feminists did occasionally turn their attention in his direction, the judgment was usually negative and sometimes even scathing. In the last decade this stand-off has changed significantly, with many now well-known figures like Nancy Fraser and Seyla Benhabib articulating their concerns in the language of critical theory and engaging various aspects of the Habermasian *oeuvre*. On his own side, Habermas has responded to this mixed reception by going to some pains in his recent work to establish the relevance of his project to feminist concerns.[1] The following chapter will review the extent to which main formulations in Habermas' mature work have responded to feminist objections to early versions of his critical theory. I will use this discussion as a prism through which to draw up a balance sheet of some of the achievements and some of the limitations of Habermas' framework. In particular, I want to suggest that Habermas' developed account of the modern public sphere offers itself as a clarification of those dimensions of liberal normativity that a Western feminist movement has been able to appropriate via its own creative reinterpretations. The chapter will also explore the source of an ongoing alienation between certain feminist accounts of the meaning of emancipation and Habermas' commitment to the idea of completing the democratic project of Enlightenment. Feminism is a complex and internally divided social movement that has been vitalized by Romantic as well as Enlightenment hopes. These former critical motivations have clearly felt unable to achieve full recognition within the limited terms set by Habermas' construction of emancipatory hopes.

* * *

Joan Landes played a leading role in shaping the feminist critique of early Habermas. We saw that she argued that *The Structural Transformation of the Public Sphere* offered an idealized description of the bourgeois public sphere that was too uncritical of the gender ideologies that sustained it. The central claim raised in her *Women and the Public Sphere* was that 'the bourgeois public sphere is essentially, not just contingently, masculinist, and that this characteristic serves to determine both its self-representation and its subsequent "structural transformation" '.[2] Habermas supposed that the exclusion of women and others from the bourgeois public that took shape in eighteenth-century Europe had not fundamentally affected the significance of its idealizing self-description as an open arena of unconstrained discussion and debate. Landes protested that the masculinity, no less than the class positions, of the participants had been by no means incidental to the mode of interaction upheld by the bourgeois public. The argumentative style of dialogue articulated into the norms of the public sphere suggested the confident assertion of an already achieved autonomy by its participants. According to Nancy Fraser, these are biases that continued to infect the tools of the critical theory as outlined in *The Theory of Communicative Action*.

These feminist critics did not simply suppose that specific formulations of Habermas' account of the normativity of the public sphere blocked its capacity to enter into a clarifying relationship with the wishes and struggles that inspired contemporary feminism. They thought that his whole approach was too contaminated with the ideological justifications of conventional gender roles to be worth rescuing for feminist purposes. The sticking point was that, because 'Habermas stops short of developing a new, post-bourgeois model of the public sphere' he never 'problematises some dubious assumptions that underlie the bourgeois model'.[3] Far from offering a reconstruction of procedures through which neglected private concerns could seek to establish a society-wide recognition of their significance, exclusionary assumptions are built into the discursive constraints upheld in Habermas' construction of the norms of a modern public sphere. For the feminist critics, Habermas' account of the 'open' procedures of a public permitted general recognition to the needs and identity claims of only certain kinds of subjects armed with particular kinds of motivations, capacities and histories. According to Landes

> Habermas's formulation fails to acknowledge the way the symbolic contents of the bourgeois public sphere worked to rule out all interests that could not or would not lay claim to their own universality. If only what is universal may wear the mantle of truth and reason, then it is precisely everything else that is reduced to the sphere of what Habermas calls 'mere opinions, cultural assumptions, normative attitudes, collective prejudices and values'.[4]

This familiar feminist critique of Habermas' version of the public sphere has never been entirely fair. He has always rejected the liberal model that counterposed a public of disinterested citizens to privately acting individuals. *The Structural Transformation* had wanted to find a way of recapturing an eighteenth-century model of the public conceived as the formation of rational solidarities by private individuals. The feminist critique appears to be even less accurate as an assessment of the construction of the relations of the private and public domains that informs Habermas' mature formulations. I want to argue that in fact the broader significance of feminism's own successes in exploiting the potentials of liberal democratic societies for self-reform can be clarified by referring to Habermas' developed model of the complex functioning of a decentred public sphere. It needs to be stressed, though, that feminism has not simply invested its critical energies in the capacities of liberal democracies for self-reform. Feminism has also been receptive to a Romantic construction of emancipatory needs that envisage an endless process of experimentation with novel descriptions of the self. The last part of the chapter will argue that the distinctive and complementary constructions of the quest for autonomy that have shaped the pluralism of motivations in contemporary feminism need to be acknowleged if the systematic distortions of its communications with Habermas' critical theory are to be overcome.

Feminist complaints/Habermasian responses

Fraser is particularly mindful of the insights that Habermas' diagnosis of modernity's rationalizing potentials can bring to the self-understanding of feminist struggles.[5] An autonomous women's movement has faced the task of conceptualizing the self-reforming capacities of liberal democracies in terms that do not simply evoke the aspirations and needs of a hegemonic subjectivity. A shift from a critical theory that focused on social labour as the real bearer of social evolution to one that gave priority to the emancipatory potentials of communicative interactions promised a sympathetic relevance to Western feminism's own search for a way of describing liberatory trends that were free from the hold of ideological, masculinist conventions. Habermas' efforts to pin an immanently critical theory on a reconstruction of the procedural norms through which needs, problems and identity descriptions might seek wider recognition had helpful potentials. However, according to Fraser, the promise was betrayed. It turned out that the critical intentions of Habermas' theory were marred by an ideological contamination that ascribed normativity to a mode of interaction that had also been shaped by gendered expectations and histories.[6] It seemed that *The Theory of Communicative Action* upheld as its critical standard a mode of interaction that idealized a pre-scribed gendered way of doing things. Habermas' distinction between system and lifeworld that lay at the heart of this critical diagnosis of modernity was not only 'gender blind' but was 'in important respects androcentric and ide-ological'.[7] It was ideological because it seemed to rely on a public/private bifurcation that locked a conventional femininity into the role of guardian of lifeworld relations in which expectations of a social integration based on mutuality and care were reproduced as a site of contest against the hegemonic ambitions of 'media steered' market and bureaucratic systems.[8]

Marie Fleming confirmed this construction of the normative commitments that underpinned Habermas' critical social theory.[9] As she saw it, his account of the pathological consequences of the penetration of strategic imperatives into the internal dynamics of the lifeworld, was 'conservative insofar as it works on an argument for resistance to fundamental change at the level of family structures'.[10] She agreed with Fraser's view that the critical thrust of the colonization thesis rested on an idealized portrait of domestic life in which social integration is supposed to be secured through communicative processes rather than as the engineered outcome of instrumentalizing imperatives. The colonization thesis, which described the 'desiccation of communicative contexts' and the 'depletion of non-renewable cultural resources' by the intrusion of system imperatives into the lifeworld, apparently reproduced a repressive gender ideology. This critical perspective on the invasiveness of strategic modes of integration throughout bureaucratic capitalism failed to recognize the extent to which women in bourgeois society had been relegated to the status of custodians of communicative interactions in vulnerable lifeworld contexts. It seemed that feminist struggles against the oppressive expectations of conventional gender roles could expect no support from a critical theory that relied upon the normativity of precisely those modes of integration that conventional bourgeois femininity was supposed to keep intact. Fleming was persuaded that Habermas' account of the pathological impact of the encroachment of formal/legal imperatives into the informally regulated lifeworld structures of the family (juridification) failed to recognize the extent to which bourgeois domesticity is organized around relations of domination and subordination. She considered that a programme aimed at the decolonization of the lifeworld would do nothing to advance the interests of modern women and would actually claw back that range of significant achievements in social justice that had been ushered in by welfare state policies.

In response to this construction of the normative underpinnings of his critical social theory, an increasingly guarded note crept into Habermas' explanations about the way the theory employed the concept of the 'lifeworld'.[11] He insisted that he had always meant that this category would not refer to a particular sphere or domain of social life but to a mode of cultural reproduction in which the weight of co-ordination fell upon a background consensus of overlapping conventional expectations. The lifeworld of communicatively acting subjects is a part of the *is*, not the *ought*, of Habermas' dualistic social theory. System co-ordination between strategically acting subjects, the other of the structural duality, introduces deliberative dimensions into co-ordination processes. We saw in earlier chapters that Habermas' theory intended to analytically engage with the communicative rationality set in motion as lifeworlds are opened up by the intrusions of system imperatives, submitting their traditional contents to critiques, communicative dialogue and negotiation. By viewing Habermas' account of rationalization processes simply in the light of the pathological consequences of system intrusions into the lifeworld, a feminist reading overlooked Habermas' earlier discussed assessment of the *paradox* of rationalization that was supposed to give 'rise to both the reification of the lifeworld *and* the utopia perspective'.[12]

However, some of the formulations and emphases in *The Theory of Communicative Action* did offer plausibility to the feminist critique. We have seen that Habermas has since rejected the concept of colonization as a framework of critique because it neglected to 'utilize the whole range of potential contributions of the theory'.[13] In particular, this formulation failed to insist that the question of whether the communicatively rationalized lifeworld might impose limits on the intrusions of strategic imperatives or find itself thwarted and suppressed by these incursions had to be recognized as 'an empirical question which cannot beforehand be decided on the analytical level in favour of the systems'.[14] Yet Habermas has admitted to less than what is required by the feminist critique. His self-criticism recognized no limits to the capacity of the theory itself. As he saw it, the theory could be elaborated to produce a complex and comprehensive account of the range of system/lifeworld relations at play in any specific conjuncture. By contrast, the feminist critics considered the blindness of the theory with respect to the specific circumstances of modern women was an index to the prejudicial normative anchorage of his critical theory in a lifeworld closed around conventional contents. Habermas has always protested his particular sympathy with feminism as a new social movement and has represented his reconstruction of the complex cultural potentials of modernizing processes as a thematization of the processes and normative self-understandings of liberal democracies that feminism has exploited. In *Between Facts and Norms*, Habermas elaborated on his theory's potentials as a clarification of feminism's wider significance as a practical appropriation of the critical normativity dormant in liberal democratic institutionality.

Chapter 5 described Habermas' efforts in the early 1990s to systematically reconstruct the normative framework of contemporary legal constitutionalism and political institutions. This was an attempt to demonstrate that the ideal of a democratic public sphere is not merely a utopian hope but exists as a powerful normative demand within existing institutional structures of liberal democracies. Habermas asserted that the normative claims raised by major politico-legal institutions in modern democracies had not been well understood and he tried to redress the one-sidedness of both liberal and republican models. *Between Facts and Norms* did not just limit itself to a reworking of the idealized self-interpretations of modern democracies but also considered the social arrangements and the political structures that could be engineered into realizing these normative demands. Habermas appeared to hope that the feminist movement might recognize in his account of the complex functions of a decentred public sphere a reconstruction of the liberal democratic potentials that its own progress towards the democratization of welfare agendas had utilized.[15]

Between Facts and Norms devoted considerable efforts to clarifying the distance Habermas' discourse theory of democracy had travelled from the limitations of a liberal model that appealed one-sidedly to the ideal of private right. His account of the centrality of the public sphere to liberal democratic normativity refers to the private individual not simply as the bearer of fundamental rights but as a potential participant in discursive processes through which public will is given content. This is a theory of liberal democratic normativity that emphasized the co-originality of private and public autonomy. The rule of law claims legitimacy, not by appealing to a supposedly already achieved private or public right, but by referring to procedures of democratic decision-making in which enfranchised citizens as equally entitled authors of the legal order, must ultimately decide on the criteria of equal treatment.[16] *Between Facts and Norms* described the communicative procedures through which public and private enter into co-constitutive relations to build a modern public sphere.[17] In doing so, an account of the processes of cultural rationalization was moved from the periphery to the centre of the analysis of modernization processes. Released from their earlier preoccupation with the mechanisms that reproduce reifying relations and rebalancing their interest in modernizing potentials towards a determination of the structural possibilities of a critical public, Habermas' later formulations appear better able to demonstrate the potentials of the theory as a clarification of the procedures through which the legitimacy of need and identity claims raised by marginalized populations might seek recognition.

We have seen that a commitment to the democratization of the post-war welfare project is central to Habermas' developed account of the self-transforming capacities of liberal democratic nation states and that he considers an active women's movement has suggested some concrete prospects for desired developments.[18] In *Between Facts and Norms* Habermas made the point that women had been particularly caught in the contradictions of the post-war welfare compromises:

> [e]ach special regulation intended to compensate for the disadvantages of women in the labor market or the workplace, in marriage or after divorce, in regard to social security, health care, sexual harassment, pornography, and so forth, rests on an interpretation of differences in gender-specific living situations and experiences. To the extent that legislation and adjudication in these cases are oriented by traditional interpretive patterns, regulatory law consolidates the existing *stereotypes of gender identity*. In producing such 'normalising effects', legislation and adjudication themselves become part of the problem they are meant to solve.[19]

To the extent that paternalistic welfare policies described women's needs for them, the primary tendency of these programmes saw the reinforcement of gender stereotypes. However, juridification processes, the penetration of administrative and legal imperatives into the domains of civil society, have two distinct implications. On the one hand, the structure of juridification involves the intervention of juridical and administrative controls into social relations that become formalized and reconstructed as 'cases'. This administrative penetration of civil society pre-empted the emergence of discursive processes of will formation and the capacity of needs for autonomy, galvanized around particular self-interpreted goods, gaining recognition of their legitimacy by the decision-making centres of the liberal democratic states. Yet at the same time, juridification meant the extension of basic legal principles to women who were formerly denied personhood by law and swept issues formerly exempted from the testing function of the law up into the jurisdiction of a democratic construction of its legitimacy. This latter tendency has been exploited by feminism which has tried to push welfare state programmes to respond to problem and need descriptions funneled up from an active civil society to decision-making agencies.[20] Habermas described this as a new 'reflexive attitude' in feminist politics that learnt to reject

> the *overgeneralized classifications* used to label disadvantaging situations and disadvantaged groups of persons... The feminist movement objects to the premise underlying both the social-welfare and the liberal politics of equality, namely, the assumption that the equal entitlement of the sexes can be achieved within the existing institutional framework and within a culture dominated and defined by men.[21]

Habermas has attempted, then, to use his mature and more elaborated conception of the operations of the public sphere to reflect on the self-reforming capacities of liberal democracies that have been activated by some of feminism's achievements. According to him, feminist activism has suggested that a progressive response to the contradictions of the welfare state can be achieved. It has done so by contesting the ascription of needs and identities to women and by placing the chosen dimensions of gendered subjectivities on the social agenda. As he sees it,

> [i]nstitutionally defined gender stereotypes must not be assumed without question. Today these social constructions can be formed only in a conscious, deliberate fashion; they require *the affected parties themselves* to conduct public discourses in which they articulate the standards of comparison and justify the relevant aspects.[22]

There has been no widespread concession within recent feminist literature that the outlook of Habermas' more recent writings might constitute a significant breakthrough. However, some feminists are now describing the achievements of the movement in terms that echo Habermas' account of an emancipatory democratic politics in which the goals of private and public autonomy coalesce. Jean Cohen stresses that the various political and legal successes of Western feminism had as their 'precondition success in the cultural sense – in the prior spread of feminist consciousness'.[23] In the effort that has been required to bring so-called 'private' or 'civil society' issues of, for example, abortion, violence against women, sexual coercion and sexual stereotyping into the domain of politics, a feminist quest for social justice has required not just a reform of institutions to reflect women's concerns, it has also involved, both as its prerequisite and as its outcome, the spread of a new determination that, for women, liberation requires neither a release from conventional feminine lifeworlds nor their uncritical affirmation, but an institutionally supported right to choose what needs to be changed and what is to count as making justifiable claims upon public recognition.

The ambiguities of feminism

Some feminists have recognized that Habermas' mature dialectical interpretation of the relation between private and public autonomy can help to clarify some of the potentials in liberal democracies that a modern feminist movement has taken advantage of. Jodi Dean, for instance, has used a Habermasian model of the relationship between formal and informal dimensions of a decentred public sphere to talk about aspects of the significance of feminist struggles.[24] She points out that feminist politics has exploited the capacity of a formal public sphere to redescribe an interpretation of shared commitments in response to new demands emanating from informal publics sited at the periphery of political power. Feminist struggles have revealed

> the biases within the fiction of the subject of the law. If claiming their status as legal subjects meant that women had to deny their femininity – that is their biological potential for motherhood or their position in the home as child-rearer – then the legal subject itself was not universal, but particular – particularly masculine.[25]

Dean agrees with Habermas that critical pressure from organized feminism has occasionally seen an activation of the self-reforming capacities of some of the political and legal structures in liberal democracies.[26]

Yet feminism is no united singular and hegemonic ideology and no general acknowledgement of the sympathetic relevance of Habermas' description of the potentials of a liberal democratic system for self-reform to a feminist 'project' can be expected. While there might be some grounds for suggesting that his recent clarifications of the normativity invested in the modern public sphere do offer the basis for a new conversation with some of his erstwhile critics, this seems an elective affinity born of a shared view that the goal of autonomy is tied to the quest for social justice. For this construction of feminist motivations, Habermas' account of the processes through which the goal of self-determining autonomy can, without distortion, achieve public recognition would seem to have real pertinence. Yet divisions run deep in feminism's understanding of its objectives. Some aspects of a feminist alienation from Habermas' critical social theory call, not simply for a clarified negotiation of shared interests, but an acknowledgement of a non-antagonistic difference in the ways in which the goal of emancipation is being interpreted.

Iris Young is a vigorous critic of Habermas' efforts to tie the quest for autonomy to an undertaking to build the grounds in terms of which the reasonableness of need claims and problem descriptions can be determined.[27]

She insists that the interest in building rational consensus that underpins the normativity of the modern public sphere suggests a coercive dimension that is inappropriate to the radicalism of a contemporary feminist interest in the representation of gender difference. According to her, an alternative construction of the quest for recognition, one that does not demand a resolution of intractable difference, is required. Using terminology developed by Luce Irigaray, Young insists that a respectful attitude of 'wonder' towards irreducible difference is the ethic appropriate to the quest for recognition in a radically democratic polity. For her,

> [a] respectful stance of wonder toward other people is one of openness across, awaiting new insight about their needs, interests, perceptions or values. Wonder also means being able to see one's own position, assumptions, perspectives as strange because it has been put in relation to others.[28]

Young goes on to say that, if the attitude of wonder at the irreducible difference of the other is infused with the idea of a respect which remains sensitive to and 'awaits insights into' the other's needs, it can avoid the 'dangerous' implications of the concept of wonder which might otherwise be interpreted as a 'kind of distant awe before the other that turns their transcendence into an inhuman inscrutability'.[29]

Does the imported category of respect adequately address Young's reasonable concerns about the essentializing dimensions of an ethics based on wonder at cultural difference? The point was made in Chapter 8 that an agonistic construction of the quest for recognition does not suggest any grounds upon which the legitimacy of contesting claims might be arbitrated and is, therefore, unable to offer any account of a quest for recognition that would constitute itself as a call for justice. 'Wonder' offers itself as a particular version of such an agonistic construction of self-other relations. The problem, then, from a feminist viewpoint, is to try and equip the ethical framework with a dimension that takes into account oppressive dimensions of attributed cultural difference. However, it does not seem that this function is adequately filled by simply qualifying 'wonder' with the need for respect. Young betrays a mixture of commitments in her description of the need for 'respect' for a difference that is not, however, invited to participate in building the grounds of a mutual understanding. She considers that the demand for respect for culturally marked difference is necessary to avoid the repressive application of ascribed mis-recognitions of that difference. So, this call for a respectful attitude of wonder suggests the aspirations of selves who desire to be accepted on their own terms, who would feel denigrated if their self-interpretations were simply over-looked. Respect requires that the adequacy of the recognition process be negotiated and so it seems that the task of elaborating the grounds through which misidentified differences can seek to clarify their motivations and aspirations cannot be circumvented.

Seyla Benhabib responds differently to the supposed inadequacy of Habermas' account of the discursive norms through which concrete particularity can seek recognition.[30] She insists that a supplementation of his account of the procedural norms through which understanding between those who are different can be developed is required if the process is to be made fully adequate to the recognition of singularity. Habermas needs to graft onto his account of the procedures through which private needs and objectives seek public acknowledgement an account of discursive actors as located selves with particular histories and competencies. Each claim for recognition needs to be viewed not simply as a demand for the extension of formal rights to cover the claims of previously neglected subjectivities but also as a demand that these settled principles be opened up to re-interpretation on the basis of the specific histories and emotional – affective identities of new claimants.[31] However, this proposal for an internal reconstruction of Habermas' account of the norms of public reason in order to respond to feminist objections about its supposed obtuseness towards the realities of concrete difference does not seem to introduce anything not already explicitly affirmed in Habermas' own recent formulations. Maeve Cooke also contests Benhabib's view that it is necessary to add another principle to Habermas' proceduralism. Cooke points out that the requirements of reciprocity and symmetry, embedded in Habermas' reconstruction of discursive rationality, already carry a commitment to the recognition of concrete differences.[32] The norms of reciprocity and symmetry between discursive partners require that participants be

> [w]illing (in principle) to consider the arguments of *everyone* no matter how poorly they are articulated, and to attach (in principle) equal weight to all these arguments ... In addition, since argumentative willingness to reach understanding requires a genuine openness not just to new arguments but also to the needs, desires, anxieties, and insecurities – whether expressed or unexpressed – of the other participants, at times this will require a special sensitivity and a willingness to look beyond explicit verbal expressions and deficiencies in argumentative skills.[33]

Habermas has himself defended the discourse ethics in similar terms. We saw earlier that he argues that sensitivity to diverse points of view and to the multifarious claims of private individuals is built into the richness of the theory's communicative and intersubjective presuppositions.[34] Yet reassurances about the capacity of a normatively charged conception of public reason to constantly penetrate through the ideological prejudices that encrust settled descriptions of its procedures seem unlikely to persuade some of Habermas' critics of his capacity to theorize a feminist investment in autonomy. Some critics hold that feminism embraces a construction of emancipatory hopes that eludes Habermas' democratic Enlightenment commitments.

Maria Pia Lara suggests that Habermas' account of the rationalizing procedures of struggle for recognition is too narrow to be able to bring into view the variety of strategies that women have used in their efforts to achieve acknowledgement of chosen descriptions of gender differences.[35] She considers that Habermas' account of the consensus-building interactions of the public sphere remains blind to the importance of the expressive/ communicative practices that have been used to explore the meanings of modern femininity. In particular, Habermas neglects the role of emancipatory narratives in mediating 'between particular group identities and universalistic moral claims, providing new frameworks that allow those who are not members of the group to expand their own-self conceptions and their definitions of civil society'.[36] Lara supposes that Habermas' account of the entwinement of the principles of private and public autonomy suggests an instrument that is too blunt to record some of the main paths of communication between private explorations of gender difference and their representations in public domains. On this view, Hannah Arendt's notion of 'storytelling' has a better capacity to capture the modes through which 'the normative and the aesthetic contents of narratives allow the multiple projects of women's identity to express themselves positively in the public sphere'.[37]

On the one hand, Lara has no dispute with Habermas' proceduralist account of the normativity that underpins the public sphere. Yet, as she sees it, he does not give a sufficiently flexible description of the processes through which private individuals might attempt to communicate a self-interpretation of their identities and needs without sacrificing investments in their distinctiveness. Her thesis is that it was through the aesthetic, particularly through literary self-presentations, that modern women first learnt to set their lifeworlds communicatively in motion. Women 'used works of art because presenting themselves within the realm of aesthetics allowed them to express themselves without the impediments of liberal theories that excluded women from the public sphere'.[38] Using narrative form, women by-passed the necessity of appealing to narrow, prejudicial conceptions of justice in their efforts to make their needs and experiences understood. Via such imaginative self-clarifications, women have succeeded in slowly pushing back the limited terms in which claims for private autonomy might be publicly recognized. However, Lara does not make clear enough the sense in which this interest in the power of the aesthetic in communicating neglected dimensions of a feminine self-consciousness suggests a *critique* of the adequacy of Habermas' interpretation of the communicative processes of a public sphere. While the aesthetic invites a playful participation in an evocation of particular 'worlds', this communicative process does not, as Habermas himself has stressed, necessarily offer itself as a competitor to the rational solidarities of a public sphere. As already noted, Habermas consistently acknowledges an important role for aesthetic self-exploration as a mechanism through which new contents, born of struggles to achieve personal autonomy, enter communicative interactions in the political public sphere. As he sees it, problems voiced in the public sphere first become visible when they are mirrored in personal life experience.[39] To the extent that these experiences find their concise expression in the languages of religion, art and literature, the 'literary' public sphere in the broader sense, which is specialized for the articulation of values and world disclosure, is intertwined with the political public sphere.[40]

Habermas does allow that the aesthetic has a distinct capacity to explore and imagine the concreteness of novel identity claims and he notes that this mode of cultural reflection assumes a special communicative power that can play a significant role in delivering new demands for justice to the deliberations of a political public. It does not seem, then, that Lara, Pieter Duvenage and others are justified in supposing that Habermas simply overlooks the importance and the specificity of the aesthetic as a communicative form.[41] It could be argued, though, that Habermas might have usefully made rather more of the significant function the communicative power of the aesthetic can play in building attitudes and aptitudes central to the construction of democratic interactions in modern pluralistic societies. Martha Nussbaum supposes that the underestimation of the role of the aesthetic communication is a deficiency that is common to many conventional versions of democratic theory. She points out that because the norm of the literary work require receptors to develop a testing appreciation of the horizons of the worlds that are inhabited by others, it promotes aptitudes that are vital to the democratic imagination. 'The greatest contribution literature has to make to the life of the citizen is', she tells us, 'its ability to wrest from our frequently obtuse and blunted imaginations an acknowledgement of those who are other than ourselves, both in concrete circumstances and even in thought and emotion'.[42]

There might be some truth in the claim that Habermas downplays the contribution to a democratic imagination that can be provided by the communicative power of the aesthetic in rendering meaningful the strangeness of the worlds inhabited by others. A stronger objection, though, is that he overlooks the role of the specificity of the aesthetic, not just in deepening capacities required by democratic Enlightenment commitments, but in evoking a distinctive construction of the need for liberty that could not accept being described as simply an immature, imaginative version of the rationalizing attitudes required by our interactions in the public sphere.

Luce Irigaray has been among the most influential and long-wearing of feminist writers who have engaged in the search for a language able to communicate the specialness of a feminine experience while evading the supposedly distorting generalizations required by the categories of theory. She has attempted to deconstruct a wide range of texts to explore the sites through which feminine difference, particularly the difference of the feminine body, can be re-imagined.[43] This has been a controversial project with its success disputed by other prominent feminist writers. Judith Butler, for example, has argued that the literary strategies that French feminism generally has employed in its efforts to explore the novelty of plural feminine identities have typically betrayed an essentializing temper that has finally only confirmed the normalizing cultural impositions that it has tried to resist.[44] Butler remains engaged with the task of articulating gendered experiences in terms that confound any imposed constructions of gendered identities, however, she is not blind to the paradoxes of a politics that is guided by gestures of refusal. The threat is that: 'the "I" becomes to a certain extent unknowable, threatened with unviability, with becoming undone altogether'.[45]

There are dangers, then, even in its own terms, in a postmodern attempt to constitute a feminist interest in emancipation as a preoccupation with the task of constructing ideational spaces for gender identities that elude all normalizing constructions. This is a project that must not only be on guard against the entwinement of its experimental imagery with conventional norms, it is also, as Butler points out, in danger of being overwhelmed by an introverted, hyper-critical agenda that can provide no positive orientations. It seems that the peculiarities of a postmodern appropriation of Romantic legacies need to be brought into view here. A postmodern suspiciousness of the conventions of the everyday has never appeared to construe itself as an exalted project that can afford either to be disdainful of the practical needs for positive orientations or disinterested in the question of how the marginalized can achieve recognition. The hybrid temper of postmodernism, which wanders across democratic Enlightenment commitments to egalitarian justice and Romantic sensibilities hostile to the rationalizing character of Enlightenment, was referred to in the previous chapter. This mixture of legacies and commitments becomes evident in postmodernism's feminist versions. On the one hand, Romantic expressions of unbounded frustration at the power of the everyday to domesticate and entrap have had a particular resonance for contemporary feminism. Yet this impatience also draws powerful incentives from a democratic Enlightenment commitment to the universalization of the conditions of autonomy in a pluralistic social world. In this chapter and in the last I have tried to identify some of the strains that arise from the attempt to interpret these latter commitments through the critical impulses of a Romantic consciousness.

It is important to draw attention to the hybrid character of postmodernism so that the sources of some of its confusing formulations can be identified. However, recognition of postmodernism's intermixture of cultural affiliations is also significant because it suggests something of the complexity of its potentials. As the heat seems to be subsiding from postmodern attachments, some harsh constructions of its supposed essential political tendencies are to be coming in. The previous chapter mentioned the strength of Richard Wolin's conviction that, seduced by unreason, postmodernism has unwittingly helped to channel the authoritarianism of counter-Enlightenment thinking. In a different way, Habermas has occasionally been severe also. He has made the connection between a neo-liberal agenda that interprets the demand for autonomy as only the willful self-promotion of private individuals and a postmodern attack on the supposed repressive dimensions of any attempt to interpret the ideal of autonomy through rationalizing Enlightenment commitments.[46] There seems to be some credibility to this, at least as an account of one contemporary appropriation of postmodern themes.

Disinclined to philosophize, the advocates of a neo-liberal 'realism' might be supposed happy to rely on postmodern theory that discovers in the ideal of rational solidarities just another attempt to tame the risk-taking personalities required by the present. In his recent title *Reclaiming the Enlightenment: Towards a Politics of Radical Engagement* Stephen Bronner also joins the critique of a postmodern politics. He blames postmodernism for cloaking the critical and democratic impulses of an Enlightenment legacy.[47] For Bronner, the overwhelming inheritance of postmodernism has been a debilitating pessimism and a politically conservative identification of resistance with the mere expression of subjectivity.

However, there might be some overkill in these assessments of the essentially compliant temper and dubious political affiliations of a postmodern theory. We saw earlier that Axel Honneth has indicated that a more moderate evaluation might be appropriate.[48] While acknowledging dimensions of the performative contradiction that result from a postmodern attempt to both embrace a democratizing interpretation of the ideal of autonomy while repudiating as essentially repressive an appeal to the concept of the public use of reason through which needs and claims might be legitimated, Honneth, nonetheless finds critical motivations in the frustrated sensibilities that have inspired a postmodern scepticism. On this point of view, a postmodern wariness at the hopes for 'reasonable consensus' is not just viewed as a narcissistic preoccupation with the singularity of unrepeatable personalities. As a brief discussion of the tensions within a postmodern feminism appears to confirm, this suspiciousness can also be a response to the, sometimes great, difficulties that can be encountered by us in our efforts to communicate without distortion across cultural and personal differences. Postmodern feminism has been a register of problematic dimensions of a modern quest for recognition that appear to pass under the radar of Habermas' framework. Concerned only with distortions that interfere with a mutual interest in creating rational solidarities, Habermas has always supposed that in the really difficult cases the appeal could always be made to the principled commitments upheld in the procedures of the communicative action itself. But there are times when the struggle to register unease with the conventional pathways of everyday communication seems to take centre stage; in such contexts the difficult case appears to be the one in which encrusted prejudices effectively block capacities for an imaginative reworking of identity and need descriptions. The self-conscious, parodic style of a postmodern culture, attentive to the spaces for imaginative reconfigurations available through a playful mistreatment of the conventional, seems an apt tool for the excavation of these kind of critical sensibilities. Perhaps we need to be as discriminating about the ambiguous potentials of the complexity of Romantic and democratic Enlightenment inclinations in postmodernism as Habermas has always maintained we should be about the ambiguities within our complex Enlightenment histories.

10 Conclusion

Right from the start, Habermas' diagnosis of modernity and its prospects has worked in the shadow of two, apparently competing, paradigms. Marx's critical theory was a necessary legacy for this student of Adorno and Horkheimer and liberal ideals have had considerable allure for a man who has lived through the dislocation of German post-War reconstruction. Has he managed to rescue the emancipatory, universalizing and practical commitments of critical theory through a project that seeks to excavate liberal democratic normativity? Habermas is convinced that liberalism does not allow us to fully grasp the potentials of liberal democratic societies for substantial self-reform and for further democratization. He insists that 'the liberal interpretation is not wrong. It just does not see the beam in its own eye'.[1] Habermas' determination to capture the elusive beam missed by a liberal interpretation of liberal democratic normativity is an undertaking that has had some real achievements; it has also failed in some important respects.

Habermas calls upon us to seriously reflect on the potentials and on the dangers of the field of possibilities bequeathed by an ambiguous Enlightenment legacy. There are no 'laws of history in the strict sense' and we can't avoid the necessity of making choices. All the same, Habermas tells us, we can draw courage from the fact that 'human beings, even whole societies, are capable of learning'.[2] Nowadays, he forcefully advocates the need to make political choices that might secure a civilized and peaceable future amidst the heightened risks of a world that has been divided into winners and losers by globalizing markets, that has been seared by the blight of warring fundamentalisms and that confronts the risks of virtually unchecked environmental degradation. His particular hope is that an exemplary European political identity might be forged 'in the daylight of the public sphere' using the structural potentials of the European Union.[3] He invests in the ideal of a rational confederacy of nations drawn together by a shared resistance to the catastrophic prospect of an undermining of the efficacy of democratic structures of authority at the national and at the transnational level by the assertion of corporate power. This is not a situation in which intellectuals can afford to sit by in the gloomy comfort of their own sense of impotence. Habermas urges fellow intellectuals across the globe to recognize and to respond to the urgency of the task at hand.[4] In his view, concerned intellectuals have in recent times tended to collude with a fatalistic 'realism' that sustains the unimpeded agenda-setting capacities of neo-liberal corporate power and have neglected their important role of reflecting upon the fault-lines and on the progressive potentials in the ambiguous histories of liberal democratic societies. The award to Habermas in 2004 of the prestigious International Kyoto Prize for Lifetime Achievement underlines the global reach of this intellectual's decades of devoted service to the mission of clarifying humanity's best chances for saving and further developing the emancipatory potentials of democratic Enlightenment traditions.

Habermas insists that the task of rescuing the balance of our Enlightenment legacies is a rationally justifiable undertaking. Because he represents his project as a reworking of the rational and humanistic commitments of a critical theory tradition, he sees it as inheriting a particularly onerous burden of proof. Habermas considers that the task of establishing the reasonableness of the value commitments that anchor his critical theory requires a type of justification that can guarantee their universal character. Habermas has not only been encumbered by a critical theory expectation that the universal status of underpinning normative values can be confirmed, his project has also taken on the challenge of trying to demonstrate the engaged and practical capacities of theory. Critical theory needs not only to seek to justify its value commitments universally but also to persuade concretely located actors that it can help make better sense of the everyday than can competing ideological frameworks. In particular, Habermas has attempted to expose the limitations of a liberal interpretation of ethical ideals and he has contested liberal and republican constructions of the idealizations that are embedded in liberal democratic institutions.

This draws us back to the centrality of the public sphere to his whole conception of the task of critical theory. Habermas has always been persuaded that liberalism has never fully grasped the democratic meaning of the modern public sphere. He has underlined the ideological assumptions of a conventional liberal ethics that universalizes the specific aspirations of subjects who call upon the use of public reason only to defend a purportedly already attained autonomy. We have seen that the discourse theory of ethics interprets liberal democratic normativity in a profoundly different way. This is an ought that is carried by the norms of a mode of interaction in which concrete, sociable subjects seek recognition as legitimate interpreters of their own needs. Habermas is not interested in conducting a mere disputation within the domain of ethical philosophy. For him, the point is to clarify the sense in which a better understanding of the significances of liberal ethical commitments can help us to appreciate the entwinement of the goals of public and private autonomy within our liberal tradition.

The discourse theory of law and democracy took Habermas' critical project further down this path. The great work of the early 1990s explored the incompletely theorized normativity that is both evident in, and betrayed by, the usual functioning of liberal democratic institutionality (the law and the Constitutional state). We saw that its central theme was that competing liberal and republican paradigms have not grasped the codependency of their separate accounts of the reference point of liberal democratic legitimacy. Each in its own way offered a truncated version where an emphasis on either 'rights' or popular sovereignty monopolized its vision. For the discourse theory, the most adequate point of reference for legal and political authority in contemporary democracies are the procedures of discursive interaction that aim at building rational solidarities between particular subjects. This is not a reference to an abstract principle but to living democratic processes of collective opinion and will formation that are alleged to be the dynamic heart of an active civil society.

However, his critics have not generally accepted the extent to which Habermas' reconstruction of liberal democratic normativity breaks from a liberal conception. In the 'Introduction' to their 2004 collection titled *After Habermas: New Perspectives on the Public Sphere*, John Roberts and Michael Crossley equate Habermas' version of the public sphere with a liberal model in which the constitution of a shared interest is seen to require the bracketing of all disruptive minority 'private' interests.[5] The publication date is significant because it suggests that, despite the elaborated account in *Between Facts and Norms* of the distinction between Habermas' conception of the public sphere and a liberal account, the view persists that Habermas looks upon the public as the domain of the disinterested citizen. Accordingly Roberts and Crossley suppose that Nancy Fraser's postmodern account of the public sphere as a composite of 'subaltern counterpublics' through which particular needs and points of view seek representation still offers an essential corrective to Habermas' model.[6] Habermas, it is asserted, ascribes normativity to a mode of interaction that privileges the aspirations and the attributes of a particular type of subjectivity and hence a 'new' account of the public sphere, construed as a matter of 'parallel discursive arenas where members of subordinated social groups invent and circulate counterdiscourses',[7] is deemed necessary. Subaltern counterpublics permit their members 'to formulate oppositional interpretations of their identities, interests and needs'.[8] It needs to be said that this supposedly new perspective on the public sphere actually only recaptures one of the important dimensions of Habermas' own mature standpoint. We saw in the earlier discussion of *Between Facts and Norms* that his worked up account of the dialectical possibilities in the relations between system and lifeworld describes the public sphere as a decentred network of communicative processes that is structured around the intertwined opinion and decision-making functions of informal and formal publics. Clustered in the associational networks of civil society, the informal public sphere offers a sounding board where problems are interpreted, signalled and dramatized and a public will is shaped and configured in a range of different constitutencies.

This model of a decentred public sphere offers a specific framework for considering the trajectories of the dramatizations of identity and need descriptions that characterize an active civil society. For Habermas, the attention seeking efforts of particular subjectivities in a vibrant civil life can only claim participation in a public sphere if they, at the same time, seek recognition of the society-wide significance, hence reasonableness, of their specific concerns. Underpinned only by a conception of the expressive, performative purposes of a quest for recognition, the paradigm of subaltern counterpublics omits the essentially rationalizing political purpose that, for Habermas and Dewey, constructs the public as a sphere. According to them, the public refers to the norms of mode of interaction in which particular subjectivities express, not merely their distinctiveness, but also their persuasion that their quest for self-determination can be secured only if they are permitted to establish the justice of their claims upon resources that are held in common. A post-liberal conviction of the essentially sociable and intersubjectively constituted character of human subjectivity informs Habermas' account of the purpose-built specificity of the norms of a modern public sphere.

Fraser and others properly stress that democratic politics can only expect to galvanize needed loyalties if it offers itself as a procedure for reflecting upon the local concerns of particular publics. However, the promise that the democratic process can offer itself, not just as forum for endless discussion, but as a particular account of how attempts at resolving problems can seek legitimation also has its attractions. If democratic politics offers itself only as a forum for the expressive release of identity and need claims, it cannot contest a technocratic determination to 'manage' problems with an alternative account of problem resolution that makes the interpretations of those who are affected central to an interpretation of its success. There is further reason to prefer Habermas' account of the specific purposes of decentered public over the more inclusive agendas of a conception of the public as a confederation of 'counter publics'. Only a model of the public sphere that requires that participants be willing to establish a case for the justice of their claims makes it possible to consider the proposals of sectional interests in terms of considerations of their public worth. Particular need claims have to be required to negotiate the legitimacy of their claims on shared resources, including the resource of toleration, if democratic politics is to be sustained as a value commitment that is rationally opposed to the racist, sexist and elitist dimensions of various confederacies that also spring up in an active civil society.

Habermas offers his reclamation of the radical potentials of the public sphere as the grounds for a critical politics that is appropriate to our times. He has given up the hopes for a revolutionary transformation of an alienated social life that were nursed by a Marxian tradition. This is rejected by Habermas as a solution that undercuts the communicative, democratic commitments that are, to him, the key to the self-transformative potentials of modernity. Nevertheless, from a contemporary point of view, Habermas' project does have claims to be a radical venture. His excavation of the critical normativity that undergirds the principles that are advocated by key institutions in liberal democratic regimes confronts both the powerful fatalism of neo-liberal ideologies as well as the limitations of classical liberal and republican versions of this normativity. The normative defeatism of neo-liberalism stems from its impoverished construction of the ideal of private autonomy understood only as the achievements of *homo economicus*, the rationally calculating economic individual. At least conventional liberalism had asserted that the defence of the conditions of private autonomy was a responsibility of a public of (supposedly disinterested) citizens. A neo-liberal construction has withdrawn from even this limited account of autonomy as a shared ideal, construing it instead as the burden of self-interested actors whose task it is to make their own way in a competitively structured social world. Habermas tries to unseat this increasingly hegemonic 'realism' by unmasking it as a particular cultural choice that affirms a limited interpretation of only one dimension of ambiguous rationalizing legacies. His recent works challenge a neo-liberal project committed to the suppression of the history of democratic Enlightenment as a rival interpretation of the goal of autonomy.

We do, Habermas stresses, have choices but our major traditions of political reflection have given us inadequate guidance as to what they are. Chapter 5 noted that he considers that the republican and the liberal traditions have both offered one-sided reconstructions of the idealizations embedded in the complex realities of liberal democratic arrangements. Habermas suggests that the limitations of each of these classical paradigms have been historically demonstrated, sometimes with catastrophic force. Marginalized and disadvantaged populations have dramatically tested the ideological character of a conventional liberal version of democratic politics that undertakes only to defend a, supposedly already achieved, private autonomy. Habermas insists that we also need to face up to the barbaric consequences of a republican conviction that rationality can only ground itself as an articulation of the collective will and learn to invest instead in the rationality of interactions aimed at the formation of a common will. The practical outcomes of this learning process are registered in tentative indications in liberal democratic states that a democratization of welfare programmes might be possible. Such developments demonstrate the capacity of such societies to utilize the complexly decentered structures of the modern public sphere to emancipatory effect. The democratization of welfare programmes requires that the politico-legal centres function to test out and respond to the reasonableness of claims that are initiated at the peripheries of an informal public. A systematic programme aimed at the democratization of the welfare project would, Habermas emphasizes, require an overhaul of the normal functioning of communicative flows in capitalist democracies. We saw that, in recent times, Habermas has not balked at the necessity of a trans-nationalization of a democratized welfare project as the only basis from which an undertaking to globalize the public sphere could be made meaningful.

A commitment to reinvent the terms under which an objectively grounded and practically motivated critical theory might survive in the contemporary context is evident in all of Habermas' work. Ever since *The Structural Transformation* he has determined that the ideology critique intentions that describe the engaged character of critical theory require an explicit defence of the universality of its core value commitments. Yet this would also have to be a post-metaphysical grounding adequate to the anti-essentializing ethos of a pluralistic and historicizing age. The linguistic turn was supposed to dislodge a practically motivated critical theory from the failed search for an expressive relationship with the frustrated aspirations of a historical agent whose 'cause' might be attributed with universal human significance. Instead, critical theory was to ground the objectivity of its judgments in the counterfactual presumptions raised by users of language in their efforts to reach mutual understanding. In particular, critical theory was to locate itself as a critique of the ideological frameworks and the structural forces that undermine the conditions necessary for building rational solidarities between differently placed subjects.

Not surprisingly, the secondary literature has tended to focus on the shortcomings of Habermas' attempt to analytically ground the objectivity of the commitments raised by his critical theory. However, this systematic undertaking has also produced some real insights. The attempt in *The Theory of Communicative Action* to conceptually elaborate the procedural norms of a mode of interaction that takes reaching understanding as its rationalizing goal has permitted Habermas to excavate and precisely describe some far-reaching cultural achievements of Enlightenment societies. His systematic reconstruction of these discursive procedures allows us to appreciate a democratic mode of integration, not just as a matter of some frozen institutional principles, but as a set of norms that regulate the everyday practices of private individuals as they seek to build the grounds of mutual understanding. This is an analysis that substantially clarifies the complex and living character of a modern public sphere. On this account, the 'public' does not constitute a sphere in any sense that can be narrowly identified with particular social sites and political institutions. Habermas' elaboration of the procedural norms of a communicative mode of rational action brings the public sphere into view as a variegated network of interactions interconnected by a shared interest in the achievement of rational solidarities. This systematization and idealization of the norms of an everyday communicative form of rationality has also allowed Habermas to frame a powerful critique of the pathological character of those tendencies in modern capitalism that appear to attack the lifeworld conditions necessary to its reproduction.

There has been substantial development in the complexity of Habermas' critique of the systemic blockages that frustrate the quest to make the demand for private and public autonomy into a universal and practical claim. Still in the shadow of a theory of reification, *The Theory of Communicative Action* stressed one-sidedly the extent to which instrumentalizing market imperatives and administrative power thwarts attempts to assert the authority of rival communicatively achieved modes of integration. From the major work of the early 1980s, it appeared that the outcome of this contestation had been determined in favour of the power of the systems. The point has already been made that in *Between Facts and Norms* Habermas elaborated in greater empirical detail the double-sided potentials in the lifeworld/ systems relations forged in liberal democracies. This more recent version suggested the pathways that can be exploited to set the communicative processes of a public sphere in motion. It insisted that a project committed to wresting agenda-setting power away from a bureaucratic and corporate network of authority would require a radical reanimation of key institutions and their interactions in capitalist democratic states. According to Habermas, this is no pie in the sky fancy. The complex political histories of liberal democracies themselves have demonstrated that dissenting publics can, occasionally, achieve some effective resonance at the centre for agendas that have been forged at the margins and have, under some circumstances, been able to ignite a mode of problem solving that cuts across the routine of bureaucratic decision-making. The non liberal conviction at the centre of *Between Facts and Norms* is that the defence of the principle of autonomy as a universal right would require not simply the protection of already achieved capacities but a commitment to secure the practical, material, as well as the discursive, conditions that make self-determination into an effective demand. In the end, it seems that Habermas' attempt to theorize a commitment to autonomy as a universal and practical right through the prism of the theory of communicative rationality yields a more inclusive and more attractive, certainly a more demanding, construction of this normative idea than liberalism has suggested. It is also a construction of liberal democratic normativity that cuts much deeper as a critique of the pathologies of really existing liberal democratic states.

It is finally not possible, though, to concede Habermas' claim that 'the theory of communicative action is not a metatheory but the beginning of a social theory concerned to validate its own critical standards'.[9] I have argued that, if his lifelong attempt to propose an engaged critical theory that is relevant to the future of humanity can be said to have succeeded, this is not because he has been able to validate philosophically the universality of its critical standards. Rather, it is because he has helped us to formalize, to grasp the complexity, and to better appreciate the embattled and tentative achievements, of liberal democratic histories. Habermas has always claimed that he intended to ground the universality of the emancipatory interests raised in his theory, not in an account of supposed invariant human aspirations, but as a reconstruction of the significance of what people actually do when they use language to communicate. However, the difficulty has always been that, if this analytic reconstruction is to add anything meaningful to his critical theory, it has to be moved out of the shadows of the counterfactual and endowed with the substance of a reconstruction of supposed explicit universal human potentialities. A quasi-anthropological foundation is imported into Habermas' philosophical attempt to anchor the commitment of his social theory in a post-metaphysical universalism. He has not, it seems, managed to successfully marry his reconstructive project to a critical theory with universalist aspirations.

Many have argued that Habermas also fails to adequately preserve the emancipatory and practically motivated character of a critical theory legacy. Perhaps the question of what the demand for an engaged critical theory can usefully mean in a contemporary pluralistic context comes better into focus if we look again at the concept of a post-metaphysical philosophy. Stephen Bronner has pointed out that a 'genuinely "postmetaphysical" philosophy must begin neither with the deconstruction nor the reconstruction of "truth," but concern itself with the specification of those material conditions which inhibit and best foster its quest'.[10] Here the postmetaphysical philosopher is called upon to present a systematic account of the conditions that confound, and those that facilitate, our struggles to realize the historical truth of modern longings for self-determination. Habermas has never presented his theory as a traditional utopianism that offers to interpret for us the desired character of the self-determined life. His restrained utopianism offers itself only as a reconstruction and as a clarification of neglected potentials and meanings that we have invested in these aspirations. It has also represented itself as an aid to our reflections on the systemic obstacles to the realization of these hopes.

However, critics have suggested that Habermas' project is both too implicitly legislative about what our need for autonomy means and is too normatively weak to constitute itself as a worthy inheritor of the commitments of a critical theory tradition. They suppose that his proceduralism idealizes and tries to universalize the terms in which a certain type of subject constructs its emancipatory needs The familiar criticism that Habermas endows normativity on the aspirations of particular types of subjects who are concerned only with the protection of an already constituted capacity for self-determination appears to miss the real distance that Habermas travels from a liberal conception of the goals of the public use of reason. We have seen that, for Habermas, communicative rationality is a value that tries to connect up with the claims of the 'damaged life'. His critical theory offers itself as a formulation of the need for autonomy that can be pressed by those who are disadvantaged and by those who are marginalized against settled descriptions of right and just conduct. Habermas seems to be correct when he strenuously defends the inclusiveness of his proceduralist construction of the ideal of self-determination appropriate to a pluralistic and egalitarian epoch against critiques of the substantive liberal prejudices that cling to his model of the public sphere.

Nevertheless, it appears that Habermas' efforts to revive the emancipatory, universalizing and practical commitments of critical theory by reconstructing a misunderstood liberal democratic normativity has won a more generally respectful rather than a warmly sympathetic reception. At least in the English-speaking world, he is generally known more as the last great systematic thinker about modern social life than as someone who is likely to attract a significant and enthusiastic following of those drawn to his delineation of the prospects for self-reform of capitalist democracies. Why is this? The uneven reception of Habermas cannot simply be put down to the technical difficulty of his writing. Other comprehensive attempts to theorize our problems and options have managed despite the daunting aspects of some of their prose to win a more enthusiastic reception amongst a critical intelligentsia. Foucault and Derrida come to mind here.

Clearly the systematic intent of Habermas' *oeuvre* jars an Anglo-Saxon intellectual tradition steeped in analytical empiricist skepticism and suspicious of grand philosophical systems. At the same time, the reformist ambitions of Habermas' project might seem to have little charm for the avant-gardist temper of much recent cultural critique. Historical sensibilities that are deeply distrustful of all grand narratives that ascribe progressive potentials to Western civilization have also played a part in muting the cultural resonance of Habermas' project. The particular terms in which Habermas himself has represented his programme for re-appropriation of the neglected humanist and democratic meanings of over-determined Enlightenment histories cannot be absolved either. In seeming tension with his own commitment to widening our appreciation of the ambiguity of modern ideals of self-determining futures, Habermas himself has actually supplied an only one-sided account of the interests in emancipation that are evident in post-Enlightenment societies. I have argued that his neglect of the irreducible significance that clings to Romantic longings for an unmediated self-expression of concrete particularity has in some part provoked the reserve that is evident within, for example, a feminist reception. Like other important manifestations of a contemporary radical politics, modern feminism has drawn on a broader range of distinctive utopian energies than is given due recognition by Habermas' reflections on the emancipatory potentials of modern culture.

A systematic attempt to rethink the emancipatory heritage of Enlightenment is the central achievement of Habermas' legacy. However, while he has helped to make some crucial distinctions about the diverse meanings of Enlightenment rationalism, a certain blurring of these trajectories also seems evident in the teleological overtones that cling to Habermas' call for an on-going engagement with modernity's 'incomplete project'. Perhaps we can get some insight into the conflation of separable strands in Enlightenment legacies that are betrayed in Habermas' account of modernity's project by looking at Tzvetan Todorov's recent attempt to distinguish distinctive ideological components of the historical Enlightenment.[11] Todorov challenges those who attempt to reduce Enlightenment to a seamless ideology bent on an instrumentalizing subjugation of the world to governing human purposes. To him, while Enlightenment thinking has certainly authored an ultra-rationalist conviction that the real can be made fully transparent, knowable and hence completely mastered, this has been accompanied by an alternative humanist interpretation of the ideal of human self-fashioning that accepts that this is a context-bound undertaking that always works within certain limited horizons. This critical humanist reading invests in the capacity of human beings to reflect, reassess and re-negotiate what they have made of themselves. The human world, Todorov says, is unique because we are able to become self-aware and to act against expectations.[12] In particular, a humanist tradition conceives this capacity for self-awareness as a communicative competence. Relinquishing the idea that humanity can ever become God-like in its all-knowing self-transparency, humanism reconciles the ideal of self-reflection with acceptance of the partial character of understandings of concrete and mutually dependent subjects. While a humanist interpretation of the ideal of a self-determining humanity has insisted on the conditionedness of our choices, this recognition that we are deeply implicated in the horizons supplied by the contingencies of our contexts does not at all suggest that we are locked within a prison-house of settled expectations. For Todorov, humanism is an essentially critical conviction that we can learn to build the self-awareness necessary to our freedom through the communicative interactions that take place between a plurality of subjects.

On this account, Habermas appears as a powerful advocate of a critical humanist tradition. His *oeuvre* has idealized the self-awareness that can be built through the communicative interactions of concrete sociable subjects. However, even though the conviction that we can become rationally aware of our options in argumentative dialogue centres Habermas' account of the ideal of a self-legislating humanity, an alternative, exacting, description of the demands of rationally justifiable knowledge also influences the terms of his allegiance to the legacies of Enlightenment reason. This is an interpretation that expects that a theory that undertakes a rational critique of prevailing ideological worldviews must be fully self-clairvoyant about its own foundational commitments. Habermas has never relinquished the determination to secure the universality and objectivity of the values upheld by his critical theory in terms that do not rely on the contingency of historical valuations. Perhaps, in the end, Habermas' attempt to anchor the commitments of his theory in the counterfactual assumptions implicit in the communicative purposes of language is a signal of his inability to ever shake free a sense of the truth of Adorno's despair at the chances of an emancipatory self-consciousness emerging in concrete history. As Habermas has said, it might be that we will never find the critical energies that will allow us to hack through the 'Gordian knots' of our problems. It should be said, though, that his lifetime project of attempting to rescue the modern public sphere has at least offered us a finer appreciation of what the stakes are.

Notes

1 Introduction: the plight of the public sphere

1 P. Self, *Rolling Back the Market: Economic Dogma & Political Choice*, London, Macmillan Press, 2000. p. 226.
2 M. Walzer, *On Toleration*, New Haven, CT and London, Yale University Press, 1997.
3 A. Touraine, *Beyond Neoliberalism*, Cambridge, UK, Polity Press, 2001.
4 J. Dewey, *The Public and its Problems*, Chicago, MA, Gateway Books, 1946, pp. 15–16.
5 R. Putnam, *Bowling Alone: The Collapse and Revival of American Community*, New York, Simon and Schuster, 2000.
6 Putnam, *Bowling Alone*, p. 22.
7 Ibid.
8 R. Sennett, *The Corrosion of Character: The Personal Consequences of Work in the New Capitalism*, New York, London, W. W. Norton & Company, 1998.
9 Sennett, *The Corrosion of Character*, p. 99.
10 Ibid., p. 138.
11 Ibid., p. 139.
12 L. Coser, *The Functions of Social Conflict*, New York, Free Press, 1976, cited by Sennett, *The Corrosion of Character*, p. 143.
13 Z. Bauman, *The Individualised Society*, Cambridge, UK, Polity, 2001, p. 14.
14 M. Walzer, *On Toleration*, New Haven and London, Yale University Press, 1997.
15 Walzer, *On Toleration*, pp. 111–112.
16 A. Giddens, *The Third Way: The Renewal of Social Democracy*, Cambridge, UK, Polity, 1998.
17 Giddens, *The Third Way*, p. 78.
18 M. Latham, *From the Suburbs: Building a Nation From Our Neighbourhoods*, NSW, Pluto Press, 2003, p. 37.
19 N. Birnbaum, *After Progress: American Social Reform and European Socialism in the Twentieth Century*, Oxford, Oxford University Press, 2001, pp. 326–327.
20 J. Dean, 'Why the Net is not a Public Sphere', *Constellations*, 10 (1), 2003, p. 96.
21 The decentred model is particularly spelt out by Habermas in *Between Facts and Norms: Contributions to a Discourse Theory of Law and Democracy*, Cambridge, MA, The MIT Press, 1996.
22 A. de Tocqueville, *Democracy in America*, Volume 2, New York, Vintage Books, 1945, p. 149.
23 de Tocqueville, *Democracy in America*, Volume I, p. 205.

24 T. Lemke, 'The Birth of bio-politics': Michel Foucault's lecture at the College de France on neo-liberal governmentality', *Economy and Society*, 30(2) May 2001, pp. 190–207, 203.

25 Lemke, 'The Birth of bio-politics', p. 200.

26 Ibid.

27 Ibid.

28 Bauman, *The Individualised Society*, p. 196.

29 R. W. Connell 'Rage Against the Dying of the Light', *The Australian*, Wednesday October 23, 2002, pp. 30–31.

30 Bauman, *In Search of Politics*, Stanford, CA, Stanford University Press, 1999.

31 Bauman, *The Individualised Society*, p. 13.

32 Ibid., pp. 9–10.

33 Ibid., p. 11.

34 N. Chomsky, *Power and Terror in Our Times*, a film by John Junkerman , 2002.

35 Heller, 'Modernity and Terror', *Constellations*, 9(1), 2002, pp. 53–65.

36 Heller, 'Modernity and Terror', p. 56.

37 J. Habermas, 'Interpreting the Fall of a Monument', *Constellations*, 10(3), 2003, pp. 364–371, 365.

38 J. Habermas, 'Afterward (May 1993)', in *Jurgen Habermas: The Past as Future*, interviews with Michael Haller, Lincoln and London, The University of Nebraska Press, 1994. pp. 143–167, 152.

39 M. Hardt, 'The Withering of Civil Society', *Social Text*, 14(4), 1995, pp. 27–44.

40 Ibid.

41 S. E. Bronner, *Reclaiming the Enlightenment: Toward a Politics of Radical Engagement*, New York, Columbia University Press, 2004.

42 Cited by Habermas in 'Walter Benjamin: Consciousness Raising or Rescuing Critique?' in *Philosophical and Political Profiles*, Cambridge, MA, The MIT Press, 1983, pp. 129–165, 137.

43 Habermas, 'Walter Benjamin: Consciousness Raising or Rescuing Critique?', p. 13.

44 Bauman, *In Search of Politics*.

45 Hardt, 'The Withering of Civil Society', p. 28.

46 R. C. Holub, *Jurgen Habermas: Critic in the Public Sphere*, London and New York, Routledge, 1991.

47 J. Habermas, *Toward a Rational Society: Student Protest, Science and Politics*, Boston, MA, Beacon Press, 1970.

48 J. Habermas, 'What Theories can Accomplish – and What they Can't', *Jurgen Habermas: The Past as Future*, interviews with Michael Haller, Lincoln and London, The University of Nebraska Press, 1994, pp. 99–121, 113–114.

49 J. Habermas, 'The Asylum Debate', Paris Lecture, January 14, 1993, in Habermas, *Jurgen Habermas: The Past as Future*, pp. 121–141.

50 J. Habermas, 'Interpreting the Fall of a Monument'.

51 J. Habermas, 'The German Idealism of the Jewish Philosophers', *Philosophical and Political Profiles*, Cambridge, MA, The MIT Press, 1983, cited in Michael Pusey, *Jurgen Habermas*, UK, Ellis Harwood and Tavistock, 1987, p. 13.

52 J. Habermas, 'The European Nation-State: On the Past and Future of Sovereignty and Citizenship', in *The Inclusion of the Other: Studies in Political Theory*, Cambridge, MA, The MIT press, 1998, pp. 105–129.

53 See for example, Martin Morris, *Rethinking the Communicative Turn: Adorno, Habermas, and the Problem of Communicative Freedom*, New York, State University of New York Press, 2001; Omid A. Payrow Shabani, *Democracy, Power and*

Legitimacy: The Critical Theory of Jurgen Habermas, Toronto, Buffalo, NY, London, University of Toronto Press, 2003.

54 O. P. Shabani, *Democracy, Power and Legitimacy: The Critical Theory of Jurgen Habermas*, Toronto, Buffalo, NY, London, University of Toronto Press, 2003.

55 M. Morris, *Rethinking the Communicative Turn: Adorno, Habermas, and the Problem of Communicative Freedom*, New York, State University of New York, 2001.

56 M. Matustik, *Jurgen Habermas: A Philosophical-Political Profile*, New York, Rowman and Littlefield, 2001, p. 281.

57 J. Whitebook, *Perversion and Utopia: A Study in Psychoanalysis and Critical Theory*, Cambridge, MA, The MIT Press, 1995, p. 84.

58 J. Habermas, 'The New Obscurity: The Crisis of the Welfare State and the Exhaustion of Utopian Energies', in *The New Conservatism: Cultural Criticism and the Historian's Debate*, Cambridge, MA, The MIT Press, 1989, pp. 48–71.

59 Habermas, 'The New Obscurity', p. 50.

60 J. Habermas, 'What Does Socialism Mean Today?', in Robert Blackburn (ed.), *After the Fall: The Failure of Communism and the Future of Socialism*, London, Verso, 1991, pp. 25–47, 39.

2 The structural transformation of the public sphere

1 This is a postdoctoral thesis required of those wishing to gain teaching status at German University.

2 J. Habermas, *The Structural Transformation of the Public Sphere: An Inquiry into a Category of Bourgeois Society*, Cambridge, MA, The MIT Press, 1989, p. 232. (Hereafter *The Structural Transformation*).

3 M. B. Matustik, *Jurgen Habermas: A Philosophical-Political Profile*, New York, Rowman and Littlefield Publishers, 2001, p. 144.

4 R. Wiggershaus, *The Frankfurt School: Its History, Theories, and Political Significance*, Cambridge, MA, The MIT Press, 1994, p. 537.

5 R. C. Holub, *Jurgen Habermas: Critic in the Public Sphere*, London and New York, Routledge, 1991, p. 2.

6 Habermas, *The Structural Transformation*, pp. 43–51.

7 H. C. Boyte, 'The Pragmatic Ends of Popular Politics', in C. Calhoun (ed.), *Habermas and the Public Sphere*, Cambridge, MA, The MIT Press, 1992, pp. 340–359, 343.

8 Habermas, *The Structural Transformation*, p. 29.

9 Ibid., p. 28.

10 Ibid., p. 46.

11 Ibid., p. 85.

12 Ibid., pp. 46–47.

13 Ibid., pp. 48–49.

14 Ibid., p. 49.

15 Ibid.

16 Ibid. p. 50.

17 J. L. Cohen and A. Arato, *Civil Society and Political Theory*, Cambridge, MA, The MIT Press, 1992, p. 214.

18 J. van Horn Melton, *The Rise of the Public in Enlightenment Europe*, Cambridge, UK, Cambridge University Press, 2001, pp. 200–201.

19 Habermas, *The Structural Transformation*, p. 56.

20 Ibid., p. 53.

21 Ibid., pp. 36–37.

22 Ibid., p. 36.

23 Ibid., p. 37.
24 Ibid., p. 52.
25 Ibid., p. 66
26 Ibid.
27 Ibid., p. 83 (original emphasis).
28 Ibid., p. 85.
29 Ibid., pp. 124–125.
30 Ibid., p. 47.
31 Ibid., p. 48.
32 See J. B. Landes, *Women and the Public Sphere in the Age of the French Revolution*, Ithaca, NY, Cornell University Press, 1988.
33 Habermas, *The Structural Transformation*, pp. 232–233.
34 Ibid., p. 176.
35 Ibid., p. 179.
36 Ibid., p. 86.
37 Ibid., p. 195.
38 Ibid., p. 175.
39 Ibid., p. 127.
40 Ibid., pp. 146–147.
41 Ibid., p. 147.
42 Ibid.
43 Ibid., p. 148.
44 Ibid., p. 200.
45 See N. Garnham, 'The Media and the Public Sphere', in C. Calhoun (ed.), *Habermas and the Public Sphere*, Cambridge, MA, pp. 359–377.
46 Habermas, *The Structural Transformation*, p. 193.
47 Ibid., p. 131.
48 Ibid., pp. 133–134.
49 Ibid., p. 88.
50 Ibid., p. 227.
51 Ibid., p. 232 (original emphasis).
52 Ibid., pp. 231–232.
53 Ibid., p. 234.
54 Ibid., p. 209.
55 Ibid., p. 237.
56 Ibid., p. 211.
57 Ibid., p. 247.
58 Habermas, 'Further Reflections on the Public Sphere' in C. Calhoun (ed.), *Habermas and the Public Sphere*, Cambridge, MA, The MIT Press, 1992, p. 430.
59 Cohen and Arato, *Civil Society and Political Theory*, also S. Benhabib, 'Models of Public Space: Hannah Arendt, the Liberal Tradition and Jurgen Habermas' in *Situating the Self: Gender Community and Postmodernism in Contemporary Ethics*, New York, Routledge, 1992, pp. 89–121.
60 J. B. Landes, *Women and the Public Sphere in the Age of the French Revolution*, Ithaca, NY, Cornell University Press, 1988, especially chapters 2 and 3; also N. Fraser, 'Rethinking the Public Sphere: A Contribution to the Critique of Actually Existing Democracy' in Calhoun (ed.), *Habermas and the Public Sphere*, Cambridge, MA, The MIT Press, 1992, pp. 109–143.
61 S. Benhabib, 'Communicative Ethics and the Claims of Gender', in S. Benhabib, *Situating the Self*, pp. 1–23; J. B. Landes, 'The Public and the Private Sphere: A Feminist Reconsideration', in Landes (ed.), *Feminism: the Public and the Private*, Oxford: Oxford University Press, 1998, pp. 135–164.

62 Landes, *Women and the Public Sphere*.
63 G. Eley, 'Nations, Publics, and Political Cultures', in Calhoun (ed.), *Habermas and the Public Sphere*, pp. 289–340; M. Ryan, 'Gender and Public Access: Women's Politics in Nineteenth Century America', in Calhoun (ed.), *Habermas and the Public Sphere*, pp. 259–289.
64 M. Ryan, 'Gender and Public Access: Women's Politics in Nineteeth Century America', in C. Colhoun (ed.), *Habermas and the Public Sphere*, Cambridge, MA, The MIT Press, 1992, p. 7.
65 Fraser, 'Rethinking the Public Sphere', in Calhoun, *Habermas and the Public Sphere*, pp. 109–143.
66 N. Fraser, 'Politics, Culture, and the Public Sphere: Toward a Postmodern Conception', in L Nicholson and S. Seidman (eds), *Social Postmodernism: Beyond Identity Politics*, Cambridge, Cambridge University Press, 1995.
67 D. Goodman, *The Republic of Letters: A Cultural History of the French Enlightenment*, Ithaca, NY and New York, Cornell University, 1994.
68 Goodman, *The Republic of Letters*, p. 271.
69 J. Habermas, 'Further Reflections on the Public Sphere' in Calhoun, *Habermas and the Public Sphere*, pp. 446–447, 421–461.
70 J. Habermas, 'Lawrence Kohlberg and Neo-Aristotelianism', *Justification and Application*, Cambridge, MA, The MIT Press, 1993, pp. 113–133, 130–131.
71 Habermas, 'Further Reflections on the Public Sphere', p. 440.
72 Cohen and Arato, *Civil Society and Political Theory*.
73 J. Habermas, 'Walter Benjamin: Consciousness-Raising or Rescuing Critique?', *Philosophical and Political Profiles*, Cambridge, MA, The MIT Press, 1983, pp. 129–165.

3 The theory of communicative action

1 J. Habermas, *Towards a Rational Society: Student Protest, Science and Politics*, Boston, MA, Beacon Press, 1970, pp. 107–120.
2 J. Habermas, *Theory and Practice*, Boston, MA, Beacon Press, 1973, pp. 254–255.
3 S. Benhabib, 'Modernity and the Aporias of Critical Theory' in *Telos*, 49, 1981, pp. 39–59, 49.
4 J. Habermas, *Towards a Rational Society*, p. 90.
5 J. Habermas, *Communication and the Evolution of Society*, Boston, MA, Beacon Press, 1979.
6 See T. McCarthy, 'Translator's Introduction', in J. Habermas, *Communication and the Evolution of Society*, Boston, MA, Beacon Press, 1979, p. xvi.
7 J. Habermas, *Knowledge and Human Interests*, Boston, MA, Beacon Press, 1971.
8 Ibid., p. 53.
9 Ibid., p. 194.
10 Ibid., pp. 312–313.
11 Ibid., p. 314.
12 R. Roderick, *Habermas and the Foundations of Critical Theory*, London, Macmillan, 1986, p. 64.
13 R. C. Holub, *Jurgen Habermas: Critic in the Public Sphere*, London and New York, Routledge, 1991, p. 10.
14 See J. Habermas, 'What is Universal Pragmatics?' in *Communication and the Evolution of Society*, pp. 1–68.
15 J. Habermas, 'Critical Hermeneutics', in J. Bleicher (ed.), *Contemporary Hermeneutics*, London and Boston, MA, Routledge & Kegan Paul, 1980, pp. 141–213, 205.

16 Horkheimer cited by Michael Theunissen 'Society and History: A Critique of Critical Theory', P. Dews (ed.), *Habermas: A Critical Reader*, UK, Blackwell, 1999, pp. 241–272, 245.

17 J. Habermas, 'A Conversation About Questions of Political Theory', *Jurgen Habermas: A Berlin Republic: Writings on Germany*, Cambridge, UK, Polity Press, 1998, p. 132.

18 O. P. Shabini, *Democracy, Power and Legitimacy: The Critical Theory of Jurgen Habermas*, Toronto, London, University of Toronto Press, 2003, p. 78.

19 J. Habermas, *Legitimation Crisis*, trans. T. Mc Carthy, Boston, Beacon Press, 1975, p. 16.

20 T. McCarthy, *The Critical Theory of Jurgen Habermas*, Cambridge, MA, The MIT Press, 1978, p. 369.

21 Habermas, *Legitimation Crisis*, p. 76.

22 McCarthy, *The Critical Theory of Jurgen Habermas*, p. 385

23 Ibid., p. 378.

24 Ibid., p. 385.

25 D. Bohler cited by T. McCarthy, *The Critical Theory of Jurgen Habermas*, p. 97.

26 Habermas, *Communication and the Evolution of Society*, pp. 8–9.

27 J. Habermas, 'Further Reflections on the Public Sphere', in C. Calhoun (ed.), *Habermas and the Public Sphere*, Cambridge, MA, The MIT Press, 1992, pp. 421–462, 442.

28 Ibid.

29 J. Habermas, 'What Theories Can Accomplish and What They Can't', *The Past as Future* (interviews with Michael Haller), Lincoln and London, University of Nebraska Press, 1994, pp. 99–121, 111.

30 Habermas, *The Legitimation Crisis*, pp. 4–5.

31 J. Habermas, 'A Reply to My Critics', in J. B. Thompson and D. Held (eds), *Habermas and Critical Debates*, Cambridge, MA, The MIT Press, 1982, pp. 196–219, 217.

32 A. Honneth and H. Joas, 'Introduction', *Communicative Action: Essays on Habermas' Theory of Communicative Action*, Cambridge, MA, The MIT Press, 1991, p. 1.

33 Ibid.

34 J. Habermas, 'The Dialectics of Rationalisation: An Interview with Jurgen Habermas', *Telos*, 49, Fall, 1981, pp. 5–33, 17.

35 J. Habermas, *The Theory of Communicative Action*, Volume I, Boston, MA, Beacon Press, 1984, pp. 282–283.

36 T. McCarthy, *The Critical Theory of Jurgen Habermas*, p. 19.

37 Habermas, *Theory of Communicative Action*, Volume I, p. 218.

38 Ibid., pp. 273–274.

39 Ibid., p. 280.

40 Ibid., p. 249.

41 Ibid., p. 286.

42 Ibid., pp. 388–389.

43 J. Habermas, *The Theory of Communicative Action*, Volume 2, Boston, MA, Beacon Press, 1984, p. 333.

44 Ibid.

45 Habermas, *Communication and the Evolution of Society*, p. 96.

46 J. E. Grumley, 'Two Views of the Paradigm of Production', *Praxis International*, 12 (2), July 1992, pp. 181–205, 182.

47 Habermas, *Toward a Rational Society*, p. 118.

48 Habermas, *The Theory of Communicative Action*, Volume 1, p. 1.

49 J. Habermas, *The Philosophical Discourses of Modernity: Twelve Lectures*, Cambridge, MA, The MIT Press, 1987, p. 63.
50 See Habermas, *The Theory of Communicative Action*, Volume 2, pp. 4–42.
51 T. McCarthy, 'Introduction', *The Theory of Communicative Action*, Volume 1, p. xx.
52 Habermas, *The Theory of Communicative Action*, Volume 2, p. 97.
53 Ibid., Volume 2, p. 395.
54 Ibid., Volume 1, p. 115.
55 Ibid., p. 383.
56 Ibid., p. 70.
57 Ibid., Volume 2, p. 133.
58 Ibid., p. 182.
59 Ibid., p. 183.
60 Ibid., p. 319.
61 Ibid., p. 173.
62 Habermas, 'Concluding Remarks', in C. Calhoun (ed.), *Habermas and the Public Sphere*, p. 466.
63 Ibid.
64 Habermas, 'Concluding Remarks', p. 154.
65 J. Habermas, *Between Facts and Norms: Contributions to a Discourse Theory of Law and Democracy*, Cambridge, MA, The MIT Press, 1996, p. 39.
66 Habermas, *The Theory of Communicative Action*, Volume 2, p. 395.
67 Ibid., p. 357.
68 Ibid., p. 361.
69 Ibid., pp. 363–373.
70 J. Habermas, 'A Conversation about Questions of Political Theory', in *Jürgen Habermas: A Berlin Republic: Writings on Germany*, Cambridge, Polity Press, 1998, p. 154.
71 Habermas, *The Theory of Communicative Action*, Volume 2, p. 327.
72 Ibid., p. 333.
73 Ibid., p. 375 (emphasis in original).
74 Ibid., p. 328.
75 Ibid.
76 Ibid., Volume 1, p. 121.
77 Ibid., p. 391.
78 Ibid., p. 392.
79 Ibid., p. 393.
80 Ibid., p. 395.
81 Ibid., p. 393.
82 Ibid., p. 395.
83 Ibid., p. 393.
84 Ibid.
85 C. Lafont, *The Linguistic Turn in Hermeneutic Philosophy*, Cambridge, MA, The MIT Press, 1999, p. 175.
86 A. Honneth and H. Joas, 'Introduction', *Communicative Action: Essays on Habermas's Theory of Communicative Action*, Cambridge, MA, The MIT Press, 1991, p. 1.
87 J. Habermas, *Theorie des kommunikativen Handelns*, Band 1, 'Vorwart zur dritten Auflage', Frankfurt, 1985, pp. 3–5.
88 T. H. Nielsen, 'Jurgen Habermas: Morality, Society and Ethics', An Interview with Torben Hviid Nielsen, *Acta Sociologica*, 33, 1990, pp. 93–114, 109.

4 Discourse ethics and the normative justification
of tolerance

1 J. Habermas, 'Morality, Society and Ethics, an Interview with Torben Hviid Nielsen', *Acta Sociologica*, 33 (2), 1990, pp. 93–114, p. 95.
2 J. Habermas, 'Concluding Remarks', in C. Calhoun (ed.), *Habermas and the Public Sphere*, Cambridge, MA, The MIT Press, 1992, pp. 466–479, 477–478.
3 J. Habermas, 'Remarks on Discourse Ethics', in *Justification and Application*, Cambridge, MA, The MIT Press, 1993, pp. 19–111, 53 and 55.
4 W. Outhwaite, *Habermas: A Critical Introduction*, Stanford, CA, Stanford University Press, 1994, p. 44.
5 C. P. Cronin, 'Introduction', in Habermas (ed.), *Justification and Application*, Cambridge, MA, The MIT Press, 1993, pp. xxi.
6 J. Habermas, 'Concluding Remarks', p. 476.
7 J. Habermas, 'Morality and Ethical Life: Does Hegel's Critique of Kant Apply to Discourse Ethics?' in *Moral Consciousness and Communicative Action*, Cambridge, MA, The MIT Press, 1990, pp. 195–217, 205; J. Habermas, 'Concluding Remarks', MA, 1992, pp. 466–479, 476.
8 Habermas, 'Concluding Remarks', p. 467.
9 Ibid.
10 J. Habermas, 'Discourse Ethics: Notes on a Program of Philosophical Justification' in *Moral Consciousness and Communicative Action*, pp. 43–116, 66 (emphasis in original).
11 J. Habermas, 'Justice and Solidarity: On the Discussion Concerning Stage 6', in T. E. Wren (ed.), *The Moral Domain: Essays in the Ongoing Discussion Between Philosophy and the Social Sciences*, Cambridge, MA, The MIT Press, 1990, pp. 225–251, 246–247.
12 Habermas, 'Remarks on Discourse Ethics', p. 52.
13 Ibid.
14 See J. L. Cohen, 'Heller, Habermas and Justice: A Review of Agnes Heller's Beyond Justice', *Praxis International*, 8 (4), 1989, pp. 491–497, 496.
15 J. Habermas, 'A Genealogical Analysis of the Cognitive Content of Morality', in *The Inclusion of the Other: Studies in Political Theory*, Cambridge, MA, The MIT Press, 1998, pp. 3–46, pp. 39–41.
16 Habermas, 'A Genealogical Analysis', p. 40 (emphasis in original).
17 Habermas, 'Remarks on Discourse Ethics', p. 91.
18 Habermas, most recent works still appeal to the centrality of this distinction: see *Between Facts and Norms*, pp. 108–109.
19 J. Habermas, 'Reply to Symposium Participants, Benjamin N. Cardozo School of Law', in E. B. Warren (ed.), *Habermas on Law and Democracy: Critical Exchanges*, New York, Cardozo School of Law Review 1996, pp. 1477–1559, 1500–1501.
20 Habermas, 'Reply to Symposium', pp. 1500–1501.
21 J. Raz, *The Morality of Freedom*, Oxford, Clarendon Press, 1986, p. 407.
22 J. S. Mill, *Utilitarianism, Liberty and Representative Government*, London, J. M. Dent & Sons Ltd, 1910, p. 73.
23 H. Marcuse, 'Repressive Tolerance', in R. P. Wolff, B. Moore, and H. Marcuse (eds), *A Critique of Pure Tolerance*, Boston, MA, Beacon Press, 1965, pp. 81–123.
24 Marcuse, 'Repressive Tolerance', p. 85.
25 Ibid., p. 95.
26 Habermas, 'A Genealogical Analysis of the Cognitive Content of Morality', p. 40 (emphasis in original).

27 T. McCarthy, *Ideals and Illusions: On Reconstruction and Deconstruction in Contemporary Critical Theory*, Cambridge, MA, The MIT Press, 1991, p. 192.
28 Cohen, 'Heller, Habermas and Justice', p. 496.
29 A. Heller, 'The Discourse Ethic of Habermas: Critique and Appraisal', *Thesis Eleven*, No. 10/11, November–March 1984–85, pp. 5–18, 9.
30 W. Outhwaite, *Habermas: A Critical Introduction*, Stanford, CA, Stanford University Press, 1994, p. 54.
31 Outhwaite, *Habermas: A Critical Introduction*, p. 9.
32 Habermas, 'Remarks on Discourse Ethics', p. 33.
33 J. Habermas, 'Political Liberalism: A Debate with John Rawls', in *The Inclusion of the Other: Studies in Political Theory*, Cambridge, MA, The MIT Press, 1998, pp. 49–101.
34 J. Habermas, ' "Reasonable" versus True", or the Morality of Worldviews', in *The Inclusion of the Other: Studies in Political Theory*, Cambridge, MA, The MIT Press, 1998, pp. 75–101.
35 Habermas, 'Remarks on Discourse Ethics', p. 92 (emphasis in original).
36 S. Benhabib, 'In the Shadow of Aristotle and Hegel', in *Situating the Self: Gender, Community and Postmodernism in Contemporary Ethics*, New York, Routledge, 1992, pp. 23–68, 34.
37 S. Benhabib, 'The Generalised and the Concrete Other', in *Situating the Self*, pp. 148–177.
38 Benhabib, 'The Generalised and the Concrete Other', p. 158.
39 Ibid., p. 159.
40 J. Habermas, 'Lawrence Kohlberg and Neo-Aristotelianism', in *Justification and Application*, Cambridge, MA and London, 1993, pp. 113–132, 130–131.
41 Habermas, 'Remarks on Discourse Ethics', p. 105.
42 Habermas particularly challenges MacIntyre's attempt to rehabilitate a strong concept of tradition see 'Remarks on Discourse Ethics', pp. 96–105.
43 Habermas, 'Remarks on Discourse Ethics', p. 105 (emphasis in original).
44 Ibid., 105.
45 Ibid., 103.
46 R. Dees, 'Establishing Toleration', *Political Theory*, 27(5), 1999, pp. 667–693, 688.
47 J. L. Cohen and A. Arato, *Civil Society and Political Theory*, Cambridge, MA, The MIT Press, 1992, p. 390.

5 A discourse theory of law and democracy

1 J. Habermas, *Between Facts and Norms: Contributions to a Discourse Theory of Law and Democracy*, Cambridge, MA, The MIT Press, 1996, 287.
2 Ibid.
3 Ibid.
4 Habermas, *Between Facts and Norms*. Cited in William Outhwaite, *Habermas: A Critical Introduction*, Stanford, CA, Stanford University Press, 1994, p. 139.
5 J. Habermas, 'What Theories Can Accomplish – and What They Can't', in *Jurgen Habermas: The Past as Future*, interviews with Michael Haller, Lincoln and London, University of Nebraska Press, 1994, pp. 99–121, 110.
6 Habermas, 'Preface', *Between Facts and Norms*, p. xlii.
7 Ibid., pp. xlii–xliii.
8 J. Habermas, 'A Conversation about Questions of Political Theory', *Jurgen Habermas: A Berlin Republic: Writings on Germany*, Cambridge, UK, Polity Press, 1998, pp. 131–161, 132.

9 W. E. Scheuerman, 'Between Radicalism and Resignation: Democratic Theory in Habermas's *Between Facts and Norms*', in *Discourse and Democracy: Essays on Habermas's Between Facts and Norms*, R. von Schomberg and K. Baynes (eds), Albany, NY State University of New York Press, 2002, pp. 61–89, p. 62. See also J. Sitton, *Habermas and Contemporary Society*, New York, Palgrave, Macmillan, 2003.

10 J. Habermas, 'Three Normative Models of Democracy', *Constellations*, 1(1), April 1994, 1–11.

11 Habermas, *Between Facts and Norms*, pp. 268–269, 296–302, 308–314.

12 Habermas, 'Three Normative Models of Democracy', pp. 3, 11.

13 Habermas, *Between Facts and Norms*, pp. 268–272, 454–457.

14 Ibid., pp. 244–246; 389–391, 395–401. See also J. Habermas, 'The New Obscurity: The Crisis of the Welfare State and the Exhaustion of Utopian Energies', *The New Conservatism: Cultural Criticism and the Historian's Debate*, Cambridge, MA, The MIT Press, 1989.

15 See M. B. Matustik, *Jurgen Habermas: A Philosophical-Political Profile*, New York, Oxford, Rowman & Littlefield Publishers, 2001.

16 Habermas, *Between Facts and Norms*, pp. 296–302.

17 Ibid., pp. 101–104, 118–129.

18 Ibid., pp. 408–418.

19 Ibid., pp. 100–103.

20 J. Habermas, 'Hannah Arendt: On the Concept of Power', *Philosophical-Political Profiles*, Cambridge, MA, The MIT Press, 1983, p. 172.

21 Habermas, *Between Facts and Norms*, pp. 244–245, 269–270, 297–300, 430–436.

22 Habermas, 'Hannah Arendt: On the Concept of Power', p. 171.

23 Habermas, *Between Facts and Norms*, p. 440.

24 Ibid., p. 360.

25 Ibid., p. 358.

26 Ibid., p. 360 (original emphasis).

27 Ibid., p. 363.

28 Ibid., p. 440.

29 Ibid., pp. 454–457.

30 Ibid., p. 448.

31 Ibid., p. 449.

32 Ibid.

33 Ibid., p. 402.

34 Ibid.

35 Ibid.

36 Ibid.

37 Ibid., p. 403.

38 Habermas, 'The New Obscurity', pp. 48–71, 59.

39 Ibid.

40 Ibid.

41 Habermas, *Between Facts and Norms*, pp. 350–351.

42 Ibid., pp. 429–430.

43 Ibid., p. 430.

44 Ibid., p. 374

45 Ibid., p. 420.

46 Ibid., p. 351.

47 Ibid., p. 354.

48 Ibid., pp. 354–359.

49 Ibid., p. 354.

50 Habermas, *Between Facts and Norms*, p. 355.
51 Ibid.
52 Ibid., pp. 354–356.
53 Ibid.
54 Ibid., p. 385.
55 Ibid., p. 445.
56 Ibid., p. 368.
57 Ibid., p. 356.
58 Ibid., p. 358.
59 Ibid., p. 357.
60 Ibid., p. 358.
61 Ibid., p. 359; see also Habermas, 'Three Normative Models of Democracy', pp. 239–253, 251.
62 Ibid.
63 Habermas, *Between Facts and Norms*, p. 360.
64 Ibid. (original emphasis).
65 Ibid., p. 377.
66 Ibid., p. 376.
67 Ibid., p. 377.
68 Ibid.
69 Ibid., p. 378.
70 Ibid., p. 381.
71 W. Rehg, 'Translator's Introduction', in Habermas, *Between Facts and Norms*, pp. ix–xxxix, xxxi–ii.
72 Ibid., p. 368.
73 Ibid., pp. 368–369.
74 Ibid., p. 368.
75 Ibid., p. 408.
76 Ibid.
77 Scheuerman, 'Between Radicalism and Resignation', pp. 61–89, 62. See also Sitton, *Habermas and Contemporary Society*.
78 Habermas, *Between Facts and Norms*, p. 307, cited in Scheuerman, 'Between Radicalism and Resignation', p. 66.
79 Scheuerman, 'Between Radicalism and Resignation', p. 69.
80 Ibid.
81 Ibid.
82 J. Habermas, 'Further Reflections on the Public Sphere', in C. Calhoun (ed.), *Habermas and the Public Sphere*, Cambridge, MA, The MIT Press, 1992, pp. 421–461, 444.
83 Habermas, 'Questions of Political Theory', pp. 131–158, 150.
84 Ibid., p. 142.
85 J. Habermas, 'What does Socialism Mean Today?' in Robin Blackburn (ed.), *After the Fall: The Failure of Communism and the Future of Socialism*, London, Verso, 1991, pp. 25–47, 39.
86 J. Sitton, *Habermas and Contemporary Society*, p. 156.
87 A. Honneth 'Patterns of Intersubjective Recognition: Love, Rights and Solidarity', *The Struggle For Recognition: The Moral Grammar of Social Conflicts*, 1995, pp. 92–131.
88 S. E. Bronner, *Of Critical Theory and Its Theorists*, Cambridge, MA, Blackwell, 1994, p. 285.
89 T. McCarthy, 'Legitimacy and Diversity: Dialectical Reflections on Analytical Distinctions', *Cardozo Law Review*, 17(4–5), March 1996, pp. 1083–1127, and

J. Bohman, *Public Deliberation: Pluralism, Complexity and Democracy*, Cambridge, MA and London, England, The MIT Press, 1996.

90 J. S. Brady, 'No Contest? Assessing the Critiques of Jurgen Habermas's Theory of the Public Sphere', *Philosophy and Social Criticism*, 30(3), 2004, pp. 331–354, 336.

91 J. Dean, 'Civil Society: Beyond the Public Sphere', in D. Rasmussen (ed.), *The Handbook of Critical Theory*, Oxford, Blackwell, 1999.

92 McCarthy, 'Legitimacy and Diversity', p. 1117.

93 Ibid., p. 1123.

94 J. Habermas, 'The Unity of Reason in the Diversity of its Voices', *Postmetaphysical Thinking: Philosophical Essays*, Cambridge, MA, The MIT Press, pp. 115–148, p. 140.

95 Ibid.

96 Habermas, *Between Facts and Norms*, pp. 445–456.

97 Ibid.

6 Globalizing the public sphere

1 J. Habermas, 'Learning from Catastrophe? A Look Back at the Short Twentieth Century', *The Postnational Constellation: Political Essays*, UK, Polity Press, 2001, pp. 58–113.

2 J. Habermas, 'The Postnational Constellation and the Future of Democracy', *The Postnational Constellation: Political Essays*, Cambridge Mass, The MIT Press, 2001, pp. 56–112, 78–79.

3 Habermas, 'The Postnational Constellation', p. 79.

4 Ibid., p. 84.

5 Ibid.

6 Ibid., p. 88.

7 J. Habermas, 'The European Nation-State: On the Past and Future of Sovereignty and Citizenship', *The Inclusion of the Other: Studies in Political Theory*, Cambridge, MA, The MIT Press, 1998, pp. 105–129.

8 Ibid., p. 106.

9 Ibid., p. 111.

10 Ibid., p. 112.

11 Ibid.

12 Ibid., p. 118.

13 J. Habermas, 'Yet Again: German Identity – A Unified Nation of Angry DM-Burghers', in H. James and M. Stone (eds), *When the Wall Came Down: Reactions to German Unification*, New York and London, Routledge, 1992, pp. 86–102.

14 Habermas, 'The European Nation-State', p. 113.

15 R. Fine and W. Smith, 'Habermas's Ambivalent Modernism', *Constellations*, 10(4), December 2003, pp. 469–488, p. 474.

16 Habermas, 'The European Nation-State', pp. 118–119.

17 Ibid.

18 Ibid.

19 Habermas, 'Learning from Catastrophe?', p. 51.

20 J. Habermas 'Does Europe Need a Constitution? A Response to Dieter Grimm, *The Inclusion of the Other: Studies in Political Theory*, Cambridge, MA, The MIT Press, 1998, pp. 155–161, 160.

21 Habermas, 'The Postnational Constellation and the Future of Democracy', p. 70.

22 J. Habermas, 'Why Europe Needs a Constitution', *New Left Review*, 11, September/October 2001, pp. 5–27, 8.

23 Habermas, 'Why Europe Needs a Constitution', pp. 17–18.

24 Habermas, 'Does Europe Need a Constitution? Response to Dieter Grimm', p. 160.
25 Habermas, 'The European Nation-State', p. 127.
26 Habermas, 'The Postnational Constellation and the Future of Democracy', p. 97.
27 J. Habermas and J. Derrida, 'February 15, or What Binds Europeans Together: A Plea for a Common Foreign Policy, Beginning in the Core of Europe', *Constellations*, 10(3), 2003, pp. 291–297, 291.
28 Habermas, 'The European Nation-State'.
29 Habermas, 'The Postnational Constellation and the Future of Democracy', p. 67.
30 U. Beck, *World Risk Society*, Cambridge, Polity Press, 1999, p. 2.
31 Ibid.
32 U. Beck, *The Reinvention of Politics: Rethinking Modernity in the Global Social Order*, Cambridge, UK, Polity, 1997, p. 25.
33 Ibid.
34 U. Beck, *Conversations with Ulrich Beck: Ulrich Beck and Johannes Willms*, Cambridge, UK, Polity, 2004, p. 11.
35 Beck, *World Risk Society*, pp. 1–2.
36 Habermas, 'The Postnational Constellation and the Future of Democracy', p. 67.
37 U. Beck, 'The Reinvention of Politics: Towards a Theory of a Reflexive Modernisation', in U. Beck, A. Giddens and S. Lash, *Reflexive Modernisation: Politics, Tradition and Aesthetics in the Modern Social Order*, Stanford, CA, Stanford University Press, 1994, pp. 1–55, 9.
38 Habermas, 'The Postnational Constellation and the Future of Democracy', p. 101.
39 Beck, *World Risk Society*, p. 13.
40 U. Beck, *What is Globalisation?*, Cambridge, UK, Polity Press, 2000, p. 147.
41 J. Goebel and C. Clermont, 'Die Tugend der Orientierungslosigkeit', manuscript, Berlin 1997, pp. 22ff., cited by U. Beck, *What is Globalization?*, p. 149.
42 Beck, *What is Globalization?* p. 149.
43 Ibid., pp. 152–155.
44 Beck, *World Risk Society*, p. 9.
45 Habermas, 'The Postnational Constellation and the Future of Democracy', p. 87.
46 Ibid.
47 J. Habermas, 'Remarks on Legitimation through Human Rights', *The Postnational Constellation: Political Writings*, Cambridge, MA, The MIT Press, 2001, pp. 113–129, 122.
48 H. Arendt, *The Origins of Totalitarianism*, London, George Allen and Unwin, 1958, pp. 290, 296.
49 Habermas, 'Remarks on Legitimation through Human Rights', p. 122.
50 Habermas, 'Postscript', *Between Facts and Norms*, p. 456 (emphasis in original).
51 Habermas, The European Nation-State', p. 126.
52 Habermas and Derrida, 'February 15, or What Binds Europeans Together', p. 291. Habermas and Derrida do not record the extent to which such demonstrations were a global phenomenon with major protests occurring in the United States, Australia and elsewhere.
53 Ibid.
54 J. Habermas, 'Fundamentalism and Terror: A Dialogue with Jurgen Habermas', G. Borradori, *Philosophy in a Time of Terror: Dialogues with Jurgen Habermas and Jacques Derrida*, Chicago and London, The University of Chicago Press, 2003, pp. 25–43, 35.
55 Habermas, 'Fundamentalism and Terror', p. 29.
56 A. Heller, 'Modernity and Terror', *Constellations*, 9(1), March 2002, pp. 53–66.
57 Heller, 'Modernity and Terror', p. 56.

58 G, Borradori, 'Introduction', *Philosophy in a Time of Terror: Dialogues with Jurgen Habermas and Jacques Derrida*, Chicago, IL and London, The University of Chicago Press, 2003, pp. 18–19.

59 Habermas cited by Borradori 'Reconstructing Terrorism', *Philosophy in a Time of Terror*, pp. 45–81, 63.

60 Habermas 'Fundamentalism and Terror', p. 35.

61 Ibid.

62 Habermas, 'Remarks on Legitimation through Human Rights', p. 128.

63 Habermas, 'Coping With Contingencies', in J. Niznik and J. T. Sanders (eds), *Debating The State of Philosophy: Habermas, Rorty, and Kolakowski*, Westport, Connecticut, London, Praeger, 1996, pp. 1–29, 17.

64 Borradori in Habermas 'Fundamentalism and Terror', p. 36.

65 J. Baudrillard, *The Spirit of Terrorism*, London, Vergo, 2002, and J. Derrida, 'Deconstructing Terror', in Borradori, *Dialogues with Jurgen Habermas and Jacques Derrida*, pp. 85–137.

66 M. Moody-Adams, *Fieldwork in Familiar Places: Morality, Culture and Philosophy*, Cambridge, MA, Harvard University Press, 1997, p. 27.

67 C. Geertz, *Available Light: Anthropological Reflections on Philosophical Topics*, Princeton, NJ, Princeton University Press, 2000, p. 260.

68 C. Geertz, *Available Light*, p. 249.

69 Ibid., p. 260.

7 The utopian energies of a radical reformist

1 J. Habermas, 'The New Obscurity: The Crisis of the Welfare State and the Exhaustion of Utopian Energies', *The New Conservatism: Cultural Criticism and the Historian's Debate*, Cambridge, MA, The MIT Press, 1989, pp. 48–70.

2 Ibid., pp. 50–51.

3 L. Lowenthal, 'The Utopian Motif in Suspension: A Conversation with Leo Lowenthal (Interview with Martin Luddke)', in M. Jay (ed.), *An Unmastered Past: The Autobiographical Reflections of Leo Lowenthal*, Berkeley, CA, University of California Press, 1987, 237 (interview recorded in 1980).

4 Habermas, 'The New Obscurity', p. 51.

5 Ibid.

6 A. Touraine, *Beyond Neoliberalism*, Cambridge, UK, Polity Press, 2001, p. 1.

7 J. Alexander, 'Robust Utopias and Civil Repairs', *International Sociology*, 16(4), December 2001, pp. 579–591, 584; R. Jacoby, *The End of Utopia: Politics and Culture in an Age of Apathy*, New York, Basic Books, 1999.

8 J. Habermas, 'Learning from Catastrophe? A Look Back at the Short Twentieth Century', *The Postnational Constellation*, Cambridge, UK, Polity, 1998, pp. 38–58, 48.

9 J. Habermas, 'Europe's Second Chance', in *Jurgen Habermas: The Past as Future*, interviews with Michael Haller, Lincoln and London, The University of Nebraska Press, 1994, p. 97.

10 Habermas, 'The New Obscurity', p. 50.

11 Ibid., p. 48.

12 Ibid., p. 50.

13 Ibid.

14 Ibid., p. 53.

15 J. Grumley, 'Two Views of the Paradigm of Production', *Praxis International*, 12(2), July 1992, pp. 181–205, 182.

16 A. Honneth, 'Work and Instrumental Action: On the Normative Basis of Critical Theory', *Thesis Eleven*, 5/6, 1982, p. 165.
17 Habermas, *Toward A Rational Society*, Boston, MA, Beacon Press, 1970, pp. 118–119.
18 Habermas, 'The New Obscurity', p. 52.
19 J. Habermas, *The Philosophical Discourse of Modernity: Twelve Lectures*, Cambridge, MA, The MIT Press, 1987, p. 315.
20 J. Habermas, *A Berlin Republic: Writings on Germany*, Cambridge, UK, Polity, 1998, p. 92.
21 Habermas, 'The New Obscurity', p. 54.
22 Ibid.
23 Ibid., p. 55.
24 C. Offe, 'Some Contradictions of the Modern Welfare State', in T. Deane (ed.), *Contradictions of the Welfare State*, Cambridge, MA, The MIT Press, 1984, pp. 147–162.
25 Habermas, 'The New Obscurity', p. 59.
26 S. Benhabib, *Critique, Norm and Utopia: A Study of the Foundation of Critical Theory*, New York, Columbia University Press, 1986, p. 235.
27 Habermas, 'The New Obscurity', p. 57.
28 Ibid.
29 Benhabib, *Critique, Norm and Utopia*, p. 235.
30 J. Habermas, *Legitimation Crisis*, Boston, MA, Beacon Press, 1975, pp. 45–46.
31 Ibid., p. 46.
32 Touraine, *Beyond Neoliberalism*, p. 5 (emphasis added).
33 J. Habermas, 'Globalism, Ideology and Traditions: Interview with Jurgen Habermas' by Johann Arnason', *Thesis Eleven*, 63, November 2000, pp. 1–11, 1.
34 Ibid., p. 2.
35 J. Habermas, 'The Postnational Constellation and the Future of Democracy', *The Postnational Constellation: Political Essays*, Cambridge, UK, Polity Press, 2001, pp. 88 ff.
36 Habermas, 'The New Obscurity', p. 67.
37 Habermas, 'The Postnational Constellation', p. 100.
38 Ibid., p. 111.
39 Habermas, 'Europe's Second Chance', p. 97.
40 Ibid.
41 Ibid.
42 Habermas, 'The New Obscurity', p. 52.
43 Habermas, *Communication and the Evolution of Society*, p. 96.
44 Benhabib, *Critique Norm and Utopia*, p. 60.
45 A. Heller and F. Feher, 'On Being Satisfied in a Dissatisfied Society 1', *The Postmodern Political Condition*, Cambridge, UK, Polity Press, 1988, pp. 14–30, 17.
46 T. W. Adorno, *Negative Dialectics*, New York, Seabury Press, 1973, p. 173.
47 Cited by Lowenthal, 'The Utopian Motif in Suspension', p. 237.
48 Habermas, 'Globalism, Ideology and Traditions', p. 2.
49 Ibid.
50 P. Self, *Rolling Back the Market: Economic Dogma and Political Choice*, London, Macmillan Press, 2000, pp. 34–38.
51 Habermas, 'Learning from Catastrophe?', p. 49.
52 J. Habermas, 'Walter Benjamin: Consciousness Raising or Rescuing Critique', *Philosophical and Political Profiles*, Cambridge, MA, The MIT Press, 1983, pp. 129–165, 158.
53 J. Habermas, 'Why Europe Needs A Constitution', *New Left Review*, 11, September/October 2001, pp. 5–27, 6.
54 Habermas, 'The New Obscurity', p. 50.

55 Ibid., p. 54.
56 Habermas, 'The Postnational Constellation', p. 87.
57 Ibid., p. 88.
58 Ibid.
59 Ibid.
60 Alexander, 'Radical Utopias and Civil Repairs', p. 582.
61 M. Morris, *Rethinking the Communicative Turn: Adorno, Habermas and the Problem of Communicative Freedom*, New York, State University of New York Press, 2001, p. 196.
62 Lowenthal, 'The Utopian Motif in Suspension', p. 245.
63 Ibid., p. 246.
64 M. B. Markus, 'Decent Society and/or Civil Society?', *Social Research*, 68(4), Winter 2001, pp. 1011–1029, 1024.
65 See E. Laclau and C. Mouffe, *Hegemony and Socialist Strategy: Towards a Radical Democratic Politics*, London, Verso, 1985, and T. McCarthy, 'Legitimacy and Diversity: Dialectical Reflections on Analytical Distinctions', *Cardozo Law Review*, 17(4–5), March 1996, pp. 1083–1127.
66 M. B. Matustik, *Jurgen Habermas: A Philosophical-Political Profile*, New York, Rowman and Littlefield, 2001, p. 151.
67 Matustik, *Jurgen Habermas*, p. 122.
68 Ibid., p. 90.
69 See J. Habermas, *The Theory of Communicative Action*, Volume 2, Boston, MA, Beacon Press, 1984, and J. Habermas, *Autonomy and Solidarity: Interviews with Jurgen Habermas*, P. Dews (ed.), London, Verso, 1986, pp. 177 ff.
70 Matustik, *Jurgen Habermas*, p. 122.
71 J. Whitebook, *Perversion and Utopia: A Study in Psychoanalysis and Critical Theory*, Cambridge, MA, The MIT Press, 1995, pp. 80–81.
72 Morris, *Rethinking the Communicative Turn*, p. 29.
73 Benhabib, *Critique, Norm and Utopia*, p. 277.
74 Ibid.
75 J. Whitebook, *Perversion and Utopia: A Study in Psychoanalysis and Critical Theory*, Cambridge, MA, The MIT Press, 1995, p. 84.
76 Ibid.
77 Habermas, 'Walter Benjamin: Consciousness Raising or Redemptive Critique', p. 157.
78 Ibid., p. 158, and Whitebook, *Perversion and Utopia*, p. 84.
79 M. Krygier, 'The Quality of Civility: Post-Anti-Communist Thoughts on Civil Society and the Rule of Law', in A. Sajo (ed.), *From and to Authoritarianism*, Dordrecht, Kluwer Acadmeic publishers, 2001. Cited in M. Markus 'Decent and/or Civil Society?', p. 1020.
80 Matustik, *Jurgen Habermas*, p. 139.
81 Ibid., p. 151.
82 Ibid., p. 184.
83 J. Habermas, 'Modernity's Consciousness of Time and the Need for Reassurance', *The Philosophical Discourse of Modernity*, Cambridge, UK, Polity Press, 1987, pp. 1–23, 15.
84 J. Habermas, 'The Asylum Debate' in *Jurgen Habermas; The Past as Future* interviews with Michael Haller, Lincoln and London, The University of Nebraska Press, 1994, pp. 121–143, 136 ff.
85 J. Habermas, 'A Reply to my Critics', J. B. Thompson and D. Held (eds), *Habermas: Critical Debates*, Cambridge, MA, The MIT Press, 1982, p. 235.
86 See S. K. White, *Political Theory and Postmodernism*, Cambridge, UK, Cambridge University Press, 1991, p. 22, and J. Butler, *Excitable Speech: A Politics of the Performative*, New York, Routledge, 1997, pp. 86 ff.

87 See for example, Young, 'Communication and the Other'.
88 I. M. Young, 'Communication and the Other', *Intersecting Voices: Dilemmas of Gender, Political Philosophy and Politics*, Princeton, NJ, Princeton University Press, 1997, pp. 60–75, 64.
89 Matustik, *Jurgen Habermas*, pp. 114–115, 122, 128.
90 Ibid., p. 114.
91 Alexander, 'Robust Utopias and Civil Repairs', p. 586.
92 J. Habermas, 'Further Reflections on the Public Sphere', C. Calhoun (ed.), *Habermas and the Public Sphere*, Cambridge, MA, The MIT Press, 1992, pp. 421–467, 422.
93 L. Kolakowski, 'The Death of Utopia Reconsidered', in *Modernity on Endless Trial*, Chicago, IL and London, University of Chicago Press, 1983, p. 136.

8 Romantic and Enlightenment legacies: the postmodern critics

1 J. Arnason, 'Modernity as Project and as Field of Tensions', in A. Honneth and H. Joas (eds), *Communicative Action: Essays on Habermas' Theory of Communicative Action*, Cambridge, MA, The MIT Press, 1991, pp. 181–214.
2 I. Berlin, *The Roots Of Romanticism*, Princeton, NJ, Princeton University Press, 1999.
3 Ibid., p. 141.
4 Ibid., p. 23.
5 Ibid., p. 141.
6 Ibid., p. 117.
7 See for example: A. W. Gouldner, 'Romanticism and Classicism: Deep Structures in Social Science', *For Sociology: Renewal and Critique in Sociology Today*, New York: Basic Books, Inc., 1973, pp. 300–323.
8 Arnason 'Modernity as Project and as Field of Tensions'.
9 G. Markus, 'The Paradoxical Unity of Culture: The Arts and the Sciences', *Thesis Eleven*, 75, 2003, pp. 7–24. See also G. Markus, 'Antinomies of "Culture"', Collegium Budapest/Institute for Advanced Study, Discussion Paper No. 38, February 1997, pp. 1–20.
10 J. Habermas, 'Habermas' Modernity: an Unfinished Project', in M. Passerin d'Entreves and S. Benhabib (eds), *Habermas and the Unfinished Project of Modernity*, Cambridge, MA, The MIT Press, 1997, pp. 38–55, 44.
11 J. Habermas, 'The Dialectics of Rationalisation: An Interview with Jurgen Habermas', by A. Honneth E. Knodler-Bunte, A. Widmann, *Telos*, 49, Fall 1981, pp. 5–31, 9.
12 C. Schmitt, *Political Romanticism*, Cambridge, MA, The MIT Press, 1986.
13 F. R. Ankersmit, *Aesthetic Politics: Political Philosophy Beyond Fact and Value*, Stanford, CA, Stanford University Press, 1996, p. 128.
14 D. R. Villa, 'Postmodernism and the Public Sphere', *American Political Science Review*, 86(3), September 1992, pp. 712–721.
15 See J. F. Lyotard, *The Postmodern Condition: A Report on Knowledge*, Minneapolis, University of Minnesota Press, 1984; J. F. Lyotard, *The Differend: Phrases in Dispute*, Minneapolis, University of Minnesota Press, 1998; J. F. Lyotard, *The Postmodern Explained: Correspondence 1982–1985*, Minneapolis and London, University of Minneapolis Press, 1992.
16 C. Schmitt, *Political Theology: Four Chapters on the Concept of Sovereignty*, Cambridge, MA, The MIT Press, 1988, pp. 16–35.
17 C. Schmitt, *The Crisis of Parliamentary Democracy*, Cambridge, MA, The MIT Press, 1988.

18 L. Strauss, 'Comments on Carl Schmitt's *Der Begriff des Politischen*', in C. Schmitt (ed.), *The Concept of the Political*, New Brunswick, NJ, Rutgers University Press, 1975, pp. 81–105, 101.

19 Schmitt, *Political Romanticism*, p. 125.

20 G. Oakes, 'Translator's Introduction', C. Schmitt, *Political Romanticism*, Cambridge, MA, The MIT Press, p. xxvii.

21 Ibid.

22 J. Habermas, 'The Horrors of Autonomy: Carl Schmitt in English', *The New Conservatism: Cultural Criticism and the Historians Debate*, Cambridge, MA, The MIT Press, 1989.

23 J. Habermas, 'Reply to Symposium Participants', *Cardozo Law Review*, 17, March 1996, pp. 1477–1557, 1493.

24 Ibid., p. 1491.

25 Habermas, 'The Horrors of Autonomy', p. 137.

26 Lyotard, *The Postmodern Condition*, p. xxiv.

27 T. McCarthy, 'Legitimacy and Diversity: Dialectical Reflections on Analytical Distinctions', *Cardozo Law Review*, 17(4–5), March 1996, pp. 1083–1127; J. Bohman, *Public Deliberation: Pluralism, Complexity, and Democracy*, Cambridge, MA, and London, UK, The MIT Press, 1996, pp. 180–181.

28 McCarthy, 'Legitimacy and Diversity', p. 1122.

29 Ankersmit, *Aesthetic Politics*, p. 128.

30 Ibid., pp. 128–129.

31 Ibid., p. 129.

32 Ibid., p. 145.

33 Ibid.

34 J. Habermas, 'The Entry into Postmodernity: Nietzsche as Turning Point', *The Philosophical Discourse of Modernity*, Cambridge, MA, The MIT Press, 1987, pp. 83–106.

35 Habermas, 'The Entry into Postmodernity', p. 95.

36 Ibid., pp. 95–6.

37 J. Habermas, 'The Unity of Reason in the Diversity of its Voices', *Postmetaphysical Thinking: Philosophical Essays*, Cambridge, MA, The MIT Press, 1992, pp. 115–148, 140.

38 A. Honneth, 'The Other of Justice: Habermas and the ethical challenge of postmodernism', in S. K. White (ed.), *The Cambridge Companion to Habermas*, Cambridge, UK, Cambridge University Press, 1995, pp. 239–325.

39 Ibid., p. 295.

40 Ibid., p. 297.

41 Habermas, 'The Unity of Reason in the Diversity of its Voices', p. 140.

42 Ibid.

43 J. Habermas, 'Reconciliation Through The Public Use of Reason: Remarks on John Rawls' "Political Liberalism"', *The Journal of Philosophy*, 92, 1995, pp. 109–131, p. 117.

44 J. Habermas, 'Lawrence Kohlberg and Neo-Arististotelianism', *Justification and Application*, Cambridge, MA, The MIT Press, 1993, pp. 113–132, 130–131.

45 See J. Habermas, *Between Facts and Norms: Contributions to a Discourse Theory of Law and Democracy*, Cambridge, MA, The MIT Press, 1996, pp. 420, 422.

46 J. F. Lyotard, 'Answering the Question: What is Postmodernism?', *The Postmodern Condition*, pp. 71–82, 72, 82.

47 Lyotard, *The Postmodern Condition*, p. 47.

48 Villa, 'Postmodernism and the Public Sphere', p. 716.

49 S. K. White, *Political Theory and Postmodernism*, Cambridge, UK, Cambridge University Press, 1991, p. 22.

50 See J. Whitebook, *Perversion and Utopia: A Study in Psychoanalysis and Critical Theory*, Cambridge, MA, The MIT Press, 1995, p. 84. Whitebook thinks that Habermas is finally advocating a kind of 'joyless reformism' that assumes that human beings have forgotten how to dream after the linguistic turn. See also M. Morris, *Rethinking the Communicative Turn: Adorno, Habermas and the Problem of Communicative Freedom*, USA, State University of New York Press, 2001, 7. Morris suggests that Habermas' turn to a linguistic and intersubjective-centred approach has abandoned critical theory's fixations with 'the aesthetic and a "new sensibility" – that is, with a substantially new ability to perceive and experience that would help constitute a liberated society'.

51 Lyotard, 'Answering the Question: What is the Postmodernism?', pp. 77–79.

52 E. Kant, *Critique of Judgment*, cited by Michael Halberstam, *Totalitarianism and the Modern Conception of Politics*, New Haven, CT, and London, Yale University Press, 1999, p. 195.

53 J. F. Lyotard, 'Postscript to Terror and the Sublime', *The Postmodern Explained*, pp. 67–75, 67–68, 72.

54 Villa, 'Postmodernism and the Public Sphere', p. 719.

55 Habermas, *Between Facts and Norms*, p. 365.

56 Ibid., p. 359.

57 Honneth, 'The Other of Justice', p. 300.

58 R. Wolin, *The Seduction of Unreason: The Intellectual Romance with Fascism From Nietzsche to Postmodernism*, Princeton, NJ, Princeton University Press, 2004, p. 8.

59 Ibid.

60 See Habermas, *Between Facts and Norms*, pp. 445–446.

61 Ibid., p. 446.

62 Wolin, *The Seduction of Unreason*, p. 13.

63 J. Habermas, 'Learning From Catastrophe? A Look Back at the Short Twentieth Century', *The Postnational Constellation*, Cambridge, UK, Polity 1998, pp. 35–58, 48.

64 See M. B. Matustik, *Jurgen Habermas: A Philosophical-Political Profile*, New York, Rowman and Littlefield, 2001, p. 151.

65 M. Halberstam, *Totalitarianism and the Modern Conception of Politics*, New Haven, CT and London, Yale University Press, 1999, pp. 117–129.

66 Ibid., p. 190.

67 Ibid., p. 48.

68 N. Elias, *The Germans*, New York, Columbia University Press, 1996, pp. 224–225.

69 C. Lamore, *The Romantic Legacy*, New York, Columbia University Press, 1996, p. 57.

70 Ibid., p. 56.

71 Ibid.

72 Ibid., p. 58.

73 Wolin, *The Seduction of Unreason*, p. 14.

74 Markus, 'The Paradoxical Unity of Culture', p. 21.

75 Ibid., p. 21.

76 Ibid., p.22.

77 Ibid.

78 Ibid., p. 23.

79 Ibid.

9 Distorted communications: Habermas and feminism

1 J. Habermas, *Between Facts and Norms: Contributions to a Discourse Theory of Law and Democracy*, Cambridge, MA, The MIT Press, 1996.
2 J. B. Landes, *Women and the Public Sphere in the Age of the French Revolution*, Ithaca, NY and London, Cornell University Press, 1988, p. 7.
3 Ibid., p. 111.
4 Ibid., p. 45.
5 N. Fraser, 'What's Critical about Critical Theory?', in J. Meehan (ed.), *Feminists Read Habermas: Gendering the Subject of Discourse*, New York and London, Routledge, 1995, pp. 21–57.
6 Ibid., pp. 21–22.
7 Ibid., p. 31.
8 Ibid., pp. 32–33.
9 M. Fleming, *Emancipation and Illusion: Rationality and Gender in Habermas' Theory of Modernity*, PA, Pennsylvania State University Press, 1997; M. Fleming, 'Women and the "Public Use of Reason"', in J. Meehan (ed.), *Feminists Read Habermas: Gendering the Subject of Discourse*, New York and London, Routledge, pp. 117–139.
10 Fleming, 'Women and the "Public Use of Reason"', p. 118. Fleming supposes that the idea of colonization, with its range of conservative implications, remains central to Habermas' critical perspective. See Fleming, *Emancipation and Illusion*, pp. 95–97.
11 J. Habermas, 'What Theories Can Accomplish – and What They Can't', *Jurgen Habermas, The Past as Future*, interviews with Michael Haller, Lincoln and London, University of Nebraska Press, 1994, pp. 99–120, 111.
12 J. Habermas, *The Theory of Communicative Action*, Volume 2, Boston, CA, Beacon Press, 1984, p. 329.
13 J. Habermas, 'Jurgen Habermas: Morality, Society and Ethics, an interview with Torben Hviid Nielsen', *Acta Sociologica*, 33(2), 1990, pp. 95–115, 106.
14 Ibid.
15 Habermas, *Between Facts and Norms*, pp. 419–426.
16 Ibid. p. 449.
17 Ibid., pp. 424–426.
18 Ibid., pp. 419–426.
19 Ibid., p. 423 (original emphasis).
20 See D. L. Rhode, *Justice and Gender*, Cambridge, Harvard University Press, 1989.
21 Habermas, *Between Facts and Norms*, pp. 422–423 (original emphasis).
22 Ibid., p. 425 (original emphasis).
23 J. L. Cohen, 'Critical Social Theory and Feminist Critiques', in J. Meehan (ed.), *Feminists Read Habermas: Gendering the Subject of Discourse*, pp. 57–90, 78.
24 J. Dean, *Solidarity of Strangers: Feminism After Identity Politics*, Berkeley, CA, University of California Press, 1996, p. 4.
25 Ibid.
26 Dean, *Solidarity of Strangers*, p. 105. Dean makes the point that '[q]uestioning is already contained within the notion of an abstract norm, which must be interpreted for its meaning to be realised'.
27 I. M. Young, 'Asymmetrical Reciprocity: On Moral Respect, Wonder and Enlarged Thought', *Constellations*, 3(3), January 1997, pp. 340–364. See also I. M. Young, 'Communication and the Other: Beyond Deliberative Democracy', in S. Benhabib (ed.), *Democracy and Difference*, Princeton, NJ, Princeton University Press, 1996, pp. 120–137.

28 Young, 'Asymmetrical Reciprocity'.

29 Ibid., pp. 341–342.

30 S. Benhabib, 'Communicative Ethics and the Claims of Gender, Community and Postmodernism', and S. Benhabib, 'The Generalised and Concrete Other', in *Situating the Self*, New York, Routledge, 1992.

31 Benhabib, 'The Generalised and the Concrete Other', p. 158.

32 M. Cooke, *Language and Reason: A Study in Habermas' Pragmatics*, Cambridge, MA, The MIT Press, 1994.

33 Ibid., p. 160.

34 J. Habermas, 'Lawrence Kohlberg and Neo-Aristotelianism', *Justification and Application*, Cambridge, MA, The MIT Press, 1993, pp. 113–133, 130–131.

35 M. P. Lara, *Moral Textures: Feminist Narratives in the Public Sphere*, Cambridge, Polity Press, 1998.

36 Ibid., p. 3.

37 Ibid., p. 7.

38 Ibid., p. 59.

39 Habermas, *Between Facts and Norms*; see Chapter 8, 'Civil Society and the Political Public Sphere' especially pp. 351, 354, 359, 360–361.

40 In his 'Further Reflections on the Public Sphere', Habermas emphasizes the key place that the *Structural Transformation of the Public Sphere* gave to literary publics (J. Habermas, 'Further Reflections on the Public Sphere', in C. Calhoun (ed.), *Habermas and the Public Sphere*, Cambridge, MA, The MIT Press, 1992, pp. 421–462, 423).

41 P. Duvenage, *Habermas and Aesthetics: The Limits of Communicative Reason*, Cambridge, UK, Polity Press, 2003.

42 M. Nussbaum, *Cultivating Humanity: A Classical Defence of Reform in Liberal Education*, Cambridge, MA, Harvard University Press, 1997, pp. 111–112.

43 See L. Irigary, *This Sex Which is Not One*, Ithaca, NY, Cornell University Press, 1980, L. Irigaray *Speculum of the Other Woman*, Ithaca, NY, Cornell University Press, 1985.

44 J. Butler, *Gender Trouble*, New York, Routledge, 1997.

45 J. Butler, *Undoing Gender*, New York and London, Routledge, 2004, p. 3.

46 J. Habermas, 'The Postnational Constellation and the Future of Democracy', in M. Pensky (ed.), *Jurgen Habermas: The Postnational Constellation*, Cambridge, MA, The MIT Press, 2001, pp. 58–112, 88.

47 S. E. Bronner, *Reclaiming the Enlightenment: Towards a Politics of Radical Engagement*, New York, Columbia University Press, 2004, pp. x–xi.

48 A. Honneth, 'The Other of Justice: Habermas and the Ethical Challenge of Postmodernism', in S. K White (ed.), *The Cambridge Companion to Habermas*, Cambridge, UK, Cambridge University Press, 1995, pp. 239–325.

10 Conclusion

1 J. Habermas, 'What Does Socialism Mean Today?', in Robert Blackburn (ed.), *After the Fall: The Failure of Communism and the Future of Socialism*, London, Verso, 1991, pp. 25–47, 31.

2 J. Habermas 'The European Nation-State', *The Inclusion of the Other: Studies in Political Theory*, Cambridge, MA, The MIT Press, 1995, pp. 105–129, p. 123.

3 J. Habermas and J. Derrida 'February 15, or What Binds Europeans Together: A Plea for a Common Foreign Policy, Beginning in the Core of Europe', *Constellations*, 10(13), 2003, pp. 291–297, 293.

4 Habermas and Derrida, 'February 15, or What Binds Europeans Together', p. 295.
5 *After Habermas: New Perspectives on the Public Sphere*, Crossley and Roberts (eds), Oxford, Blackwell Publishing/The Sociological Review, 2004, p. 15.
6 N. Fraser, 'Rethinking the Public Sphere: A Contribution to the Critique of Actually Existing Democracy', in C. Calhoun (ed.), *Habermas and the Public Sphere*, Cambridge, MA, MIT Press, 1992.
7 N. Fraser, 'The Uses and Abuses of French Discourse Theories for Feminist Politics', in N. Fraser and S. L. Bartky (eds), *Revaluing French Feminism: Critical Essays on Difference, Agency and Culture*, Bloomingdale Indiana, Indiana University Press, 1995, p. 291.
8 Ibid.
9 J. Habermas, *The Theory of Communicative Action*, Volume 1, Boston, MA, Beacon Press, 1984, p. xxxix.
10 S. E. Bronner, *Of Critical Theory and Its Theorists*, Cambridge, MA, Blackwell Publishers, 1994, p. 306.
11 T. Todorov, *Hope and Memory: Lessons from the Twentieth Century*, Princeton, NJ, Princeton University Press, 2003, pp. 19–26.
12 Todorov, *Hope and Memory*, p. 24.

Bibliography

T. W. Adorno, *Negative Dialectics*, New York, Seabury Press, 1973.

J. Alexander, 'Robust Utopias and Civil Repairs', *International Sociology*, 16(4), December 2001, pp. 579–591.

F. R. Ankersmit, *Aesthetic Politics: Political Philosophy Beyond Fact and Value*, Stanford, CA, Stanford University Press, 1996.

H. Arendt, *The Origins of Totalitarianism*, London, George Allen and Unwin, 1958.

J. Arnason, 'Modernity as Project and as Field of Tensions', in A. Honneth and H. Joas (eds), *Communicative Action: Essays on Habermas' Theory of Communicative Action*, Cambridge, MA, The MIT Press, 1991.

——, 'Globalism, Ideology and Traditions: Interview with Jurgen Habermas', *Thesis Eleven*, 63, November 2000, pp. 1–11.

J. Baudrillard, *The Spirit of Terrorism*, London, Vergo, 2002.

Z. Bauman, *In Search of Politics*, Stanford, CA, Stanford University Press, 1999.

——, *The Individualised Society*, Cambridge, UK, Polity, 2001.

U. Beck, 'The Reinvention of Politics: Towards a Theory of a Reflexive Modernisation', in U. Beck, A. Giddens and S. Lash (eds), *Reflexive Modernisation: Politics, Tradition and Aesthetics in the Modern Social Order*, Stanford, CA, Stanford University Press, 1994, pp. 1–55.

——, *The Reinvention of Politics: Rethinking Modernity in the Global Social Order*, Cambridge, UK, Polity, 1997.

——, *World Risk Society*, Cambridge, Polity Press, 1999.

——, *What is Globalization?*, Cambridge, UK, Polity Press, 2000.

——, *Conversations with Ulrich Beck: Ulrich Beck and Johannes Willms*, Cambridge, UK, Polity, 2004.

U. Beck, A. Giddens and S. Lash, *Reflexive Modernisation: Politics, Tradition and Aesthetics in the Modern Social Order*, Stanford, CA, Stanford University Press, 1994.

S. Benhabib, 'Modernity and the Aporias of Critical Theory', *Telos*, 49, 1981, pp. 39–59.

——, *Critique, Norm and Utopia: A Study of the Foundation of Critical Theory*, New York, Columbia University Press, 1986.

——, *Situating the Self: Gender Community and Postmodernism in Contemporary Ethics*, New York, Routledge, 1992.

——, *Democracy and Difference*, Princeton, NJ, Princeton University Press, 1996.

I. Berlin, *The Roots Of Romanticism*, Princeton, NJ, Princeton University Press, 1999.

N. Birnbaum, *After Progress: American Social Reform and European Socialism in the Twentieth Century*, Oxford, Oxford University Press, 2001.

R. Blackburn (ed.), *After the Fall: The Failure of Communism and the Future of Socialism*, London, Verso, 1991.

J. Bleicher (ed.), *Contemporary Hermeneutics: Hermeneutics as Method, Philosophy and Critique*, London and Boston, MA, Routledge and Kegan Paul, 1980.

J. Bohman, *Public Deliberation: Pluralism, Complexity, and Democracy*, Cambridge, MA, and London, UK, The MIT Press, 1996.

G. Borradori, 'Introduction', *Philosophy in a Time of Terror: Dialogues with Jurgen Habermas and Jacques Derrida*, Chicago, IL and London, The University of Chicago Press, 2003.

H. C. Boyte, 'The Pragmatic Ends of Popular Politics', in C. Calhoun (ed.), *Habermas and the Public Sphere*, Cambridge, MA, The MIT Press, 1992, pp. 340–359.

J. S. Brady, 'No Contest? Assessing the Critiques of Jurgen Habermas's Theory of the Public Sphere', *Philosophy and Social Criticism*, 30(3), 2004, pp. 331–354.

S. E. Bronner, *Of Critical Theory and Its Theorists*, Cambridge, MA, Blackwell, 1994.

——, *Reclaiming the Enlightenment: Toward a Politics of Radical Engagement*, New York, Columbia University Press, 2004.

J. Butler, *Excitable Speech: A Politics of the Performative*, New York, Routledge, 1997.

——, *Gender Trouble*, New York, Routledge, 1997.

——, *Undoing Gender*, New York and London, Routledge, 2004.

C. Calhoun (ed.), *Habermas and the Public Sphere*, Cambridge, MA, The MIT Press, 1992.

N. Chomsky, *Power and Terror in Our Times*, a film by John Junkerman, 2002.

J. L. Cohen, '*Heller, Habermas and Justice: A Review of Agnes Heller's* Beyond Justice', *Praxis International* 8(4), 1989, pp. 491–497.

——, 'Critical Social Theory and Feminist Critiques', in J. Meehan (ed.), *Feminists Read Habermas: Gendering the Subject of Discourse*, New York and London, Routledge, 1995, pp. 57–90.

J. L. Cohen and A. Arato, *Civil Society and Political Theory*, Cambridge, MA, The MIT Press, 1992.

R. W. Connell, 'Rage Against the Dying of the Light', *The Australian*, Wednesday, October 23, 2002, pp. 30–31.

M. Cooke, *Language and Reason: A Study in Habermas' Pragmatics*, Cambridge, MA, The MIT Press, 1994.

L. Coser, *The Functions of Social Conflict*, New York, Free Press, 1976.

C. P. Cronin, 'Introduction', in J. Habermas (ed.), *Justification and Application*, Cambridge, MA, The MIT Press, 1993.

J. Dean, *Solidarity of Strangers: Feminism After Identity Politics*, Berkeley, CA, University of California Press, 1996, pp. 95–113.

——, 'Civil Society: Beyond the Public Sphere', in D. Rasmussen (ed.), *The Handbook of Critical Theory*, Oxford, Blackwell, 1999.

——, 'Why the Net is not a Public Sphere', *Constellations*, 10(1), 2003.

R. Dees, 'Establishing Toleration', *Political Theory*, 27(5), 1999, pp. 667–693.

M. Passerin d'Entreves and S. Benhabib (eds), *Habermas and the Unfinished Project of Modernity*, Cambridge, MA, The MIT Press, 1997.

J. Derrida, 'Deconstructing Terrorism', in G. Borradori, *Philosophy in a Time of Terror: Dialogues with Jurgen Habermas and Jacques Derrida*, Chicago, IL and London, the University of Chicago Press, 2003.

J. Dewey, *The Public and its Problems*, Chicago, MA, Gateway Books, 1946.

P. Dews (ed.), *Habermas: A Critical Reader*, UK, Blackwell, 1999.

P. Duvenage, *Habermas and Aesthetics: The Limits of Communicative Reason*, Cambridge, UK, Polity Press, 2003.

G. Eley, 'Nations, Publics and Political Cultures', in C. Calhoun (ed.), *Habermas and the Public Sphere*, Cambridge, MA, The MIT Press, 1992, pp. 289–340.

N. Elias, *The Germans*, New York, Columbia University Press, 1996.

R. Fine and W. Smith, 'Habermas's Ambivalent Modernism', *Constellations*, 10(4), December 2003, pp. 469–488.

M. Fleming, 'Women and the "Public Use of Reason"', in J. Meehan (ed.), *Feminists Read Habermas: Gendering the Subject of Discourse*, New York and London, Routledge, 1995, pp. 117–139.

——, *Emancipation and Illusion: Rationality and Gender in Habermas' Theory of Modernity*, PA, Pennsylvania State University Press, 1997.

N. Fraser, 'Rethinking the Public Sphere: A Contribution to the Critique of Actually Existing Democracy', in C. Calhoun (ed.), *Habermas and the Public Sphere*, Cambridge, MA, The MIT Press, 1992, pp. 109–143.

——, 'Politics, Culture, and the Public Sphere: Toward a Postmodern Conception', in L. Nicholson and S. Seidman (eds), *Social Postmodernism: Beyond Identity Politics*, Cambridge, Cambridge University Press, 1995.

——, 'The Uses and Abuses of French Discourse Theories for Feminist Politics', in Fraser and S. L. Bartky (eds), *Revaluing French Feminism: Critical Essays on Difference, Agency and Culture*, Bloomingdale Indiana, Indiana University Press, 1995.

——, 'What's Critical about Critical Theory?', in J. Meehan (ed.), *Feminists Read Habermas: Gendering the Subject of Discourse*, New York and London, Routledge, 1995, pp. 21–57.

N. Garnham, 'The Media and the Public Sphere', in C. Calhoun (ed.), *Habermas and the Public Sphere*, Cambridge, MA, The MIT Press, 1992, pp. 359–377.

C. Geertz, *Available Light: Anthropological Reflections on Philosophical Topics*, Princeton, NJ, Princeton University Press, 2000.

A. Giddens, *The Third Way: The Renewal of Social Democracy*, Cambridge, UK, Polity, 1998.

J. Goebel and C. Clermont, 'Die Tugend der Orientierungslosigkeit', manuscript, Berlin 1997, cited by U. Beck, *What is Globalization?*, Cambridge, UK, Polity Press, 2000.

D. Goodman, *The Republic of Letters: A Cultural History of the French Enlightenment*, Ithaca, NY and New York, Cornell University, 1994.

A. W. Gouldner, 'Romanticism and Classicism: Deep Structures in Social Science', *For Sociology: Renewal and Critique in Sociology Today*, New York: Basic Books Inc., 1973, pp. 300–323.

J. E. Grumley, 'Two Views of the Paradigm of Production', *Praxis International*, 12(2), July 1992, pp. 181–205.

J. Habermas, *Toward a Rational Society: Student Protest, Science and Politics*, Boston, MA, Beacon Press, 1970.

——, *Knowledge and Human Interests*, London, Beacon Press, 1971.

——, *Towards a Rational Society*, London, Heinemann, 1972.

——, *Theory and Practice*, Boston, MA, Beacon Press, 1973.

——, *Legitimation Crisis*, trans. T. McCarthy, Boston, MA, Beacon Press, 1975.

——, *Communication and the Evolution of Society*, Boston, MA, Beacon Press, 1976.

——, 'Critical Hermenuetics', in J. Bleicher (ed.), *Contemporary Hermeneutics*, London and Boston, MA, Routledge & Kegan Paul, 1980, pp. 141–213.

——, 'The Dialectics of Rationalisation: An Interview with Jurgen Habermas', by A. Honneth, E. Knodler-Bunte, A. Widmann, *Telos*, 49, Fall, 1981, pp. 5–33.

——, 'A Reply to my Critics', in J. B Thompson and D. Held (eds), *Habermas and Critical Debates*, Cambridge, MA, The MIT Press, 1982.

——, *Philosophical and Political Profiles*, Cambridge, MA, The MIT Press, 1983.

——, *The Theory of Communicative Action*, Volume I, Boston, MA, Beacon Press, 1984.

——, *The Theory of Communicative Action*, Volume 2, Boston, MA, Beacon Press, 1984.

——, *Theorie des kommunikativen Handelns*, Band 1, 'Vorwart zur dritten Auflage', Frankfurt, 1985.

——, *Autonomy and Solidarity: Interviews with Jurgen Habermas*, P. Dews (ed.), London, Verso, 1986.

——, *The Philosophical Discourse of Modernity: Twelve Lectures*, Cambridge, MA, The MIT Press, 1987.

——, *The New Conservatism: Cultural Criticism and the Historian's Debate*, Cambridge, MA, The MIT Press, 1989.

——, *The Structural Transformation of the Public Sphere: An Inquiry into a Category of Bourgeois Society*, Cambridge, MA, The MIT Press, 1989.

——, 'Jurgen Habermas: Morality, Society and Ethics, an Interview with Torben Hviid Nielsen', *Acta Sociologica*, 33(2), 1990, pp. 93–114.

——, 'Justice and Solidarity: On the Discussion Concerning Stage 6', in T. E. Wren (ed.), *The Moral Domain: Essays in the Ongoing Discussion Between Philosophy and the Social Sciences*, Cambridge, MA, The MIT Press, 1990, pp. 182–224.

——, *Moral Consciousness and Communicative Action*, Cambridge, MA, The MIT Press, 1990.

——, 'What Does Socialism Mean Today?', in Robert Blackburn (ed.), *After the Fall: The Failure of Communism and the Future of Socialism*, London, Verso, 1991, pp. 25–47.

——, 'Concluding Remarks', in C. Calhoun (ed.), *Habermas and the Public Sphere*, Cambridge, MA, The MIT Press, 1992, pp. 466–479.

——, 'Further Reflections on the Public Sphere', in C. Calhoun (ed.), *Habermas and the Public Sphere*, Cambridge, MA, The MIT Press, 1992, pp. 421–462.

——, 'The Unity of Reason in the Diversity of its Voices', *Postmetaphysical Thinking: Philosophical Essays*, Cambridge, MA, The MIT Press, 1992, pp. 115–148.

——, 'Yet Again: German Identity – A Unified Nation of Angry DM-Burghers', in H. James and M. Stone (eds), *When the Wall Came Down: Reactions to German Unification*, New York and London, Routledge, 1992, pp. 86–102.

——, 'The Asylum Debate', Paris Lecture, January 14, 1993.

——, *Justification and Application*, Cambridge, MA, The MIT Press, 1993.

——, 'Three Normative Models of Democracy', *Constellations*, 1(1), April 1994, pp. 1–11.

——, 'What Theories Can Accomplish – and What They Can't', in *Jurgen Habermas, The Past as Future*, interviews with Michael Haller, Lincoln and London, University of Nebraska Press, 1994.

——, 'Reconciliation Through The Public Use of Reason: Remarks on John Rawls' "Political Liberalism"', *The Journal of Philosophy*, 92, 1995, pp. 109–131.

——, *Between Facts and Norms: Contributions to a Discourse Theory of Law and Democracy*, Cambridge, MA, The MIT Press, 1996.

J. Habermas, 'Reply to Symposium Participants, Benjamin N. Cardozo School of Law', in E. B. Warren (ed.), *Habermas on Law and Democracy: Critical Exchanges*, New York, Cardozo School of Law Review 1996, pp. 1477–1559.

——, 'Habermas' Modernity: an Unfinished Project', in M. Passerin d'Entreves and S. Benhabib (eds), *Habermas and the Unfinished Project of Modernity*, Cambridge, MA, The MIT Press, 1997, pp. 38–55.

——, *A Berlin Republic: Writings on Germany*, Cambridge, UK, Polity, 1998.

——, 'A Conversation About Questions of Political Theory', in *Jurgen Habermas: A Berlin Republic: Writings on Germany*, Cambridge, UK, Polity Press, 1998.

——, *The Inclusion of the Other: Studies in Political Theory*, Cambridge, MA, The MIT Press, 1998.

——, 'Globalism, Ideology and Traditions: Interview with Jurgen Habermas' by Johann Arnason, *Thesis Eleven*, 63, November 2000, pp. 1–11, 1.

——, *The Postnational Constellation: Political Essays*, Cambridge, UK, Polity Press, 2001.

——, 'Why Europe Needs a Constitution', *New Left Review*, September/October 2001, pp. 5–27.

——, 'Fundamentalism and Terror: A Dialogue with Jurgen Habermas', in G. Borradori (ed.), *Philosophy in a Time of Terror: Dialogues with Jurgen Habermas and Jacques Derrida*, Chicago, IL and London, The University of Chicago Press, 2003, pp. 25–43.

——, 'Interpreting the Fall of a Monument', *Constellations*, 10(3), 2003, pp. 364–371.

J. Habermas and J. Derrida, 'February 15, or What Binds Europeans Together: A Plea for a Common Foreign Policy, Beginning in the Core of Europe', *Constellations*, 10(3), 2003, pp. 291–297.

M. Halberstam, *Totalitarianism and the Modern Conception of Politics*, New Haven, CT and London, Yale University Press, 1999.

M. Haller (interviewer), *Jurgen Habermas, The Past as Future*, interviews with Michael Haller, Lincoln and London, University of Nebraska Press, 1994.

M. Hardt, 'The Withering of Civil Society', *Social Text*, 14(4), 1995, pp. 27–44.

A. Heller, 'The Discourse Ethic of Habermas: Critique and Appraisal', *Thesis Eleven*, No. 10/11, November–March 1984–85.

——, 'Modernity and Terror', *Constellations*, 9(1), 2002, pp. 53–65.

A. Heller and F. Feher, 'On Being Satisfied in a Dissatisfied Society 1', *The Postmodern Political Condition*, Cambridge, UK, Polity Press, 1988, pp. 14–30.

R. C. Holub, *Jurgen Habermas: Critic in the Public Sphere*, London and New York, Routledge, 1991.

A. Honneth, 'Work and Instrumental Action: On the Normative Basis of Critical Theory', *Thesis Eleven*, 5/6, 1982, pp. 162–185.

——, 'The Other of Justice: Habermas and the Ethical Challenge of Postmodernism', in S. K. White (ed.), *The Cambridge Companion to Habermas*, Cambridge, UK, Cambridge University Press, 1995, pp. 239–325.

A. Honneth and H. Joas, *Communicative Action: Essays on Habermas' Theory of Communicative Action*, Cambridge, MA, The MIT Press, 1991.

L. Irigaray, *This Sex which is Not One*, Ithaca, NY, Cornell University Press, 1980.

——, *Speculum of the Other Woman*, Ithaca, NY, Cornell University Press, 1985.

R. Jacoby, *The End of Utopia: Politics and Culture in an Age of Apathy*, New York, Basic Books, 1999.

H. James and M. Stone (eds), *When the Wall Came Down: Reactions to German Unification*, Routledge, 1992.

M. Jay (ed.), *An Unmastered Past: The Autobiographical Reflections of Leo Lowenthal*, Berkeley, CA, University of California Press, 1987.

L. Kolakowski, 'The Death of Utopia Reconsidered', *Modernity on Endless Trial*, Chicago, IL, London, University of Chicago Press, 1983.

Martin Krygier, 'The Quality of Civility: Post-Anti-Communist Thoughts on Civil Society and the Rule of Law', in A. Sajo (ed.), *From and to Authoritarianism*, Dordrecht, Kluwer Academic Publishers, 2001.

E. Laclau and C. Mouffe, *Hegemony and Socialist Strategy: Towards a Radical Democratic Politics*, London, Verso, 1985.

C. Lafont, *The Linguistic Turn in Hermeneutic Philosophy*, Cambridge, MA, The MIT Press, 1999.

C. Lamore, *The Romantic Legacy*, New York, Columbia University Press, 1996.

J. B. Landes, *Women and the Public Sphere in the Age of the French Revolution*, Ithaca, NY, Cornell University Press, 1988.

——, 'The Public and the Private Sphere: A Feminist Reconsideration', in J. Meehan (ed.), *Feminists Read Habermas: Gendering the Subject of Discourse*, New York and London, Routledge, 1995, pp. 91–117.

——, 'The Public and the Private Sphere: A Feminist Reconsideration', in J. Meehan (ed.), *Feminism, the Public and the Private*, Oxford, Oxford University Press, 1998, pp. 135–164.

M. P. Lara, *Moral Textures: Feminist Narratives in the Public Sphere*, Cambridge, Polity Press, 1998.

M. Latham, *From the Suburbs: Building a Nation From Our Neighbourhoods*, NSW, Pluto Press, 2003.

T. Lemke 'The Birth of bio-politics: Michelle Foucault's lecture at the College de France on neo-liberal governmentality', *Economy and Society*, 30(2), May 2001, pp. 190–207.

L. Lowenthal, 'The Utopian Motif in Suspension: A Conversation with Leo Lowenthal (Interview with Martin Luddke)', in M. Jay (ed.), *An Unmastered Past: The Autobiographical Reflections of Leo Lowenthal*, Berkeley, CA, University of California Press, 1987 (interview recorded 1980).

J. F. Lyotard, *The Postmodern Condition: A Report on Knowledge*, Minneapolis, MN, University of Minnesota Press, 1984.

——, *The Postmodern Explained: Correspondence 1982–1985*, Minneapolis, MN and London, University of Minneapolis Press, 1992.

——, *The Differend: Phrases in Dispute*, Minneapolis, MN, University of Minnesota Press, 1998.

T. McCarthy, *The Critical Theory of Jurgen Habermas*, Cambridge, MA, The MIT Press, 1978.

——, 'Translator's Introduction', in J. Habermas, *Communication and the Evolution of Society*, Boston, MA, Beacon Press, 1979.

——, 'Introduction', in J. Habermas, *The Theory of Communicative Action*, Volume 1, Boston, MA, Beacon Press, 1984.

——, *Ideals and Illusions: On Reconstruction and Deconstruction in Contemporary Critical Theory*, Cambridge, MA, The MIT Press, 1991.

——, 'Legitimacy and Diversity: Dialectical Reflections on Analytical Distinctions', *Cardozo Law Review*, 17(4–5), March 1996, pp. 1083–1127.

H. Marcuse, 'Repressive Tolerance', in R. P. Wolff, B. Moore and H. Marcuse (eds), *A Critique of Pure Tolerance*, Boston, MA, Beacon Press, 1965, pp. 81–123.

G. Markus, 'Antinomies of "Culture"', Collegium Budapest/ Institute for Advanced Study, Discussion Paper No. 38, February 1997, pp. 1–20.

G. Markus, 'The Paradoxical Unity of Culture: The Arts and the Sciences', *Thesis Eleven*, 75, 2003, pp. 7–24.

M. B. Markus, 'Decent Society and/or Civil Society?', *Social Research*, 68(4), Winter 2001, pp. 1011–1029.

M. B. Matustik, *Jurgen Habermas: A Philosophical-Political Profile*, New York, Rowman and Littlefield Publishers, 2001.

J. Meehan (ed.), *Feminists Read Habermas: Gendering the Subject of Discourse*, New York and London, Routledge, 1995.

J. van Horn Melton, *The Rise of the Public in Enlightenment Europe*, Cambridge, UK, Cambridge University Press, 2001.

J. S. Mill, *Utilitarianism, Liberty and Representative Government*, London, J. M. Dent & Sons Ltd, 1910.

M. Moody-Adams, *Fieldwork in Familiar Places: Morality, Culture and Philosophy*, Cambridge, MA, Harvard University Press, 1997.

M. Morris, *Rethinking the Communicative Turn: Adorno, Habermas, and the Problem of Communicative Freedom*, New York, State University of New York, 2001.

L. Nicholson and S. Seidman (eds), *Social Postmodernism: Beyond Identity Politics*, Cambridge, Cambridge University Press, 1995.

T. H. Nielsen, 'Jurgen Habermas: Morality, Society and Ethics, An Interview with T. H. Nielsen', *Acta Sociologica*, 33, 1990, pp. 93–114.

M. Nussbaum, *Cultivating Humanity: A Classical Defence of Reform in Liberal Education*, Cambridge, MA, Harvard University Press, 1997.

G. Oakes, 'Translator's Introduction', in C. Schmitt (ed.), *Political Romanticism*, Cambridge, MA, The MIT Press, 1986.

C. Offe, 'Some Contradictions of the Modern Welfare State', in T. Deane (ed.), *Contradictions of the Welfare State*, Cambridge, MA, The MIT Press, 1984, pp. 147–162.

W. Outhwaite, *Habermas: A Critical Introduction*, Stanford, CA, Stanford University Press, 1994.

C. Pateman, *The Sexual Contract*, Cambridge, UK, Polity Press, 1988.

Michael Pusey, *Jurgen Habermas*, UK, Ellis Harwood and Tavistock, 1987.

R. D. Putnam, *Bowling Alone: The Collapse and Revival of American Community*, New York, Simon and Schuster, 2000.

D. Rasmussen (ed.), *The Handbook of Critical Theory*, Oxford, Blackwell, 1999.

J. Raz, *The Morality of Freedom*, Oxford, Claredon Press, 1986.

W. Rehg, 'Translator's Introduction', in J. Habermas (ed.), *Between Facts and Norms: Contributions to a Discourse Theory of Law and Democracy*, Cambridge, MA, The MIT Press, 1996, pp. ix–xxxix.

D. L. Rhode, *Justice and Gender*, Cambridge, MA, Harvard University Press, 1989.

John Roberts and Michael Crossley (eds), *After Habermas: New Perspectives on the Public Sphere*, Oxford, Blackwell Publishing/The Sociological Review, 2004.

R. Roderick, *Habermas and the Foundations of Critical Theory*, London, Macmillan, 1986.

M. Ryan, 'Gender and Public Access: Women's Politics in Nineteenth Century America', in C. Calhoun (ed.), *Habermas and the Public Sphere*, Cambridge, MA, The MIT Press, 1992, pp. 259–289.

A. Sajo (ed.), *From and to Authoritarianism*, Dordrecht, Kluwer Academic Publishers, 2001.

W. E. Scheuerman, 'Between Radicalism and Resignation: Democratic Theory in Habermas' *Between Facts and Norms*', in R. von Schomberg and K. Baynes (eds), *Discourse and Democracy: Essays on Habermas's Between Facts and Norms*, Albany State, NY, University of New York Press, 2002, pp. 61–89.

C. Schmitt, *Political Romanticism*, Cambridge, MA, The MIT Press, 1986.

——, *Political Theology: Four Chapters on the Concept of Sovereignty*, Cambridge, MA, The MIT Press, 1988.

——, *The Crisis of Parliamentary Democracy*, Cambridge, MA, The MIT Press, 1988.

P. Self, *Rolling Back the Market: Economic Dogma & Political Choice*, London, Macmillan Press, 2000.

R. Sennett, *The Corrosion of Character: The Personal Consequences of Work in the New Capitalism*, New York, London, W. W. Norton & Company, 1998.

O. P. Shabani, *Democracy, Power and Legitimacy: The Critical Theory of Jurgen Habermas*, Toronto, Buffalo, NY and London, University of Toronto Press, 2003.

J. Sitton, *Habermas and Contemporary Society*, New York, Palgrave, Macmillan, 2003.

L. Strauss, 'Comments on Carl Schmitt's *Der Begriff des Politischen*', in C. Schmitt (ed.), *The Concept of the Political*, New Brunswick, NJ, Rutgers university press, 1971, pp. 81–105.

A. de Tocqueville, *Democracy in America*, Volumes 1 and 2, New York, Vintage books, 1945.

T. Todorov, *Hope and Memory: Lessons from the Twentieth Century*, Princeton, NJ, Princeton University Press, 2003.

M. Theunissen, 'Society and History: A Critique of Critical Theory', in P. Dews (ed.), *Habermas: A Critical Reader*, UK, Blackwell, 1999.

U. Thielemann, 'Globale Konkurrenz: Socialstandards und der Zwang zum Unternehertum' cited in Habermas, 'The European Nation-State: On the Past and Future of Sovereignty and Citizenship', *The Inclusion of the Other: Studies in Political Theory*, Cambridge, MA, The MIT Press, 1998.

J. B. Thompson and D. Held (eds), *Habermas and Critical Debates*, Cambridge, MA, The MIT Press, 1982.

A. Touraine, *Beyond Neoliberalism*, Cambridge, UK, Polity Press, 2001.

D. R. Villa, 'Postmodernism and the Public Sphere', *American Political Science Review*, 86(3), September 1992, pp. 712–721.

M. Walzer, *On Toleration*, New Haven, CT and London, Yale University Press, 1997.

S. K. White, *Political Theory and Postmodernism*, Cambridge, UK, Cambridge University Press, 1991.

—— (ed.), *The Cambridge Companion to Habermas*, Cambridge, UK, Cambridge University Press, 1995.

J. Whitebook, *Perversion and Utopia: A Study in Psychoanalysis and Critical Theory*, Cambridge, MA, The MIT Press, 1995.

R. Wiggershaus, *The Frankfurt School: Its History, Theories, and Political Significance*, Cambridge, MA, The MIT Press, 1994.

R. P. Wolff, B. Moore, and H. Marcuse (eds), *A Critique of Pure Tolerance*, Boston, MA, Beacon Press, 1965.

R. Wolin, *The Seduction of Unreason: The Intellectual Romance with Fascism From Nietzsche to Postmodernism*, Princeton, NJ, Princeton University Press, 2004.

T. E. Wren (ed.), *The Moral Domain: Essays in the Ongoing Discussion Between Philosophy and the Social Sciences*, Cambridge, MA, The MIT Press, 1990.

I. M. Young, 'Communication and the Other: Beyond Deliberative Democracy', in S. Benhabib (ed.), *Democracy and Difference*, Princeton, NJ, Princeton University Press, 1996, pp. 120–137.

——, 'Asymmetrical Reciprocity: On Moral Respect, Wonder and Enlarged Thought', *Constellations*, 3(3), January 1997, pp. 340–364.

——, 'Communication and the Other', *Intersecting Voices: Dilemmas of Gender, Political Philosophy and Politics*, Princeton, NJ, Princeton University Press, 1997, pp. 60–75.

Index

Lightning Source UK Ltd.
Milton Keynes UK
13 October 2009

144914UK00002B/5/P